Aviation Security Management

Aviation Security Management

VOLUME 3

PERSPECTIVES ON AVIATION SECURITY MANAGEMENT

Edited by
Andrew R. Thomas

PRAEGER SECURITY INTERNATIONAL
Westport, Connecticut • London

Library of Congress Cataloging-in-Publication Data

Aviation security management / edited by Andrew R. Thomas.
    p. cm.
  Includes bibliographical references and index.
  ISBN-13: 978–0–313–34652–1 ((set) : alk. paper)
  ISBN-13: 978–0–313–34654–5 ((vol. 1) : alk. paper)
  ISBN-13: 978–0–313–34656–9 ((vol. 2) : alk. paper)
  ISBN-13: 978–0–313–34658–3 ((vol. 3) : alk. paper)
1. Airlines—Security measures.   I. Thomas, Andrew R.
  HE9776.A95   2008
  363.28'76068—dc22   2008018728

British Library Cataloguing in Publication Data is available.

Library of Congress Catalog Card Number: 2008018728

ISBN-13: 978–0–313–34652–1 (set)
        978–0–313–34654–5 (vol. 1)
        978–0–313–34656–9 (vol. 2)
        978–0–313–34658–3 (vol. 3)

First published in 2008

Praeger Security International, 88 Post Road West, Westport, CT 06881
An imprint of Greenwood Publishing Group, Inc.
www.praeger.com

Printed in the United States of America

The paper used in this book complies with the
Permanent Paper Standard issued by the National
Information Standards Organization (Z39.48–1984).

10   9   8   7   6   5   4   3   2   1

Contents

Preface

Because of September 11, there is an almost universal recognition that aviation security is a deadly serious business. Yet, still, today around the world, the practice of aviation security is rooted in a hodgepodge of governmental rules, industry traditions, and local idiosyncrasies. In fact, seven years after the largest single attack involving the air transport industry, there remains no viable framework in place to lift aviation security practice out of the mish-mash that currently exists. The purpose of this three-volume set is to begin to change that. It is my sincere hope that this work, written from a truly global point of view, will be the first of many on this most important topic.

The fact that over half of the contributors to this set come from outside of the United States is no coincidence. Although roughly 40 percent of all air transport today takes place within the United States, the long-term trend is for dramatic increases in global system usage, driven by high-growth emerging markets like China, India, Russia, and Brazil. It is widely estimated that the total volume of passengers and cargo moved via the international air transport system will nearly triple in the next 25 years. Although America will remain the single largest player, the surge will come from emerging markets.

This evolving reality mandates that aviation security management be viewed not merely on a country by country basis, but as a global endeavor, where best practices—regardless of where they originate—are integrated into a new paradigm that is truly global in scope and scale. With that in mind, *Aviation Security Management* is intended to serve as a foundation for researchers, practitioners, and educators around the world who are looking to develop new knowledge and pass it along to the next generation of aviation security managers.

Dishearteningly, however, there id only a handful of academic programs—currently less than a dozen—where someone can actually study transportation security management. The number of schools where an aviation security management curriculum is available is even smaller. Such a lack of educational opportunities means that unless something is done quickly, the tens of thousands of new aviation security mangers who will join the profession in the coming years will not have had the opportunity to learn the best in transportation security management research and practice.

To professionalize the field of transportation security management, in general, and, aviation security management, in particular, several requirements need to be met. First and foremost, there must be a body of knowledge and a repertoire of behaviors and skills needed in the practice of the profession, knowledge, behavior, and skills that are not normally possessed by the nonprofessional. To date, very little of that body of knowledge and repertoire exists in a clear and cogent format. While many researchers and practitioners across multiple disciplines have been engaged in their own worthwhile pursuits, there remains a deficiency in the availability of clearinghouses for that knowledge. Bluntly asked, where does one go to learn about the emerging ideas, thoughts, technologies, and best practices in transportation and aviation security management?

Clearly there is neither the need nor the desire to provide those who seek to harm transportation networks with information they can use against us. As researchers, practitioners, and educators, we must be ever vigilant, striving to balance the need for open knowledge with the necessary parameters of sensitive information. I am certain we can do both—that is, provide cutting-edge knowledge to a growing body of well-intentioned researchers and practitioners while maintaining the integrity needed to ultimately make transportation more secure.

Which brings us back to those clearinghouses. This set of volumes and with the recently founded *Journal of Transportation Security* are intended to be some of the first building blocks of a much more extensive foundation, which will ultimately serve to prepare for the arrival of a true profession: transportation security management.

Having previously set the context and identified some of the key elements of aviation security management in the previous volumes, this third volume constitutes what is intended to serve as part of the foundation for the next generation of research in the area.

The first chapter, by Ruwantissa I. R. Abeyratne, details the efforts of the International Civil Aviation Organization (ICAO) to build and foster a working culture of security among the nations of the world. In the same light, Charles M. Bumstead argues that a global aviation security management crisis team would go a long way to resolving disputes between stakeholder groups.

As passenger screening becomes seemingly more cumbersome and widespread, Anthony T. H. Chin of the National University of Singapore discusses the possible uses of scientific content analysis (SCAN), a technique that analyzes linguistic structure and content, in the aviation security realm. Terry Sheridan introduces the concept of emotive profiling. And, Adrian Schwaninger, Saskia M. Koller, and Anton Bolfing lay out principles and requirements for assessing X-ray image interpretation as it relates to the competency of aviation security screeners.

Challenging the status quo of current aviation security strategy, Professor Chien-tsung Lu puts forth his notion of constructing a comprehensive aviation security management model (ASMM). So does Jeffrey Ian Ross in his look at the growing pains faced by the U.S. Transportation Security Administration.

Looking at the cabin environment, two world-class experts lay out the future of this ever-changing area: David E. Forbes and Michael Tunnecliffe.

Reminding us that aviation security is a business component, Clinton V. Oster, Jr., and John S. Strong look at the associated funding and costs.

This volume and the entire set of volumes conclude with Mark B. Salter's analysis of the overall future of aviation security management.

The appendix contains a report from the U.S. Government Accountability Office that details progress made in aviation security since the September 11 attacks as well as the challenges that remain.

It is my heartfelt desire that this dynamic set should showcase the most current trends, issues, ideas, and practices in aviation security management, especially as the field evolves in the context of globalization and advances in technology, and address the salient issues concerning aviation security management so as to lay the foundation for the professionalization of this field of endeavor for future generations.

Andrew R. Thomas, University of Akron
Editor

CHAPTER 1

The Efforts of ICAO in Ensuring a Security Culture among States

Ruwantissa I. R. Abeyratne

THE SECURITY CRISIS

Since the events of September 11, 2001, took place, the most critical challenge facing international civil aviation has been the compelling need to ensure that the air transport industry remains continuous in its operations, and that its consumer is assured of sustained regular, safe, and secure air transport services. The Air Transport Association (ATA), in its 2002 State of the United States Airline Industry Statement, advised that, in the United States, the combined impact of the 2001 economic downturn and the precipitous decline in air travel following the September 11, 2001, attacks on the United States had resulted in devastating losses for the airline industry that were likely to exceed $7 billion and continue through 2002.[1] Of course, the overall picture, which portended a certain inevitable gloom for the air transport industry, was not the exclusive legacy of United States' carriers. It applied worldwide, as was seen in the abrupt downturn of air traffic globally during 2001. The world community's retaliation against terrorism, which is an ongoing feature in world affairs, increased the airline passenger's fear of air transport and reluctance to use it. In most instances in commercial aircraft purchasing, air carriers canceled or postponed their new aircraft requisition orders. Many carriers, particularly in developing countries, were seen revisiting their cost structures and downsizing their human resource bases. It is incontrovertible

The author is coordinator, air transport programs, at the International Civil Aviation Organization in Montreal. He has written this article in his personal capacity and the views expressed herein do not necessarily reflect those of ICAO.

that another similar event or series of events will inevitably plunge the aviation industry into similar despair and destitution.

In order to arrive at where we are at the present time with regard to the results of the global measures taken by the International Civil Aviation Organization (ICAO), it is necessary to discuss the various steps taken from a regulatory perspective by ICAO, in its role as regulator and mentor of international civil aviation, in countering imminent threats to the sustainability of the air transport industry.

The ICAO High-Level Ministerial Conference

At the 33rd Session of its ICAO Assembly, held from September 25 to October 5, 2001, ICAO adopted Resolution A33–1, entitled the *Declaration on Misuse of Civil Aircraft as Weapons of Destruction and Other Terrorist Acts Involving Civil Aviation*.[2] This resolution, while singling out for consideration the terrorist acts that occurred in the United States on September 11, 2001, and, inter alia, recognizing that the new type of threat posed by terrorist organizations requires new concerted efforts and policies of cooperation on the part of states, urged all contracting states to intensify their efforts to achieve the full implementation and enforcement of the multilateral conventions on aviation security, as well as the implementation and enforcement of the ICAO standards and recommended practices and procedures (SARPs) relating to aviation security, to monitor such implementation, and to take within their territories appropriate additional security measures commensurate to the level of threat, in order to prevent and eradicate terrorist acts involving civil aviation. The resolution also urged all contracting states to make contributions in the form of financial or human resources to ICAO's aviation security mechanism, in order to support and strengthen the combat against terrorism and unlawful interference in civil aviation; it called on contracting states to agree on special funding for urgent action by ICAO in the field of aviation security; and it directed the ICAO Council to develop proposals and take appropriate decisions for a more stable funding of ICAO action in the field of aviation security, including appropriate remedial action.

Resolution A33–1 also directed the ICAO Council to convene, at the earliest date, a high-level international ministerial conference on aviation security in Montreal with the objectives of preventing, combating, and eradicating acts of terrorism involving civil aviation; of strengthening ICAO's role in the adoption of SARPs in the field of security and the auditing of their implementation; and of ensuring the necessary financial means to strengthen ICAO's AVSEC mechanism, while providing special funding for urgent action by ICAO in the field of aviation security.

On February 19 and 20, 2002, in keeping with the requirement of Assembly Resolution A33, a high-level ministerial conference on aviation security was held in the headquarters of the International Civil Aviation Organization, Montreal. In the words of Dr. Assad Kotaite, president of the ICAO Council, who opened the conference (and later served as its chairman), the conference was being held "at a critical juncture for civil aviation and for society at large . . . and would review and develop global strategy for strengthening aviation security with the aim of protecting lives both in the air and on the ground, restoring public confidence in air travel and promoting the health of air transport in order that it can renew its vital contribution to the world economy."[3] Dr. Kotaite stated that this was a historic moment in the evolution of civil aviation.

At this conference, attended by member states of the International Civil Aviation Organization, some 714 participants from 154 contracting states and observers from 24 international civil aviation organizations endorsed a global strategy for strengthening aviation security worldwide and issued a public declaration at the conclusion of their two-day meeting.

The conference came to several conclusions and adopted numerous recommendations containing guidance for follow-up action. The conference concluded that the events of September 11, 2001, had had a major negative impact on world economies and an impact on air transport that was unparalleled in history and that the restoration of consumer confidence in air transport and assurance of the long-term health of the air transport industry were both vital, and that many states had already initiated a range of measures to this effect. It was also the view of the conference that the effective application of enhanced uniform security measures, commensurate with the threat, would help to restore confidence in air transport, but these measures would need to be passenger and cargo user friendly and not overly costly for the industry and its consumers if traffic growth was to be regenerated. Accordingly, the conference recommended that consistent with Assembly Resolution A33-1, states should intensify their efforts to achieve the full implementation and enforcement of the multilateral conventions on aviation security as well as of the ICAO standards and recommended practices (SARPs) relating to aviation security, and take within their territories appropriate additional security measures that would be commensurate with the level of threat and cost effective. Since the restoration of confidence in air transport is a collective responsibility, the conference called upon states to enhance international cooperation in aviation security and assist developing countries to the extent that this was possible.

With regard to the compelling need to strengthen aviation security worldwide, the conference concluded that a strong and viable aviation security (AVSEC) program was indispensable and that a uniform global approach to the implementation of the international aviation security standards was essential, while leaving room for operational flexibility. It was also considered useful to establish regional and subregional approaches which could make a significant contribution to ICAO's aviation security activities. The conference concluded that aviation security was a responsibility of contracting states, and states that outsourced aviation security programs should therefore ensure that adequate governmental control and supervision were in place.

The conference also observed that, since gaps and inadequacies appeared to exist in international aviation security instruments with regard to new and emerging threats to civil aviation, further study was needed in this regard. There was a need for a comprehensive ICAO aviation security plan of action for strengthening aviation security, through a reinforced AVSEC mechanism, an ICAO aviation security audit program, technical cooperation projects, and the promotion of aviation security quality control functions and appropriate performance indicators.

Based on the above conclusions, the conference recommended that states should take immediate action to lock flight deck doors for aircraft operated internationally, while maintaining measures on the ground to provide the highest level of aviation security. States were also requested to actively share threat information in accordance with the standards in Annex 17, to employ suitable threat assessment and risk management methodologies appropriate to their circumstances, based on a template to be developed by ICAO, and to ensure that aviation security measures were implemented in an objective and nondiscriminatory manner.

As for ICAO's role in this process, the conference recommended that the organization should develop, as a matter of high priority, amendments to the appropriate annexes to require protection of the flight deck door from forcible intrusion; should continue its efforts to identify and analyze the new and emerging threats to civil aviation with the purpose of assisting in the development of security measures and to actively collaborate with other associated agencies; should carry out a detailed study of the adequacy of the existing aviation security conventions and other aviation security–related documentation with a view to proposing and developing measures to close the existing gaps and remove the inadequacies, including amendments where required, so as to deal effectively with the existing as well as the new and emerging threats to international civil aviation; and should develop and take action to deal with the problem of aviation war risk insurance; and develop and implement a comprehensive aviation security plan of action and take any additional actions approved by the council, including a clear identification of priorities.

One of the key conclusions of the conference was that, in order to further enhance safety and security and to ensure the systematic implementation of the critical elements of a state's aviation security system, there was an urgent need for a comprehensive ICAO program of aviation security audits and that such a program should audit national level and airport level compliance with Annex 17 and with aviation security–related provisions of other annexes on a regular, mandatory, systematic, and harmonized basis. It was the view of the conference that the ability to determine whether an airport or state is in compliance will require that auditors have a solid aviation security background and be sufficiently trained and certified by ICAO to ensure that auditing is conducted in a consistent and objective manner. The conference was strongly convinced that such an audit program should be undertaken under the auspices of ICAO's AVSEC mechanism, which could be guided by proven and successful concepts used in viable programs already developed by the European Civil Aviation Conference (ECAC), the United States, and other states in the development of the framework for a security audit program.

It was considered that the regional approach would have many benefits and was to be considered as supplementary to local initiatives, in particular in promoting regional partnership and the activities of the ICAO regional AVSEC training centers. The AVSEC Panel, which is an instrumentality of the ICAO Council, should assist in the development of the technical requirements and guidance materials needed to administer the audits and assist in the development of an effective quality assurance program to maintain the standards of audit performance; and since an audit program could provide the security levels of audited airports only at the time of the audit, a permanent mechanism based on quality control and the regular conduct of exercises and inspections could guarantee the continuity and improvement of the security levels determined by the audits.

Arguably, the most significant and seminal recommendation of the conference was that ICAO should establish a comprehensive program of universal, regular, mandatory, systematic, and harmonized aviation security audits, with implementation beginning in 2003 based on the final work plan established by the council. It was also decided that, in order to be effective, the program should be based on an audit process that uses ICAO trained and certified audit teams, which are headed by an ICAO staff member and which consistently apply fair and objective methods to determine compliance with Annex 17 by observing measures at airports and assessing the state's capabilities to sustain those measures.

The conference was of the view that of singular importance to the audit process was the need for the audit program to be established under the auspices of ICAO's AVSEC mechanism. It recommended that, in developing the audit program, which should be transparent and autonomous, ICAO should ensure the greatest possible coordination and coherence with audit programs already established at a regional or subregional level, taking into account aviation security situation in these states. For this to become a reality, a compliance mechanism had to be built into the program, a mechanism that would delineate between minor and serious areas of improvement, ensure that immediate corrective action was taken for serious deficiencies and provide to developing states the necessary assistance to measurably improve security.

With regard to funding an aviation security audit program to be run by ICAO, an adequate and stable source of funding was to be sought for the AVSEC mechanism through increased voluntary contributions until such time that an allocation of funds could be sought through the regular program budget, which was envisioned to be as soon as possible. It was recommended that all states be notified of a completed audit, that ICAO headquarters be the repository for full audit reports, and that the sharing of audit reports between states take place on a bilateral or multilateral basis. States were required, under such a program, to commit to provide ICAO with national AVSEC findings based on a harmonized procedure to be developed by ICAO as early as possible. Of course, those states—in particular developing countries—should be provided with technical and financial assistance under technical cooperation, so that they might take remedial actions to rectify the deficiencies identified during the audit. States should also utilize the ICAO audits to the maximum extent possible and could always approach ICAO with regard to the audit findings for other states.

The conference also concluded that, in order to execute the ICAO plan of action, an indicative additional funding requirement was for a minimum of US$ 5.4 million through voluntary contributions for the triennium 2002–2003–2004, these figures to be used as a basis for further study by the council. However, for the longer term a more stable means of funding the ICAO plan of action would be either through an increase of the assessment to the ICAO General Fund for the following triennia, or by a long-term commitment, on a voluntary basis, of systematic contributions according to an approved suggested level of contribution, to be determined by the council, by all states. With regard to the recouping policies of states, the conference observed and confirmed that ICAO's policy and guidance material on the cost recovery of security services at airports in ICAO's *Policies on Charges for Airports and Air Navigation Services* (Doc 9082/6) and the *Airport Economics Manual* (Doc 9562) remained valid, although there was a need for the development of additional policy and guidance material on the cost recovery of security measures with regard to air navigation services, complementary to that which already existed with respect to airport security charges. There was also a need for further improvement of human resources, utilizing the existing training centers and the standardization of instruction materials, where appropriate, based on ICAO's TRAINAIR methodology.

On this basis, states were called upon by the conference to commit to provide adequate resources, financial, human and/or otherwise in kind, for the time being on a voluntary basis through the AVSEC mechanism, for the ICAO plan of action for the triennium 2002–2003–2004 as a matter of priority, and to be aware of the continuing needs for subsequent triennia. They were also called upon to agree to remove the existing ties they individually imposed on the expenditures of AVSEC mechanism contributions in order for ICAO to immediately utilize all funds available in the AVSEC mechanism trust funds. The conference observed that states might wish to use ICAO's technical cooperation program as one of the main instruments to obtain assistance in advancing the implementation of their obligations under relevant international conventions, and the standards and recommended practices (SARPs) of 17—"Security" and related provisions of other annexes, as well as adherence to ICAO guidance material.

As for ICAO's involvement and contribution, the organization was requested to establish an ICAO aviation security follow-up program and seek additional resources, as with the USOAP follow-up program of the Technical Co-operation Bureau, to enable states to obtain technical cooperation in the preparation of necessary documentation and in resource mobilization for aviation security. It was felt that one of the ways in which this could be achieved was by ICAO's promoting the use of the ICAO objectives implementation mechanism as a means for states to obtain technical cooperation, as required for the rectification of deficiencies identified during aviation security evaluations and audits and urgently pursuing the development and implementation of an international financial facility for aviation safety (IFFAS), to encompass not only safety but also security.[4] Another significant function of ICAO was to elaborate on its policy and guidance material on cost recovery of security services, notably to include the development of policy and guidance material on cost recovery, through charges, of security measures with regard to air navigation services and to explore the issue of using security charges as a means of recovering the cost of ICAO assistance provided to states for security development projects.

Postconference Work

In furtherance of the recommendations of the Conference, the ICAO Secretariat initiated an aviation security plan of action which was aimed at reviewing legal instruments, in particular the enhancement of Annex 17—"Security—Safeguarding International Civil Aviation against Acts of Unlawful Interference to the Convention on International Civil Aviation" (the work undertaken by the AVSEC panel and amendment 1010 to Annex 17) and the introduction or strengthening of security-related provisions in other annexes to the convention (Annex 1—"Personnel Licensing," Annex 6—"Operation of Aircraft," Annex 8—"Airworthiness of Aircraft," Annex 9—"Facilitation," Annex 11—"Air Traffic Services," Annex 14—"Aerodromes," and Annex 18—"The Safe Transport of Dangerous Goods by Air"). The plan of action also envisioned reinforcing AVSEC mechanism activities, notably in the preparation of security audits and in undertaking immediate/urgent assistance to states, and expediting work on improving technical specifications relating to and further implementing the use of machine readable travel documents (MRTDs), biometric identification, travel document security, and the improvement of border security systems. The reviewing of certain procedures for air navigation services (PANS) and revision of relevant ICAO manuals and other guidance material including further development of aviation security training packages (ASTPs), training programs, workshops, seminars, and assistance to states through ICAO's technical cooperation program were also on the program of implementation.

At that time, ICAO considered the development and execution of a comprehensive and integrated ICAO AVSEC plan of action as its highest priority. It is no less important to ICAO at the present time. The success of this plan of action was to be measured over a long period as the improvements expected in contracting would require an intensive and continuous worldwide commitment. It was expected that the full and active participation of all contracting states, as well as all technical and deliberative bodies of ICAO, would be essential for the achievement of concrete results within an acceptable period of time.

The aviation security plan of action of ICAO was to focus on the development of new training and guidance material on national quality control (NQC), system testing, auditors, and audit guidelines and forms, with urgent distribution to all states, including the training and certification of international auditors through the existing ICAO aviation security training centers (ASTCs) network, which was to be reinforced and expanded where required. It was also expected to include undertaking universal, mandatory, and regular AVSEC audits to assess the level of implementation and enforcement by states of the SARPs contained in Annex 17, together with the assessment of security measures undertaken, on a sample basis, at airport level for each state. ICAO would maintain an ICAO AVSEC findings database. The creation of aviation security regional units (ASRUs) functionally linked to the AVSEC mechanism, to be urgently implemented in Africa, the Middle East, Eastern Europe, the Americas, and Asia and the Pacific, in order to coordinate the execution of AVSEC mechanism activities and provide direct assistance to states, was also be a feature of the plan.

The seminal consideration regarding ICAO's role in sustaining the aviation industry lies in the mandate of the organization, as contained in Article 44 of the Convention on International Civil Aviation.[5] In this context, ICAO's role throughout the past 63 years has been one of adapting to the trends as civil aviation has gone through three distinct phases of metamorphosis. The first phase was the modernist era that prevailed when the Convention on International Civil Aviation was signed at Chicago on December 7, 1944, an era centered on state sovereignty[6] and the widely accepted postwar view that the development of international civil aviation could greatly help to create and preserve friendship and understanding among the nations and peoples of the world, yet that its abuse could become a threat to general security.[7] This essentially modernist philosophy focused on the importance of the state as the ultimate sovereign authority, which could overrule considerations of international community welfare if they clashed with the domestic interests of the state. This gave way, in the 1960s and 1970s, to a postmodernist era of recognition of the individual as a global citizen whose interests in public international law were considered paramount over considerations of individual state interests.

The September 11, 2001, events led to a new era that calls for a neo-postmodernist approach. This approach, as has been demonstrably seen after the events of September 11, 2001, admits of social elements and corporate interests being involved with states in an overall effort at securing world peace and security. The role of ICAO in this process is critical, since the organization is charged with regulating for safe and economic air transportation within the broad parameters of the air transport industry. The industry remains an integral element of commercial and social interactivity and a tool that could be used by the world community to forge closer interactivity between the people of the world.

In the above sense, ICAO's initiatives in the fields of aviation security in the immediate aftermath of the September 11 events have not been mere reactive responses but a visionary striving to ensure the future sustainability of the industry. Of course, this responsibility should not devolve upon ICAO alone. ICAO's regulatory responsibility can only be fulfilled through active regulatory participation by states.

SECURITY MEASURES AND SECURITY CULTURE

A Risk-Based Approach to Security

It must also be noted that a new dimension in the sabotage of aviation is damage caused by the hostile use of dirty bombs, electromagnetic pulse devices, or biochemical materials. Dirty bombs are devices that cause damage through nuclear detonation involving the spread of radioactivity to undetermined areas.[8] In recent years, man-portable air defense systems (MANPADS) have posed a serious threat to aviation security.

Studies have shown that stringent measures, when adopted against a particular type of crime belonging to a generic group (such as hijacking in the spectrum of unlawful interference against civil aviation), would be effective enough to reduce that particular type of crime. However, such measures might give rise to increase in other forms of crime belonging to that generic group. Called the spillover effect, this pattern has applied to civil aviation, as seen in the decrease in offences against aircraft after the events of September 11, 2001.

In order for basic strategies to be employed to prevent crime and to combat crime when prevention is impossible, crime prevention strategies adopt two methods of combating crime. The first method is to prevent or stop potential criminal acts. The second method is to apprehend and punish anyone who commits a criminal act. These methods follow the philosophy that the prevention of crime can be achieved by increasing the probability of apprehension and applying severe penal sanction to a crime. For example, the installation of metal detectors at airports increases the probability of detecting and apprehending potential hijackers or saboteurs. Theoretically the high risk of being apprehended decreases the potential threat, and the stringent penal sanction that may apply consequent to such apprehension compounds the ominous quality of the preventive means taken.

At the 36th Session of the ICAO Assembly (Montreal, September 18–28, 2007), a resolution. was adopted, addressing a consolidated statement of continuing ICAO policies related to the safeguarding of international civil aviation against acts of unlawful interference. The assembly took note, inter alia, of the August 2006 threat to civil aviation operations posed by an alleged terrorist plot against civil aircraft over the North Atlantic that would have involved the component parts of an improvised explosive device including a homemade liquid explosive, being taken through the passenger and cabin baggage security checkpoint for assembly airside, probably on the aircraft. The resolution recognizes new and emerging threats posed to aviation security, including those posed by the use of aircraft as a weapon of destruction, the targeting of aircraft by MANPADS, and other surface-to-air missile systems, light weapons and rocket-propelled grenades, unlawful seizure of aircraft, attacks on facilities and other acts of unlawful interference against civil aviation, acts aimed at the destruction of aircraft by carrying on board liquids, gels, and aerosols as component parts of an improvised explosive device, acts aimed at using the aircraft as a weapon of destruction, and the unlawful seizure of aircraft.

The resolution also notes that attacks on aviation facilities and other acts of unlawful interference against civil aviation have a serious adverse effect on the safety, efficiency, and regularity of international civil aviation, endangering the lives of persons on board and on the ground and undermining the confidence of the peoples of the world in the safety of international civil aviation.

It therefore concludes that all acts of unlawful interference against international civil aviation constitute a grave offence in violation of international law.

MANPADS

It is evident that various global security measures have been taken since 2001. It is also clear that, in general terms, aviation security should be centered on identifying new and emergent threats to aviation and the attendant adoption of a risk-based approach. One of the ominous threats is the use MANPADS to destroy or damage aircraft in flight. As a result of the various security measures taken by the international community following the events of September 11, 2001. to strengthen aircraft against attacks on them,[9] attacks against aircraft, although still posing a threat, are not as prolific, having given way to attacks against facilities such as airports and allied service providers.[10] Generally, however, perceived threats to civil aviation remain hijacking of aircraft; aviation sabotage, such as the causing of explosions in aircraft on the ground and in flight; missile attacks against aircraft; armed attacks on passengers, airports, and other aviation-related property; and the illegal carriage of narcotics by air and its criminal ramifications. These threats are by no means new.[11]

MANPADS are extremely effective weapons that are widely available worldwide. Introduced in the 1950s and originally meant to deter terror attacks from air to ground and meant to be used by state authorities and other protection agencies, these weapons have gotten into the wrong hands and are being used against civil and military aviation. The surface-to-air MANPAD is a light weapon that offers very little warning before impact, and is often destructive and lethal.[12] MANPADS are cheap, and easily carried, handled, and concealed. It is claimed that there are at least 100,000 and possibly in excess of 500,000 systems in inventories around the world, and several thousands of these are vulnerable to theft from state authorities.[13] It is also claimed that there is a 70 percent chance that a civil aircraft will be destroyed if hit by a MANPAD.[14] A study conducted and published in early 2005 by the Rand Corporation concludes that, based on the effects of the attacks of September 11, 2001, it is likely for air travel in the United States to fall by 15 to 20 percent after a successful MANPADS attack on a commercial airliner in the United States.[15] The international aviation community is aware that civil aircraft are particularly vulnerable to handheld ground-to-air missiles and that susceptibility avoidance techniques (calculated to avoid being hit) and vulnerability avoidance (survival after being hit) systems must be in place. This is particularly so since tracking the proliferation of MANPADS is difficult, as any intelligence gathered on this particular threat is usually ex post facto, through the recovery of launchers or fragments from expended missiles. Contrary to popular belief, the MANPAD is highly durable and can be used several years after inactivity, with recharged batteries.

The world's attention was further drawn to the deadly threat posed by MANPADS in November 2002, when there was an unsuccessful attempt to bring down a civilian aircraft leaving Mombasa, Kenya. Over the past 35 years, significant developments have taken place in dangerous weapons systems, creating more opportunities for terrorists. The ready acceptance of new technologies by the international community and our growing dependence on them have created many targets, such as nuclear and civil aircraft in flight. Similarly, developments in electronics and microelectronics, and the trend toward miniaturization and simplification have resulted in a greater availability of tactical weapons with longer ranges and more accuracy that are also simpler to operate. One of the most effective developments in individual weaponry is portable, precision-guided munitions (PGMs), which are lightweight and easy to operate. They can usually be carried and operated by a single person. The U.S.-made Stinger, the British-made Blowpipe, and the Russian-made SA-7 missiles are examples of these smaller weapons. These are shoulder-fired, antiaircraft missiles with infrared, heat-seeking sensors that guide the projectile to the heat emitted from an aircraft engine. It is known that more than 60 states possess SA-7 missiles and there is no doubt that most of them maintain strict security measures to prevent the outflow of the weapons. However, it has been alleged that some states, including Libya, have supplied PGMs to terrorist organizations. It is incontrovertible that in the hands of terrorists these missiles are not likely to be used against conventional targets such as tanks and military fighter aircraft. Of particular concern is the prospect of civilian airliners being shot at by surface-to-air missiles (SAMs) and antitank rockets as they land at or take off from airports.[16] Dr. Richard Clutterbuck summarizes the great threat of missile attacks:

Recent years have seen increasing use of expensive and sophisticated surface-to-surface and surface-to-air missiles (SSM and SAM) by terrorists, generally of Russian or East European origin and redirected by Arab Governments, notably Colonel Gadafi's. Continuing development of these weapons for use by regular armies will ensure that new and more efficient versions will become available for terrorists.[17]

With increased airport security, placing explosive devices on civil aircraft is becoming more difficult, but now the same destructive result can be achieved far more easily by using modern missiles or rockets.

United Nations (UN) General Assembly Resolution 58/241, on the illicit trade in small arms and light weapons in all its aspects, started the process that led to the adoption, on December 8, 2005, of the International Instrument to Enable States to Identify and Trace, in a Timely and Reliable Manner, Illicit Small Arms and Light Weapons. For the purpose of this instrument, "small arms and light weapons" mean any man-portable lethal weapon that expels or launches, is designed to expel or launch, or may be readily converted to expel or launch a shot, bullet or projectile by the action of an explosive, excluding antique small arms and light weapons or other replicas.

The purpose of this instrument is to enable states to identify and trace, in a timely and reliable manner, illicit small arms and light weapons. The purpose is also to promote and facilitate international cooperation and assistance in marking and tracing the illicit trade in small arms and light weapons, and to enhance the effectiveness of, and complement, existing bilateral, regional, and international agreements to prevent, combat, and eradicate this trade in all its aspects.

For the purpose of identifying and tracing illicit small arms and light weapons, at the time of manufacture of each small arm or light weapon under their jurisdiction or control, states will be required to maintain a unique marking, in order to permit identification by all states of the country of manufacture. States will also ensure that accurate and comprehensive records are established for all marked small arms and light weapons within their territory. States should also maintain the manufacturing records for at least 30 years, and all other records, including records of import and export, for at least 20 years.

The instrument contains a number of provisions relating to cooperation in tracing, which is defined as "systematic tracking of illicit small arms and light weapons found or seized on the territory of a State from the point of manufacture or the point of importation through the lines of supply to the point at which they became illicit." The instrument calls upon contracting states to consider rendering technical, financial, and other assistance in building national capacity in the areas of marking, record keeping, and tracing in order to support the effective implementation of this instrument by states. It also encourages initiatives, within the framework of the United Nations Program of Action to Prevent and Eradicate the Illicit Trade in Small Arms and Light Weapons in All Its Aspects, that mobilize the resources and expertise of, and where appropriate cooperation with, relevant regional and international organizations to promote the implementation of this instrument by states.

The United Nations General Assembly, on September 8, 2006, adopted a counterterrorism strategy that is , a unique global instrument to enhance national, regional, and international efforts to counter terrorism. The strategy emphasizes the need to combat the illicit arms trade, in particular the trade in small arms and light weapons, including MANPADS. Member states have agreed to a common strategic approach to fighting terrorism, not only by sending a clear message that terrorism is unacceptable but also resolving to take practical steps individually and collectively to prevent and combat it. These steps include a wide range of measures ranging from strengthening state capacity to counter terrorist threats to better coordinating the UN system's counterterrorism activities.

In order to strengthen joint efforts to counter the threat to civil aviation operations posed by MANPADS, the Asia-Pacific Economic Cooperation (APEC) organization, the Organization of American States (OAS), the Organization for Security and Cooperation in Europe (OSCE), and individual states have taken a number of initiatives such as the holding of seminars, workshops, and special meetings, the development of guidelines on control and security of MANPADS, and the exchange of information.

The Diverse Nature of Missile Attacks

The use of SAMs and antitank rockets by terrorists goes back to 1973. On September 5, 1973 Italian police arrested five Middle Eastern terrorists armed with SA-7s. The terrorists had rented an apartment under the flight path leading to Rome's Fiumicino Airport and were planning to shoot down an El Al airliner coming in to land at the airport.[18] These arrests proved a considerable embarrassment to Egypt, because the SA-7s were later traced back to a batch supplied to that country by the USSR. It was alleged that the Egyptian government was supplying some missiles to the Libyan army but inexplicably, the SA-7s had been directly rerouted to the terrorists. This incident also placed the USSR in an awkward position because its new missile and its proxy use of surrogate warfare against democratic states were revealed to the West.[19]

The plot of the missile attack on El Al derived from an appalling incident on February 21, 1973, when a Libyan B-727 was shot down over the Sinai Desert by an Israeli fighter, killing the 108 innocent people on board.[20] The Libyan people called for vengeance against Israel. Libya urged the other Arab states to send their warplanes against Israel's major cities and to destroy Israeli airliners wherever they could be found.[21]

On January 5, 1974, 220 soldiers and 200 police officers sealed off five square miles around Heathrow International airport in London after receiving reports that terrorists had smuggled SA-7s into Britain in the diplomatic pouches of Middle Eastern embassies and were planning to shoot down an El Al airliner.[22]

Another significant incident occurred on January 13, 1975, when an attempt by terrorists to shoot down an El Al plane with a missile was believed to have brought civil aviation to the brink of disaster. Two terrorists drove their car onto the apron at Orly Airport, where they set up a rocket launcher and fired at an El Al airliner that was about to take off for New York with 136 passengers. The first round missed the target, thanks to the pilot's evasive action, and hit the fuselage of a Yugoslav DC-9 airplane waiting nearby to embark passengers for Zagreb. The rocket failed to explode and no serious casualties were reported. After firing again and hitting an administration building, which caused some damage, the terrorists escaped by car. A phone call from an individual claiming responsibility for the attack was received by Reuters. The caller clearly implied that there would be another such operation, saying, "Next time we will hit the target."

In fact, six days later another dramatic though unsuccessful attempt did occur at Orly airport. The French authorities traced the attack to Carlos, the Venezuelan PFLP terrorist and leader of the PFLP group in Europe.[23] It is also known that once again an El Al airliner had been deliberately chosen as a target by Gadafi in an attempt to avenge the loss of the Libyan airliner shot down by Israel over the Sinai Desert.[24]

Despite there failures, on January 25, 1976 another abortive attempt made by three PFLP terrorists, who were arrested by Kenyan police at Nairobi Airport—following a tip-off by Israeli intelligence to the Kenyan General Service Unit—before they had time to fire SA-7 missiles at an El Al aircraft carrying 100 passengers. In connection with this operation, two members of the German Baader-Meinhoff Faction, Thomas Reuter and Brigitte Schultz, were also arrested. After 10 days of interrogation, the terrorists were handed over to Israel by the Kenyan government. However, it was not until March 1977, 14 months after the arrests in Kenya, that the Israelis officially announced that they were holding the three Palestinian and two German terrorists. During this period, an unsuccessful attempt to gain their release was undertaken by the PFLP in June 1976, when Palestinian terrorists hijacked an Air France aircraft to Entebbe. The names of the five being held in Israel were included on the list of prisoners whose release was demanded in exchange for the hostages. The three Palestinians were released by the Israeli government in 1985.[25]

There has been a marked increase in missile attacks since 1984. On September 21, 1984, Afghan counterrevolutionaries fired a surface-to-air missile and hit a DC-10 Ariana Airliner carrying 308 passengers. The explosion tore through the aircraft's left engine, damaging its hydraulic system and a wing containing a fuel tank. The captain of the aircraft, however, managed to land the aircraft safely at Kabul International Airport.[26] Another significant incident took place on April 4, 1985, when a member of the Abu Nidal group fired an RPG rocket at an Alia airliner as it took off from Athens Airport. Although the rocket did not explode, it left a hole in the fuselage.[27]

Advanced missiles and rockets can be found in many terrorist and insurgent armories. It is suspected that some terrorist organizations, including Iranian militia in Lebanon, the Provisional Irish Republican Army, and various African and Latin American insurgents, possess the sophisticated Russian-made RPG-7 portable rocket launcher, but it is disturbing to note that some terrorist organizations, most notably Palestinian groups, have their own RPG-7-manufacturing facilities. In addition, more than a dozen other terrorist and insurgent groups are known to possess portable surface-to-air missiles, These groups include various Cuban surrogates, Colombian drug dealers, and a number of African, European, and Palestinian terrorist organizations.[28]

The possibility of the undeterred use of missiles may be encouraged by the rapid proliferation of such weapons and the publicity to be gained by using them. The enhanced effectiveness of missiles against aircraft makes the threat of such attacks real.

Installation of an Antimissile System

The installation of a sophisticated antimissile system similar to that employed on military aircraft to divert surface-to-air missiles is an effective deterrent. One good example is the measure taken by the British government, which, immediately after the discovery of 20 SA-7s in the coaster *Eksund*, which was intercepted by French authorities off the coast of Brittany in November 1987 when bound for a rendezvous with the IRA, fitted all British Army helicopters flying in Northern Ireland with electronic and other decoy systems to confuse the missile's heat-seeking guidance system. These systems included the U.S.-made Saunders, AN/ALG 144. This system, when linked to the Tracor AN/ALE 40 chaff dispenser, works by jamming the missile's homing radar and sending infrared flares and chaff to act as a decoy for the heat-seeking device.[29] The system is used by both the U.S. and the Israeli armies, which have been well pleased with its performance. Until the British realized that the IRA might be in possession of SAMs, the Ministry of Defence hesitated to install such a system because of the high cost involved, and its decision to do so shows the seriousness of the threat. Another example of a good countermeasure is the response of El Al to the threat of such an attack, which included the installation of electronic countermeasure equipment similar to that employed on military aircraft to divert surface-to-air missiles.[30] However, the problem is that these countermeasures are not yet fully effective, although they could minimize the threat. Hence there is a need to proceed diligently with the development of systems that are guaranteed to prevent this type of attack against civil aviation.

The Perimeter Guard

For a successful missile attack against aircraft, the firing position has to be located within range of the flight path. A missile's guidance system is such that the weapon has to be fired within a few degrees of the flight path if the infrared sensor is to locate the target. Accordingly, a possible preventive measure would be to prevent terrorists from getting into a firing position with their missiles. However, it would be very difficult to cut off areas of up to 6 km wide that lie in the paths of aircraft as they land and take off. This measure is therefore impracticable if not impossible.[31] This difficulty can be overcome to an extent by patrolling the outer areas of airports in times of stringent security conditions. Even in times when no specific threat has been received, it is within the capacity of most states to monitor those strips of land from which a SAM could be launched and thus minimize the risk. At the same time, these security operations would deter terrorists from spending vital resources on buying SAMs given the limited possibilities for their use.

Although the success rate so far of Western states in preventing terrorist missile attacks against civil aviation is satisfactory, and security forces, with the help of good intelligence, have been successful in tracking down and capturing missiles before they could be used, it is not unlikely that there will be attempts to use surface-to-air missiles to attack civil aviation in the near future. As some targets are becoming more difficult for terrorists to attack, it can be anticipated that they will make efforts to overcome the enhanced security systems as well as redirecting their efforts toward less secure targets. The displacement of the increasingly ineffective system of hijacking by missile attacks against civil aviation is a real threat.

INTERNATIONAL ACCORD

In April 1996 in Vienna, state representatives of the "New Forum" held a plenary meetingto confirm the Wassenaar Arrangement,[32] earlier agreed upon in the city of Wassenaar, the Netherlands, which addresses the risks to regional and international security related to the spread of conventional weapons and dual-use goods and technologies while preventing destabilizing accumulations of weapons such as MANPADS. The Wassenaar Arrangement complements and reinforces, without duplicating, the existing control regimes for weapons of mass destruction and their delivery systems, as well as other internationally recognized measures designed to promote transparency and greater responsibility, by focusing on the threats to international and regional peace and security that may arise from transfers of armaments and sensitive dual-use goods and technologies where the risks are judged greatest. It is also calculated to enhance cooperation in order to prevent the acquisition of armaments and sensitive dual-use items for military end uses, if the situation in a region or the conduct of a state is or becomes a cause for serious concern to the participating states. It is not the intent and purpose of the arrangement to be directed against any state or group of states, nor will it impede bona fide civil transactions. Furthermore, it will not interfere with the rights of states to acquire legitimate means with which to defend themselves pursuant to Article 51 of the Charter of the United Nations.[33] The arrangement allows for participating states to control all the items set forth in a list of dual-use goods and technologies with the objective of preventing unauthorized transfers or retransfers of those items. Participating states also agree to exchange general information on the risks associated with transfers of conventional arms and dual-use goods and technologies in order to consider, where necessary, the scope for coordinating national control policies to combat the risks involved. At the tenth plenary meeting of the Wassenaar Arrangement, held in Vienna on December 8–9, 2004, participating states reaffirmed their intent and resolve to prevent the acquisition by unauthorized persons of conventional arms and dual-use goods and technologies, in particular by terrorist groups and organizations. States also exchanged information on various national measures adopted to implement the provisions of the arrangement.

The Wassenaar Arrangement is the first global multilateral arrangement on export controls concerning conventional weapons and sensitive dual-use goods and technologies. It has not been given the conventional term, "convention" or "agreement," but nonetheless carries the agreement of participating states to collaborate in complementing, without duplicating, existing regimes on the nonproliferation of weapons of mass destruction and their delivery systems. The Wassenaar Arrangement is not a treaty in the sense of Article 102 of the United Nations Charter,[34] nor is it a treaty as defined by the Vienna Convention on the Law of Treaties of 1969, Article 2 of which defines a treaty inter alia as an international agreement concluded between states in written form and governed by international law. However, it remains an agreement between sovereign states concerning the implementation of the internal law of each participating state. This does not, however, mean that the Wassenaar Arrangement cannot be considered an international agreement or that it is invalid. It merely means that the arrangement does not come within the purview of the Vienna Convention. It is worthy of note that Article 3 of that convention explicitly recognizes that international agreements between states do not lose their validity merely because they do not come within the ambit of the convention.[35]

As mentioned earlier, the ICAO Assembly,[36] at its 36th Session (Montreal, September 18–28, 2007), adopted Resolution A36, in which the assembly expressed its deep concern regarding the global threat posed to civil aviation by terrorist acts, in particular the threat posed by MANPADS, other surface-to-air missiles systems, light weapons, and rocket propelled grenades.

The assembly noted that the United Nations General Assembly, on September 8, 2006, adopted a counterterrorism strategy. The Assembly recalled United Nations General Assembly resolutions 61/66 on the illicit trade in small arms and light weapons in all its aspects, 60/77 on the prevention of the illicit transfer and unauthorized access to and use of man-portable air defense systems, 61/71 on assistance to states for curbing the illicit traffic in small arms and light weapons and collecting them and 60/288 on the UN's global counterterrorism strategy. It also noted the International Instrument to Enable States to Identify and Trace, in a Timely and Reliable Manner, Illicit Small Arms and Light Weapons (A/60/88) and the Wassenaar Arrangement on Export Controls for Conventional Arms and Dual-Use Goods and Technologies, Elements for Export Controls of MANPADS, and the Inter-American Convention against the Illicit Manufacturing of and Trafficking in Firearms, Ammunition, Explosives, and other Related Material:

Noting with satisfaction the ongoing efforts of other international and regional organizations aimed at developing a more comprehensive and coherent response to the threat to civil aviation posed by MANPADS; and [recognizing] that the specific threat posed by MANPADS requires a comprehensive approach and responsible policies on the part of States.

The assembly urged all contracting states to take the necessary measures to exercise strict and effective controls on the import, export, transfer or re-transfer, and stockpile management of MANPADS and associated training and technologies, as well as limiting the transfer of MANPADS production capabilities. It called upon all contracting states to cooperate at the international, regional, and subregional levels with a view to enhancing and coordinating international efforts aimed at implementing countermeasures carefully chosen with regard to their effectiveness and cost, and combating the threat posed by MANPADS. Furthermore, the assembly called upon all contracting states to take the necessary measures to ensure the destruction of nonauthorized MANPADS in their territory as soon as possible, while urging all contracting states to implement the international instruments to enable states to identify and trace, in a timely and reliable manner, illicit small arms and light weapons as referred to in United Nations General Assembly Resolution 61/66. All contracting states were urged to apply the principles defined in the Elements for Export Controls of MANPADS of the Wassenaar Arrangement. Finally, the assembly directed the ICAO Council to request the secretary general to monitor on an ongoing basis the threat to civil aviation posed by MANPADS and to continuously develop appropriate countermeasures to this threat and periodically request contracting states to inform the organization regarding the status of implementation of the resolution and the measures taken to meet its requirements.

Other Current Threats

Security restrictions on the carriage of liquids, aerosols, and gels (LAGs) in hand baggage were introduced on August 10, 2006, in response to the foiling of an alleged terrorist plot in the United Kingdom against aviation using improvised explosive devices containing homemade liquid explosives. An initial ban on the carriage of all hand baggage on flights leaving the United Kingdom was subsequently modified to a restriction on the amounts of LAGs that were permitted to be carried by passengers through screening points. These restrictions were adopted elsewhere in Europe and in North America. They were subsequently harmonized within the European Union by an amendment to the European Commission regulations, which came into effect on November 6, 2006.

As a global follow-up to these measures, ICAO recommended their universal adoption (no later than March 1, 2007) in a state letter. ICAO also reacted to the new threat with urgency and efficiency, calling a special meeting of the council on August 17, 2006 to explore ways of countering the new threat. As the international civil aviation industry attaches great importance to the security screening of liquids, many countries have made great efforts to study methods to detect liquids. At present and for the near future, the most effective and the safest method is a combination of regular measures, such as X-ray screening, visual examination, inspection by removing bottle lids, restrictions on carrying liquids, and so forth. ICAO temporary security control guidelines provide a uniform operation mode for liquids screening, which is helpful to the unification of international civil aviation security standards.

Bioterrorism

A bioterrorism attack is the deliberate release of viruses, bacteria, or other agents used to cause illness or death in people, animals, or plants. These agents are typically found in nature, but it is possible that they could be changed to increase their ability to cause disease, make them resistant to current medicines, or increase their ability to be spread into the environment. Biological agents can be spread through the air, through water, or in food. Terrorists may use biological agents because they can be extremely difficult to detect and do not cause illness for several hours to several days. While some bioterrorism agents, such as the smallpox virus, can be spread from person to person, some agents such as anthrax are incapable of being so spread.

There have been several noteworthy instances of bioterrorism in the past,[37] even as early as 1915,[38] which send an ominous message that it is a distinct possibility in the aviation context. Until recently in the United States, most biological defense strategies have been geared to protecting soldiers on the battlefield rather than looking after ordinary people in cities. In 1999, the University of Pittsburgh's Center for Biomedical Informatics deployed the first automated bioterrorism detection system, called RODS (Real-Time Outbreak Disease Surveillance). RODS is designed to draw collect data from many data sources and use them to perform signal detection, that is, to detect a possible bioterrorism event at the earliest possible moment. RODS, and other similar systems, collect data from various sources including clinical data, laboratory data, and data from over-the-counter drug sales. In 2000, Michael Wagner, the codirector of the RODS laboratory, and Ron Aryel, a subcontractor, conceived of the idea of obtaining live data feeds from "nontraditional" (non–health care) data sources. The RODS laboratory's efforts eventually led to the establishment of the National Retail Data Monitor, a system that collects data from 20,000 retail locations nationwide.

On February 5, 2002, President Bush visited the RODS laboratory and used it as a model for a $300 million spending proposal to equip all 50 states with biosurveillance systems. In a speech, Bush compared the RODS system to a modern "DEW" line (referring to the Cold War ballistic missile early warning system).

The principles and practices of biosurveillance, a new interdisciplinary science, were defined and described in a handbook published in 2006.[39] Data that could potentially assist in the early detection of a bioterrorism event include many categories of information. Health-related data such as those collected from hospital computer systems, clinical laboratories, electronic health record systems, medical examiner record-keeping systems, 911 call center computers, and veterinary medical record systems could be of help in the fight against bioterrorism. Researchers are also considering the utility of data generated by ranching and feedlot operations, food processors, drinking water systems, school attendance recording, and physiological monitors, among others. Intuitively, one would expect systems that collect more than one type of data to be more useful than systems that collect only one type of information (such as single-purpose laboratory or 911 call-center based systems) and be less prone to false alarms. This indeed appears to be the case.

The inherently uncontrollable nature of dangerous pathogens makes bioterrorism unattractive as a warfare strategy. However, the potential power of genetic engineering cannot be marginalized or underestimated, and the compelling need for continuing vigilance cannot be ignored.

Intelligence Gathering

The gathering of reliable intelligence remains the first line of defense. Although modern technologies clearly aid terrorists in terms of weapons and targets, technology can also be used against terrorists. Governments that are endowed with the necessary technology can keep track of terrorist organizations and their movements with the aid of computers. At the same time, electronic collection methods and signals intelligence afford the possibility of eavesdropping on and intercepting terrorist communications, leading to better predictions of their operations. One of the instances in which intelligence gathering has worked well to prevent terrorism occurred in September 1984, when the Provisional IRA spent an estimated £1.5 million in the United States on a massive shipment of seven tons of arms. With the help of an informer who warned about a forthcoming shipment of weapons, including rockets, to the Provisional IRA from the United States, the FBI informed British intelligence, which in turn contacted the Irish, and the ship carrying the arms was tracked by a U.S. satellite orbiting 300 km above the earth. The satellite photographed the transfer of the arms to a trawler. Finally, two Irish naval vessels intercepted the trawler, and British security forces arrested the crew.[40] This incident shows that intelligence gathering with the help of high technology can cut off the transfer of missiles and other weapons to terrorists.

A Risk-Based Approach?

Intelligence and the likelihood of an attack are central elements of risk management. However, the need to introduce more risk assessment is driven in part by the passenger hassle factor. The hassle factor is making air travel increasingly unpopular and contradicting the very aim of Article 22 of the

Chicago Convention, which aims to preserve the speed and convenience of air travel ("to prevent unnecessary delays to aircraft, crews, passengers, and cargo"). The need to introduce more risk assessment is also driven by increased costs for security measures and for related equipment and technology. In this context, all stakeholders in the system, that is, governments, airlines, airports, and passengers, have an interest in reflecting on how best to decide which possible measures can be introduced, and what their respective impacts, both positive and negative, are likely to be across the board.

A key principle leading toward more risk-based security is the idea that addressing all risks at the same level, regardless of their severity, is actually less efficient than concentrating the bigger part of one's resources on the most severe risks. Like everything, air transport operates in a context of limited resources, be they financial, infrastructural, or other (availability of trained staff, and so forth). In this context, and in the interest of better security, governments must carefully weigh the options that present themselves to them, and make the right decisions. The primary role of the authorities must be to centralize intelligence and threat information. Airlines are major interested parties and need to be informed in good time. Assessing and prioritizing the different risks is a typical government duty. A certain risk can be addressed or mitigated by a number of possible measures. Here the role of governments should be to assess which of these options will have the least impact on industry and passengers. This impact can be operational as well as financial.

Security management systems, particularly when applied to air carriers, provide an effective tool that would ensure a risk-based approach to aviation security. Within a security risk management environment, consideration is given to threats that are often ill defined, constantly evolving, and the result of deliberate and intentional actions. In addition, specific security threats must be considered unpredictable and likely to be indiscriminate in nature. For example, while the intelligence and law enforcement agencies involved in preventing terrorist activity may uncover information suggesting pending attacks, it is necessary and prudent to assume that they may not be able to identify and stop all possible threats all of the time.

Security measures must also be capable of being strengthened quickly at any time as a result of increased levels of security risk. In addition, by virtue of their nature, they are usually highly visible and intrusive and often conflict with passenger and air cargo facilitation needs that require ready access to facilities and services to expedite the process of air transportation. This is not the case with the vast majority of controls in a safety environment. These factors require recognition and assessment when specific preventative security controls and associated regulatory standards are considered and developed. Recognizing these factors, the need exists for an integrated systems managed approach within various organizations, at both regulatory and industry levels, that have responsibilities relating to the delivery of safety and security outcomes. Such an approach has the ability to offer a range of benefits, including the integration of existing organizational quality management systems into a comprehensive and aligned organizational structure and culture that ensures a more cohesive and standardized approach to how security processes should be implemented with overall better and more uniform standards of service delivery.

The introduction into existing processes, at both regulatory and industry levels, of effective risk assessment activity that can contribute to making security processes proactive and targeted, and therefore potentially more efficient and effective without unduly impacting on export trade and passenger movements, is certainly a proactive measure in a risk-based approach. Additionally, in order for air carriers to successfully implement security event management systems (SEMS) within their operations, it is paramount that states endorse this approach as being in compliance with the security requirements of ICAO Annex 17—"Security" as well as with individual regulators. States are also encouraged to draft regulations based on the desired outcome or standard rather than prescribe actual procedures that are necessary to be in compliance. Allowing flexibility to those entities responsible for the implementation of security measures to meet the stated standards in the best possible way will lead to a more effective and efficient use of resources.

Outcome- or performance-based regulations also facilitate the quality control oversight that a state needs to exercise on various stakeholders by limiting the oversight responsibility to ensuring that the security standards are met, without focusing on the particulars of the procedures. Finally, in order to ensure better co-operation, it is paramount that contracting states recognize various methods by which to meet security standards if an overall improved security environment is to be achieved. Mutual acceptability of security procedures prevents the mandating of security procedures extraterritorially, all the while ensuring that the same level of security is achieved globally.

The ICAO Security Audits

On the basis of Assembly Resolution A33–1 adopted in 2001 and the recommendations of the high-level ministerial conference on aviation security (Montreal, February 2002), the council adopted in June 2002 its Aviation Security Plan of Action, which included the establishment of a comprehensive program of regular, mandatory, systematic, and harmonized audits to be carried out by ICAO in all contracting states. The ICAO Universal Security Audit Program (USAP) was subsequently launched, with the objective that all contracting states should have benefited from an initial audit by the end of 2007.

Since the launch of the USAP in 2002, 169 aviation security audits and 77 follow-up missions have been conducted.[41] The audits have proven to be instrumental in the ongoing identification and resolution of aviation security concerns, and analysis reveals that the average implementation rate of Annex 17 standards in most states has increased markedly between the period of the initial audit and the follow-up mission.

A critical part of the audit process is the requirement that all audited states submit a corrective action plan to address deficiencies identified during an audit. As directed by the council, all states are notified (by state letter and on the USAP secure Web site) of those states that are more than 60 days late in submitting a corrective action plan. As of July 31, 2007, there were seven states that were more than 60 days late. In the case of late corrective action plans, repeated reminders are sent to states, including reminders at the level of the secretary general and with the involvement of the applicable regional office, and ICAO assistance is offered should the state require advice or support in the preparation of its action plan. Extensive feedback is provided to each audited state on the adequacy of its corrective action plan, and an ongoing dialogue is maintained where necessary to provide support in the implementation of proposed actions.

ICAO performs comprehensive analysis of audit results on levels of compliance with Annex 17—"Security" standards on an ongoing basis (globally, by region, and by subject matter). This statistical data is made available to authorized users on the USAP secure Web site and is shared with other relevant ICAO offices as a basis for prioritizing training and remedial assistance projects. As of July 31, 2007, 77 follow-up missions had been conducted. These missions take place two years after the initial audit with the purpose of validating the implementation of state corrective action plans and providing support to states in remedying deficiencies. These missions are normally conducted by the applicable regional office, with close coordination through headquarters. The results of the follow-up visits indicate that the majority of states have made significant progress in the implementation of their corrective action plans.

A high-level ICAO Secretariat Audit Results Review Board (ARRB) has been established as part of a coordinated strategy for working with states that are found to have significant compliance shortcomings with respect to ICAO standards and recommended practices (SARPs). The ARRB both examines the safety and security histories of specific states and also provides an internal advisory forum for coordination among ICAO's safety, security, and assistance programs.

As future measures in the audit program of ICAO, the ICAO Council in 2007 approved the practice that not all states need to be audited at the same frequency, although the USAP should always preserve the principle of universality. The council was of the view that, with a solid baseline of audit results established for all states by the end of 2007, a more effective use of resources could be achieved by developing an appropriate scheduling/frequency model to determine the priority of future audits and frequency of visits to states. It remains a requirement, however, that the principle of universality will be maintained, with all states audited at least once within a six-year period.

Another decision of the council was that future audits under the USAP should be expanded to include relevant security-related provisions of Annex 9–"Facilitation." With the recent expansion of the universal audit program to a comprehensive systems approach covering all safety-related annexes, Annex 9 is currently the only annex not included in either of ICAO's two audit programs. There are a number of security-related provisions contained in Annex 9, particularly as related to the security and integrity of travel documentation, which can be audited under the USAP along with the related standards of Annex 17.

The council also decided that wherever possible, ICAO aviation security audits should be focused on a state's capability to provide appropriate national oversight of its aviation security activities. Using the results of the initial audits and follow-up visits, the scope of future ICAO audits should be adjusted to the prevailing situation in each audited state. Those states that have demonstrated the national infrastructure necessary to oversee security activities at their airports may undergo a targeted oversight audit to verify adequate implementation of the state's national quality control program. Such oversight audits would continue to include a verification of the implementation of ICAO provisions through spot checks at the airport level.

The ICAO USAP has been implemented on schedule and within its budget allocation. The audits have proven to be instrumental in the identification of aviation security concerns and in providing recommendations for their resolution. From its inception, the USAP has enjoyed the support of contracting states and is promoting positive change as states become increasingly sensitized to the international requirements. The USAP follow-up missions have shown a markedly increased level of implementation of ICAO security standards, attesting to states' commitment to achieving the objective of the USAP, to strengthen aviation security worldwide.

CONCLUSION

A security culture, if such were to exist among ICAO's member states, would mean that the states would be aware of their rights and duties and, more importantly, assert them. Those who belong to a security culture know which conduct would compromise security and they are quick to educate and caution those who, out of ignorance, forgetfulness, or personal weakness, partake in insecure conduct. Security consciousness becomes a "culture" when all the 190 member states working together make security violations socially and morally unacceptable within the group.

All ICAO member states were to have been successfully audited by the end of 2007, with strengths and weaknesses identified, regional and global trends tracked, and recommendations made to states for improving their security regimes. However, there remains a small number of states that have made little or no progress in implementing the ICAO recommendations to correct the deficiencies identified through the audits. Although security audit information has been restricted in the past, steps should be taken to increase the transparency of the audit program and ensure that the global aviation network remain protected. It is therefore proposed that, in addition to a review of deficiencies by the Audit Results Review Board, consideration be given to the development of a process that will notify all member states when deficiencies identified during the course of a USAP audit remain unaddressed for a sustained period. A notification process could involve the use of information that does not divulge specific vulnerabilities but enables states to initiate consultations with the state of interest to ensure the continued protection of aviation assets on a bilateral basis.

Upon completion of a USAP audit, states are required to submit a corrective action plan addressing deficiencies and schedule a follow-up visit. Audit follow-up visits were initiated in mid-2005 in order to check the implementation of states' corrective action plans and to provide support in remedying identified deficiencies. These visits are normally conducted in the second year following a state's audit. According to USAP reports, follow-up visits have shown that the majority of states have made progress in the implementation of their corrective action plans. At the same time, however, follow-up visits have also revealed that a small number of states that have made little or no progress in correcting their deficiencies.

According to a progress report submitted to the ICAO Council in 2006, the ICAO Secretariat advised that in the case of states that are demonstrating little or no progress by the time of the follow-up visit, a cross analysis of the USAP audit results with those of the USOAP reveals that generally, states that have difficulty in implementing the safety-related SARPs are also experiencing difficulties with the implementation of the Annex provisions on the security side. Certain contributing factors have been identified. These often include a lack of financial and/or suitably qualified human resources, as well as frequent changes in key personnel within a state's appropriate authority. In some cases, there also appears to be a certain complacency and general lack of interest in implementing the ICAO recommendations."

In order to address the issue of states that are not responding effectively to the ICAO audit process, a high-level Secretariat Audit Results Review Board has recently been established for the purpose of examining both the safety and security histories of specific states brought to its attention by either USOAP or USAP. The objective is to highlight or raise the profile of these states within the system, in order to encourage them to take responsible actions in a measured and timely manner.

The Committee on Unlawful Interference of the ICAO Council has recommended to the council that these data and trends be made public at the assembly. Although such information has been restricted in the past, the committee believes all states and the public should be aware of the areas needing improvement without identifying specific states or vulnerabilities. Further, the council has been discussing with the Secretariat ways in which it can most effectively exercise its oversight responsibilities with respect to states that do not comply with their responsibilities under the convention and its annexes.

For those states that lack the resources to improve their security systems, new mechanisms such as ICAO's Coordinated Assistance and Development

(CAD) Program are in place to assist in directing longer-term attention to problems. For those states that remain unable to improve their security systems, bringing such problems before the Audit Results Review Board, and possibly the council, for consideration are valuable steps toward addressing the deficiencies in the longer term. However, the vulnerabilities presented by unresolved and sustained issues represent a significant weakness in the global protective network and a possible critical or urgent area of vulnerability for other member states with air carrier service at the airport of interest, particularly when combined with indications of a heightened threat.

In building a security culture within ICAO member states, it is imperative that consideration should also be given to the development of a process for ensuring that all member states are notified when deficiencies identified during the course of a USAP audit remain unaddressed for a sustained period of time. A notification process could involve the use of information that does not divulge specific vulnerabilities but enables states to initiate consultations with the state of interest. Such a notification process may result in a strengthened ability on the part of ICAO to ensure that states unwilling to meet basic security standards will be held accountable and allow for a limited amount of transparency in the security audit program without divulging specific potential security vulnerabilities.

NOTES

1. Carol B. Hallett, President and CEO, Air Transport Association, *State of the United States Airline Industry, A Report on Recent Trends for United States Carriers,* statement, 2002, www.airlines.org/news/speeches.

2. *Assembly Resolutions in Force* (as of October 5, 2001), ICAO Doc. 9790, VII-1. Also of general interest is UN General Assembly Resolution 56/88, *Measures to Eliminate International Terrorism,* adopted at the Fifty-Sixth Session of the United Nations, which calls upon states to take every possible measure in eliminating international terrorism.

3. ICAO News Release, "High-Level Ministerial Conference Approves Worldwide Manditory Aviation Security Audit Programme," February 21, 2002, PIO 02/2002.

4. For detailed information on the proposed international facility for aviation safety, see Ruwantissa I. R. Abeyratne, "Funding an International Financial Facility for Aviation Safety," *Journal of World Investment* 1, no. 2 (December 2000): 383–407.

5. Convention on International Civil Aviation (also called the Chicago Convention), signed at Chicago on December 7, 1944. See ICAO Doc. 7300/9, 9th ed., 2006.

6. Article 1 of the Chicago Convention provides that the contracting states recognize that every state has complete and exclusive sovereignty over the airspace above its territory.

7. Preamble to the Chicago Convention.

8. At the 35th Session of the ICAO Assembly (Montreal, September 28–October 8, 2004), the International Air Transport Association (IATA) brought to the attention of the assembly the fact that the aviation underwriting community had formally announced its intention to exclude all hull, spares, passenger, and third party liability claims resulting from damage caused by the hostile use of dirty bombs, electromagnetic pulse devices, or biochemical materials. For a discussion of this subject, see Ruwantissa

I. R. Abeyratne, "Emergent Trends in Aviation War Risk Insurance," *Air and Space Law* 30, no. 2 (April 2005): 117–29.

9. As has already been discussed in the first part of this chapter, at the 33rd Session of the Assembly, ICAO adopted Resolution 13/1, entitled *Declaration on Misuse of Civil Aircraft as Weapons of Destruction and Other Terrorist Acts Involving Civil Aviation.* This resolution, while singling out for consideration the terrorist acts that occurred in the United States on September 11, 2001, and, inter alia, recognizing that the new types of threat posed by terrorist organizations require new concerted efforts and policies of cooperation on the part of states, urges all contracting states to intensify their efforts in order to achieve the full implementation and enforcement of the multilateral conventions on aviation security, as well as of the ICAO standards and recommended practices and procedures (SARPs) relating to aviation security. The resolution also calls upon states to monitor such implementation, and to take within their territories appropriate additional security measures commensurate to the level of threat, in order to prevent and eradicate terrorist acts involving civil aviation. Stemming from this resolution, and subsequent ICAO action such as was contained in Resolution A35–1 (on the destruction of Russian civil aircraft on August 24, 2004), various security and facilitation measures such as biometric identification, strengthening of cockpit doors, and issuance of passenger name records have succeeded in reducing the incidents of physical human action on board, such as hijacking, over the past few years.

10. In the period from 1947 to 1996, hijacking was the most common offense against civil aviation, recording 959 incidents. During this period, hijacking constituted 87 percent of all attacks on aircraft. see Paul Wilkinson and Brian M. Jenkins, eds., *Aviation Terrorism and Security* (Frank Cass: London, 1999), 12.

11. Hijacking in the late 1960s started an irreversible trend, which was later dramatized by such incidents as the skyjacking by Shia terrorists of TWA Flight 847 in June 1985. The skyjacking of Egypt Air Flight 648 in November of the same year and the skyjacking of a Kuwait Airways Airbus in 1984 are other early examples of skyjacking. Aviation sabotage, in which explosions on the ground or in midair destroy whole aircraft, their passengers, and their crew, has also been a continuing threat in past decades. The explosion of Air India Flight 182 over the Irish Sea in June 1985 and Pan Am Flight 103 over Lockerbie, Scotland, in 1988, and the UTA explosion over Niger in 1989 are examples. Missile attacks, in which aircraft are destroyed by surface-to-air missiles (SAMs) also occurred as early as the 1970s. The destruction of the two Viscount aircraft of Air Rhodesia in late 1978/early 1979 provides two examples. Armed attacks at airports, now a reemerging threat, occurred early on in instances where terrorists opened fire in congested areas of airport terminals. Examples of this type of terrorism include the June 1972 attack by the Seikigunha (Japanese Red Army) at Ben Gurion Airport, Tel Aviv; the August 1973 attack by Arab gunmen on Athens Airport; and the 1985 attacks on the Rome and Vienna airports; Finally, the illegal carriage by air of narcotics and other psychotropic substances and crimes related to this, such as the seizure of or damage to aircraft, persons, and property, also constitute a threat that cannot be ignored in the present context. For an extensive study of the carriage of narcotics by air, see Ruwantissa I. R. Abeyratne, *Aviation Security* (London: Ashgate, 1998), 197–296.

12. The lethality of the weapon can be illustrated by the 340 MANPADS used by Afghan Mujahedeen rebels to successfully hit 269 Soviet aircraft. See http://www.janes.com/security/international_security/news/.

13. "MANPADS," *Ploughshares Monitor,* Autumn 2004, 83.

14. Ibid. The deadly accuracy and ease of handling of MANPADS were demonstrated when Somali gunmen shot down two U.S. MH-60 Black Hawk helicopters in October 1993.

15. *Infrastructure Safety and the Environment, Protecting Commercial Aviation against the Shoulder-Fired Missile Threat* (Santa Monica, CA: Rand Corporation, 2005), 9.

16. Donald J. Hanle, *Terrorism: The Newest Face of Warfare* (New York: Pergamon-Brassey's, 1989), 185; Arie Ofri, "Intelligence and Counterterrorism," *ORBIS* 28 (Spring 1984): 49; Andrew J. Pierre, "The Politics of International Terrorism," *ORBIS* 19 (1975–76): 1256; Frederick C. Dorey, *Aviation Security* (London: Granada, 1983): 142.

17. Richard Clutterbuck, *Living with Terrorism* (London: Butterworths, 1991), 175.

18. Christopher Dobson and Ronald Payne, Appendix B, "The Chronology of Terror: 1968–1987," in *War without End: The Terrorists: An Intelligence Dossier* (London: Sphere Books, 1987), 366.

19. Christopher Dobson and Ronald Payne, *The Carlos Complex: A Pattern of Violence* (London: Hodder and Stoughton, 1977), 134.

20. *Keesing's Contemporary Archives*, March 5–11, 1973, 25757.

21. Ibid.

22. Edward F. Mickolus, *Transnational Terrorism: A Chronology of Events, 1969–1979* (London: Aldwych Press, 1980), 428.

23. Dobson and Payne, *The Carlos Complex*, 53.

24. Ibid.

25. Mickolus, *Transnational Terrorism*, 581; *Al-Hadaf, Al-Hadaf mao Al-Babtal al-Muharrarin: Al-Muo taqilun hawwalu Dhallam al-Asr ila Nidhal Mushriq* (Al-Hadaf with the Liberated Heroes: The Detainees Transformed the Gloom of Imprisonment into a Shining Struggle), June 1985, 35–41.

26. U.S. Department of Transportation (FAA), *Worldwide Significant Acts Involving Civil Aviation* (Washington, DC: Federal Aviation Administration, 1984), 14.

27. U.S. Department of Defense, *Terrorist Group Profiles* (Washington, DC: U.S. GPO, 1989), 7.

28. James Adams, *Trading in Death: Weapons, Warfare and the Modern Arms Race* (London: Hutchinson, 1990), 60–61; Paul Wilkinson, "Terrorism: International Dimensions" in *The New Terrorism*, ed. William Gutteridge (London: Institute for the Study of Conflict and Terrorism, 1986), 39–40; Christopher Dobson and Ronald Payne, *The Terrorists: Their Weapons, Leaders and Tactics* (New York: Facts on File, 1982), 119.

29. *Daily Telegraph* (London), January 7, 1988.

30. Aryeh Lewis and Meir Kaplan, eds., *Terror in the Skies: Aviation Security* (Tel Aviv, Israel: ISAS, 1990), 226; William Alva Crenshaw, "Terrorism and the Threat to Civil Aviation" (PhD diss., University of Miami, 1987): 126.

31. Dorey, *Aviation Security*, 142.

32. Wassenaar Arrangement on Export Controls for Conventional Arms and Dual-Use Goods and Technologies, Elements for Export Controls of MANPADS and the Inter-American Convention against the Illicit Manufacturing of and Trafficking in Firearms, Ammunition, Explosives, and Other Related Material, available at www.wassenaar.org.

The participating states were Argentina, Australia, Austria, Belgium, Bulgaria, Canada, Croatia, Czech Republic, Denmark, Estonia, Finland, France, Germany, Greece, Hungary, Ireland, Italy, Japan, Latvia, Lithuania, Luxembourg, Malta, the

Netherlands, New Zealand, Norway, Poland, Portugal, the Republic of Korea, Romania, the Russian Federation, Slovakia, Slovenia, Spain, Sweden, Switzerland, Turkey, Ukraine, the United Kingdom, and the United States.

33. Article 51 of the United Nations Charter provides, inter alia, that nothing in the charter will impair the inherent right of individual or collective self-defense if an armed attack occurs against a member of the United Nations, until the Security Council has taken measures necessary to maintain international peace and security.

34. Infrastructure Safety and the Environment, Article 102 of the UN Charter, stipulates that every treaty and every international agreement entered into by any member of the United Nations after the charter comes into force shall be registered with the UN Secretariat as soon as possible.

35. Malcolm N. Shaw, *International Law*, 5th ed. (Cambridge: Cambridge University Press, 2003), 812.

36. The ICAO's triennial assembly, at which its 190 member states gather to evaluate policy and make new policy as necessary through resolutions, is the supreme governing body of the organization.

37. In 1984, followers of the Bhagwan Shree Rajneesh attempted to control a local election by incapacitating the local population through infecting salad bars in restaurants, doorknobs, produce in grocery stores, and items in other public areas with salmonella typhimurium in the city of The Dalles, Oregon. The attack caused about 751 people to become sick (there were no fatalities). This incident was the first known bioterrorist attack in the United States in the twentieth century. In September and October of 2001, several cases of anthrax occurred in the United States; these were reportedly caused deliberately. This was a well-publicized act of bioterrorism. It motivated efforts to define biodefense and biosecurity.

38. In 1915 and 1916, Dr. Anton Dilger, a German-American physician, used cultures of anthrax and glanders with the intention of committing biological sabotage on behalf of the German government. Other German agents are known to have undertaken similar sabotage efforts during World War I in Norway, Spain, Romania, and Argentina.

39. Michael Wagner, Andrew Moore and Ron Aryel, eds., *Handbook of Bio Surveillance* (New York: Elsevier, 2006). Bio surveillance is the science of real-time disease outbreak detection. Its principles apply to both natural and man-made (bioterrorist) epidemics. In addition to activity in this field in the United States, work is also being done in Europe, where disease surveillance is beginning to be organized on a continent-wide scale, which is needed to track biological emergencies. The system not only monitors infected persons but also attempts to discern the origin of the outbreak.

40. *Daily Telegraph*, October 16, 1984; *Times* (London), December 12, 1984.

41. The 36th Session of the ICAO Assembly was informed that there are some 150 certified auditors on the Universal Security Audit Program (USAP) roster, from 59 states in all ICAO regions. The participation of certified national experts in the audits under the guidance of an ICAO team leader has permitted the program to be implemented in a cost-effective manner while allowing for a valuable interchange of expertise.

CHAPTER 2

The Case for an Aviation Security Crisis Management Team

Charles M. Bumstead

The new wave of political violence in the Middle East and South Asia, where religious sectarianism has added a dangerous and potent factor to the problem of international terrorism, has focused attention on the real danger this brand of terrorism could pose to Western civilization and international order.

Terrorism, political or religious, can be briefly defined as "A special form of clandestine, undeclared, and unconventional warfare waged without benefit of humanitarian restraints or rules."[1] Terrorist attacks on the Western international airline industry strike at the very heart of the global economy as well as affecting individual states. The major threat at this time is *organized international terrorism*.

There has been a remarkable increase in the number and intensity of incidents in the past few years. Since the attack on the World Trade Center in September of 2001, the growing threat of extremist violence involving civil aircraft in the air and the industry's infrastructure and buildings on the ground has been looming over the international civil aviation industry. No state, it seems, is safe from this type of threat, as it appears to be ideological rather than political in nature. There are still random, individual threats to international civil aviation that do not fall into the category of international terrorism. However, organized international terrorism is the major threat facing the industry today. There is not, currently, a way to prevent all such attacks.

During the past few years, the aviation community has attempted to address the complicated issues related to preventing unlawful interference with international civil aviation. Early on, incidents in which an aircraft was destroyed were relatively rare. Usually, it was a hostage situation and the aircraft was on the ground. That scenario has changed, and the threat has grown to include devastating property damage, including the loss of aircraft and human lives, such as when an aircraft is used as a destructive missile. The other aspect of the current threat is risk of damage to the infrastructure: terminal buildings, rail transportation, and other structures. These types of attacks, even though some are directed toward the ground transportation industry, have a deleterious effect on all segments of transportation including that of the air domain.

States and international organizations have historically limited their responses and their actions to individual incidents. There was little or no recognition of the growing unrest in certain areas of the Middle East, where the roots of organized international terrorism were growing. Therefore, the actions taken by states and by international organizations tended to be reactive rather than proactive. Subsequently, actions treated only the issues specific to each individual incident. The term "incremental" can be applied to their processes. The international organizations did not recognize the growing threat posed by organized ideological entities. As a result, little or no effort was expended by the international organizations to organize a concerted effort to develop an aggressive program to forecast, prevent, or provide an emergency response during an incident or to seek measures to amend the aviation security system. That task has primarily been left to individual states. This failure to see into the future is fundamental to the problems connected with the prevention and treatment of incidents of terrorism.

Due to the increased number of incidents and the severity of the attacks, it is time to rethink the entire international aviation security management process; and that includes examining the role played by international organizations in the aviation security milieu.

A FRESH PERSPECTIVE

The international aviation organizations must take a fresh look at the problems they are now facing. There are some problems that need to be addressed on a priority basis. First; there's the inability of international aviation organizations, specifically the International Civil Aviation Organization (ICAO), to effectively deal with incidents of unlawful interference. The role of the ICAO is limited by international law to rule making and assistance to the various contracting states. There is no apparent vehicle within the ICAO to deal with an ongoing incident or to play any role in the development of preventive measures to avoid or minimize the effects of such incidents. ICAO has provided documents that provide general guidelines to the contracting states concerning aviation security. Within the documents provided by ICAO there are regulations that place the responsibility on ICAO to develop standards and recommended practices (SARPs) to govern the establishment of aviation security regulations in each contracting state.[2] It is imperative that the ICAO documents be examined with an eye to providing a more aggressive posture toward security, perhaps to include preventive measures and the ability to coordinate with the contracting states' intelligence agencies.

Second, existing regulations concerning aviation security are stated by ICAO in Annex 17, Standards and Recommended Practices, "Safeguarding International Civil Aviation against Acts of Unlawful Interference," and are expressed in very general terms.[3] The states have a great deal of leeway as to the type and kind of security regulations they promulgate. Some states have very stringent security requirements for their international and domestic air carriers. Other states do not have strict security procedures, because of the lack of a perceived threat.

There are occasions when the threat assessment organ of a contracting state may determine that a heightened security level is required, due to intelligence reports indicating a credible threat to the state or its aircraft. The security requirements may be perceived as serious enough to require the state to seek a higher level of security at an airport in another state's sovereign territory. It would be helpful to have a means provided in the ICAO documents through which such problems can be sorted out ahead of time, rather than during an incident. Such a vehicle could be made available to the international community.

In April 1996, the U.S. Congress passed the Hatch Act. This was antiterrorism legislation, requiring all airlines flying to the United States, no matter from which sovereign nation, to apply security measures similar to those imposed by the Federal Aviation Administration (FAA) on U.S. airlines. There was an adverse reaction on the part of many contracting states in ICAO over the proposed legislation. Several states alleged that the act attempted to apply U.S. law outside the territorial limits of the United States, and further, that the Hatch Act infringed upon the sovereignty of contracting states.[4] It was considered objectionable by almost the entire international aviation community. States said that the Hatch Act flew in the face of the "host state responsibility" set out in the Chicago Convention, to which the United States is a contracting party.

The Hatch Act created a firestorm of opinions from almost all of the contracting states in ICAO that operated civil aviation flights into or out of the United States. The conclusion drawn by several states was that the move was more of an economic strategy by the United States to force other states into investing large amounts of cash to help cover the cost of providing a specified level of safety. Additionally, the majority of states felt that the increased security measures required by the act would not enhance safety but, rather, would decrease the safety component by not allowing contracting states to utilize the precepts of the risk management concept.[5]

An example will illustrate the way in which the U.S. requirement for heightened security could affect the international aviation community and help to clarify the issues involved. The United States receivs information that a specific flight, departing from the United Kingdom with a destination in the

United States, has been threatened with a bomb; the United States requests that United Kingdom security should not allow curbside baggage checks but should match passengers with baggage prior to departure. The United Kingdom, not being able to comply with the request, reports this to the United States. The United States finds this position unacceptable because it considered the threat to be very credible. The United States informs the United Kingdom that the aircraft can not land in the United States. The United Kingdom is left with the option of canceling the flight or delaying it until the request from the United States could be met. Since there are no resources at the United Kingdom airport to perform the required functions, the flight is canceled by the United States. The United Kingdom objects because the United States, in effect, attempted to take U.S. security actions in the United Kingdom's sovereign airspace.

The position of the United Kingdom, as presented here, is supported in the ICAO SARPs, as the SARPs forbid a state from requiring a higher level of security than that provided for in the SARPs. It is evident that there is a major problem. No state, under threat of a potential bomb aboard an aircraft landing in its territory, is going to pay much attention to the Chicago Convention or to the ICAO SARPs. Nationalism and protection of citizens and property will be the primary motivation for the affected state. It is quite obvious that such a situation in the international arena cannot be allowed to exist. There must be provisions in current ICAO documents for states to require increased security standards, above those required by the SARPs, when a high-security situation arises.

After an initial flurry of activity, ICAO and other international organizations took action to criticize the United States for its precipitate action in passing the Hatch Act. The ensuing months led to strong comments from around the world. States were adamant in their criticism of the act, and ICAO published an official response to the United States—the "Notice of Proposed Rule Making" (NPRM)—in 1999, objecting to the stringent terms of the act, and adding a specific complaint concerning the requirement for contracting states to provide a level of security similar to that provided by the United States.[6]

All of the objections made by ICAO and the contracting states had a measure of validity, as the required standards would, in fact, cause many problems for other states. For instance, the problems of baggage handling outside of the terminal area and of matching passengers with baggage could cause problems in the United Kingdom and many other states in Europe.

While the provisions of the Hatch Act had concrete effects on the sovereign airspace of many of the contracting states, international organizations such as the International Air Transport Association (IATA) and ICAO were quick to suggest to the United States other methods of improving security standards. Unfortunately, most of the suggestions were for the United States to conform to the provisions of Annex 17 and to the language of the annex in the formulation of U.S. security regulations.

CONSIDERATION OF ICAO ACTIONS

Throughout the years, the ICAO instituted a number or measures to meet with the increased threat of "unlawful interference with civil aviation." Among those measures were the following:

Establishment of the Aviation Security Cooperation and Development Unit (ASCAD). The unit will be the focal point for assistance and for the funding of programs in the aviation security field.

- Certification of ICAO instructors. A new certification program for instructors in aviation security has been implemented.
- Aviation security training centers (ASTCs). A total of 15 facilities, at least one in each of the regional and subregional areas of ICAO were to be established.
- AVSEC training courses. Over 50 training package programs per year are being conducted in the 15 ICAO ASTCs.
- Aviation security training packages (ASTPs). A new package, ASTP/AIRLINE, has been developed jointly with the International Air Transport Association (IATA). Other ASTPs have been developed by ICAO.
- Establishment of a secure Web site to deal with man-portable air defense systems (MANPADs).
- Establishment of an aviation security regional officer (ASRO) position in three of the ICAO regional offices.

ICAO has also established an audit system called the Universal Security Audit Program (USAP). The program allows for the analysis of client states' aviation security programs with regard to Annex 17 to the Convention on International Civil Aviation Standards.[7]

Finally, one of the more important programs established by ICAO is the requirement for contacting states to develop and utilize machine readable travel documents (MRTDs). This includes new standards stating that all contracting states should begin issuing only machine readable passports (MRPs) by April 1, 2010, and that any non–machine readable passport issued before that date should have an expiration date before November, 24. 2015; and a recommended practice that all client states should incorporate biometric identification in their travel documents. The dates established for compliance seem to be quite a distance down the road (3–8 years) for the effective countering of a current terrorist threat. It becomes increasingly obvious that the steps taken by ICAO, while helpful, do not address the fundamental problem of incident prevention and mitigation, nor do they identify the SARPs, or other ICAO documents, as being deficient in providing quality security direction or procedures to the contracting states.[8]

CONSIDERATION OF ACTIONS TAKEN BY IATA

A major part of the fallout after the September 2001 attack on the World Trade Center was a marked increase in antiterrorist legislation and preventive measures initiated by the various states and by ICAO and IATA, as well as by other international organizations associated with international civil aviation. IATA, as always, was in the forefront in seeking to ensure the viability of the international aviation industry. It took very positive steps to improve safety; among the measures taken by IATA was the establishment of the security management systems (SEMS) for air transport operators.[9]

SEMS is a standardized approach to implementing the security processes outlined in IATA's air carrier security program. It is a businesslike approach to the way in which security processes should be implemented and will provide better and more uniform standards throughout the aviation industry. Essentially, SEMS is an element of corporate management responsibility, which sets out a company's security policy for the management of security as an integral part of its overall business, making security one of the company's core values by developing a security culture within the organization.

SEMS is based on ICAO Annex 17 standards and IATA operational safety audit security standards (IOSA). A major responsibility of management in SEMS is the establishment of an effective and focused threat assessment process that will contribute to making security processes proactive. SEMS provides a businesslike approach to security: goals are set and levels of authority are established, thereby ensuring that effective security matters are mandated by IATA.

IATA has established a series of training packages covering most aspects of security within its domain. The overall program is called the Aviation Security Training Package (ASTP). ICAO and IATA have partnered to provide international airlines with the most up-to-date and comprehensive security training packages available worldwide. This package is claimed to be "the answer to your aviation security training challenges." The package is designed for senior managers, middle managers, managers/supervisors, and technical staff.

The disadvantages are few but relatively important, as the package focuses only on those items that are directly associated with IATA's responsibilities to its client states. First, the package does not deal with the ground-associated infrastructure that accompanies all aviation-oriented activity—fuel storage depots, terminal buildings, airport ground transportation, visitor and passenger automobile parking, public transportation access, airport secure areas, and so forth. The fact that various states may have different security requirements makes this program less efficient than it could be. The effort is commendable, but, given the states' own security regulations and the additional requirements of ICAO, it will be very difficult for an individual state to incorporate this program into other security programs. Second, the course costs a considerable amount of money and includes over 900 slides. This constitutes an incredible amount of material for the average employee to assimilate. This criticism is not meant to cast aspersions on the program. It is merely meant to point out areas that can be modified or altered to make it easier and simpler for the average employee to assimilate the information. The greatest advantage is that it is not a correspondence course but one that is taught by ICAO and IATA personnel. For this reason alone, the program is highly recommended and applauded.

IATA did not stop with the establishment of SEMS and ASTP but took further steps to provide training for employees of the aviation community by providing for a course leading to a diploma in aviation security.[10] It is required that participants be graduates of the Senior Management of Civil Aviation Security Course and three other courses over a three-year period. Stringent grading requirements are applied to ensure that participants demonstrate knowledge of the subject.

All of the efforts on the part of ICAO and IATA serve to reinforce the perception that security education is no longer just a course of study to add to a person's resume but now requires a university level course (or the equivalent) of study that will lead to a degree in aviation security management. The education of security specialists can no longer be relegated to the sphere of supplementary education but should now be required. An airline pilot requires specialized education to do her or his job, and so does a security specialist. There is no more important job in the international aviation community than that of aviation security management, and it should be the responsibility of well-trained and educated security professionals.

THE UNITED NATIONS' APPROACH TO INTERNATIONAL TERRORISM

The United Nations (UN), as the leading international organization, embraced the challenge of international terrorism following the attack on the World Trade Center. The UN made great strides in developing a progressive program to deal with the threat of terrorism. One of the major problems with the UN effort, however, is the political ramifications of dealing with contracting states; the UN charter demands consensus in all of its decisions. The entire international community has had difficulty even in reaching a consensus on the definition of "terrorism." As an international organization, the UN could not and did not permit a definition that equates terrorism with "national liberation movements."

A challenge to the UN is that it must convince the major powers, and especially the United States, as its largest contributor, that security information will not be leaked and used for terrorist activities. The various state intelligence organs must feel secure that information shared with the UN does not warn terrorist organizations of potential operations against them.[11]

When dealing with terrorism, the international community cannot show any weakness or vacillation, because this feeds the terrorist movement, especially as the proponents of terrorism ignore the rules governing the conduct of a civilized society. Any effort against international terrorism requires total commitment if it is to be successful, which explains the U.S. position that recognizes the value of stern preventive/preemptive security measures.

The United Nations must lead the free world against terrorism, and it can only do this by adopting a very strong position against any state or group of states that support, sponsor, encourage, or abet terrorism. A strong position adopted by the UN will go a long way toward convincing the free world of its determination to join in the battle against unlawful interference in international civil aviation. Such a position would alleviate international concerns and encourage cooperation. Terrorism is an international problem, which can only be defeated with complete cooperation between all contracted states.

RAMIFICATIONS OF THE HATCH ACT

Since 1999, when the National Proposal for Rulemaking (NPRM) was published by the United States, there have been several major terrorist attacks against the United States, the United Kingdom, Spain, Indonesia, and other states; so severe were the attacks, in fact, that aviation security management has now assumed a position it has never enjoyed, that of being a primary concern in the international struggle against unlawful interference with civil aviation.

When an international organization such as ICAO is expected to provide standards for the entire international aviation community, a major problem for all of the contracting states is created, that is, the time frame associated with rule making. The contracting states must all be appraised of the proposed changes, additions, amendments, or supplements to the appropriate regional air navigation plan. This is an extremely time-consuming process and often takes literally years to go from the initial proposal to final rule making.

When technological changes are proposed to the contracting states, it must be recognized that some of the states do not have the financial or technological expertise available to implement all of the changes proposed. Some changes involve a large outlay of money or require that advanced technology be implemented immediately due to international security concerns. One example is machine readable passports. The less affluent states may not be able to comply with the standards or the time constraints required by ICAO.

ICAO has, in the past, provided the opportunity for the less affluent states to delay compliance with the standards until such time as a state can reasonably be expected to adopt the standards. The delay, however, would not just apply to the less affluent states but to all of the contracting states, as specified in Annex 17. It may well be that a particular technology has become available and the more affluent states want the standards amended to include the new technology. These states, because of the heightened international threat, will want the new technology applied immediately. The problems associated with different states having a different perceived threat level and different abilities to put into effect security measures add to the already complex problem of handling an international incident.

In order to assist in minimizing the effects of such a situation, it is suggested that some method be developed that will allow interstate coordination to take place in a much quicker and more efficient manner in order to handle security problems between states when an international incident occurs.

One step that can be taken is that a *minimum standard of aviation security* be established, and *all* contracting states be required to be in compliance, in order to receive the sponsorship of the other members of the international aviation community or to enter into interstate letters of understanding concerning state to state aircraft operations.

The most important issue is the fact that aviation security management has come into its own because of the increased security threats that now exist worldwide. In every job description in the aviation industry there appears a section on security responsibilities. It does not matter what domain, air or ground, in the vicinity of an airport or aircraft, security is a prime requirement for each and every employee in the aviation industry. It has become a necessity to have professionally trained and educated personnel in key security positions at all levels of the aviation community. ICAO has already put into effect some of the suggestions that have been made.[12]

Security cannot be relegated to online study or correspondence course study to obtain a qualification for a position as an aviation security specialist. These courses are acceptable for employees whose primary duty is nonsecurity; but positions that are directly security oriented must require professional training and extensive technical training in order to ensure that operatives are able to operate some of the existing, and soon to be existing, technological equipment.

CRISIS MANAGEMENT TEAMS

One of the most neglected counterterrorist tools is the "think tank." Academic think tanks are said to be helpful in providing a broader view of the phenomena of international terrorism. It is considered a necessity that an organization such as a think tank, a threat assessment team or a crisis management team, hereafter called simply a "team," be organized within the organizational structure of ICAO.

Annex 17, chapter 2, paragraph 2.1.3.b, SARPs, speaks directly to the development of regulations, practices, and procedures that "are capable of responding rapidly to meet any security threat."[13] This paragraph may actually provide for the formation of a crisis management team in each contracting state, with the prototype organization being organized in the ICAO's Air Transport Bureau. This organization would be able to provide a fresh, broad perspective on any international terrorist "incident," as the team would not be directly or operationally involved with the actual incident. Its members would be able to view the incident from all angles and positions.

The team would be directly involved in the examination of all existing documents relating to aviation security management; additionally, in the course of their duties, the members of the team would be "gaming" scenarios of potential terrorist threats, to determine the exact nature of the threat and to assist in establishing a risk management model to ensure that an appropriate level of response is assigned to each determined threat level.

The team would deal with actual incidents and apply the knowledge gained from them to examine existing regulations and procedures with an eye to better preparing the international community. A great deal of experience is available in the international community, and that experience should be utilized and considered in preparing for the selection of qualified personnel for participation in the team. What better way is there to utilize the skills of dedicated and experienced security specialists, who have actually been involved in combating terrorists and in countering their activities, than in a consulting or operational capacity on a crisis management team. These specialists can provide critical observations and feedback to the international community.

What is needed, and suggested, is a network of crisis management teams throughout the various regions of ICAO, to keep the international community and the various member states up to date on the latest threats and the current counterterrorist technology. It is urged that such a network among the several contracting states be considered by, and supported by, the international organizations and by state security management organizations from the international community.

There is a need for multiple international centers of competence, which will concentrate on specialized tasks as an interdisciplinary contribution to the global war on terror. It is recognized that nationalism and the possibility of compromising the security of a sovereign state is of primary importance. The suggestion of organizing a team as described above may not be realized due to political or bureaucratic problems. Official government operations and coordinated strategies are often held back by procedures, bureaucracy, and political interests.

If such a team is possible, however, the ability to be involved in all phases of an international incident would allow it to examine all aspects of any given situation, from start to finish, with an eye to applying whatever corrections, amendments, or supplements are needed to existing regulations or procedures. An additional advantage of such a team is that some basic weaknesses in procedure could be corrected quickly. The suggestion of such a team comes as a result of a study of the actions of several contracting states in their attempts to achieve a more efficient method of dealing with international terrorism and unlawful interference with civil aircraft.

In almost every state, procedures have been implemented to organize an effective method to forecast threats and develop a national threat level program that will alert the population and all security organizations within the country to the seriousness of the potential threat. Additionally, the setting of a threat level allows the identification of actions that need to be taken at each step of the threat level process. This system is very helpful when dealing with a large population and a large number of security organizations and other organizations that may be the subject of or affected by the threat.

It must be understood at the outset that ICAO has no apparent operational responsibility to perform threat assessment or to take action when an international incident is in progress. The function of ICAO, a coordinating body at best, leaves the operational handling of an incident to the contracting states for the most part. The affected states have the opportunity to employ an ongoing risk management program that is directed toward their state assets, vulnerabilities, and capabilities. A state, after an incident, has the opportunity to critique its own actions and the actions of other states involved. International organizations, like ICAO or IATA, have little opportunity to participate directly in the incident and are only able to gain access to pertinent information after the fact.

It is suggested that the team lists its first responsibility as reviewing all the international security documents for currency and applicability. It is necessary to review the existing documents to determine how to better assist the contracting states to develop, maintain, and manage a current and effective aviation security program.

POSSIBLE SOLUTIONS

First, the ICAO document, Annex 17 to the Convention on International Civil Aviation, needs to be reviewed and possibly to have portions rewritten to allow more effective coordination during an incident. Rather than concentrating on assisting the states involved after an incident, ICAO documents should be written to allow for forecasting and preventing incidents, as well as real-time coordination to effect immediate changes or alterations to existing standards and recommended practices (SARPs) to meet specific security requirements.

As an example of the need for real-time coordination, it is necessary to recall that ICAO SARPs discourage a state from requiring a security standard of another state that is in excess of the ICAO standard. If an affected state feels the necessity to demand that specific security measures be taken in another state's sovereign territory, rather than have an argument between the states over whether or not a state can require a higher standard of security, SARPs should be rewritten to reflect the ways in which real-time coordination can be used to temporarily allow for the raising of security standards. Following an incident, security measures may return to the standard called for in the SARPs.

Second, a minimum level of security must be maintained by all states. This requirement would allow each contracting state to know the level, at least the minimum level, of security to be maintained. Additionally, ICAO and other international bodies can identify more readily which states need assistance either to meet the minimum requirements or to implement current or increased requirements. There is a wide disparity among states concerning levels of security. It is not expected that a state such as Bhutan will need the same level of security that Indonesia will need; however, that being said, a minimum level of security at each and every airport in the international system is both desired and anticipated.

Third, the team should be established and organized with the ability to analyze intelligence information and assist in the development of a threat analysis program for contracting states. This program will be designed based on most of the world's threat-analysis programs, adhering to the same risk management principles and allowing for analysis and forecasting using "gaming principles," while developing real-time responses to threat levels. The responses will allow coordination during an incident on a real-time basis, and, in the aftermath, examine the entire incident with an eye to improving the international community's response to a terrorist threat. A key item in the aftermath will be to reexamine the existing documents and determine whether changes or alterations are needed or desired. The team will, of necessity, be staffed by dedicated security specialists, fully trained in every aspect of aviation security management.

The team would utilize the well-known principles of risk management. Risk management is a cardinal security principle that almost every state employs in its efforts to prepare to meet aviation security threats. Protective security measures are extremely expensive to utilize, and to apply resources when the threat does not dictate it involves a waste or, at the very least, a misuse of those resources. It is for that reason that a risk management system is the only viable way to predict threat level, thus allowing an appropriate level of response to a perceived threat.

One major problem in using risk management principles in the international arena is that two affected states or two security organizations may not see the threat in the same light, thus making an appropriate response to the threat next to impossible. A method must be developed to harmonize differing risk management programs in the international arena, to allow for an adequate response and to ensure efficient utilization of available resources. It will be impossible to arrive at a single risk management program for all states, but a minimum acceptable level of response to threats by all states can and should be achieved.

If one examines the principles involving the development of appropriate risk management procedures, it is obvious that the response can be different with each perceived threat. The reason for developing the program is to provide a vehicle for assessing the threat and devising an appropriate response to that threat. Recognizing this fact allows the state's program to be flexible, allowing for various threats to be properly assessed. There is a need, then, for every state to develop and to formally endorse, in a written document, its risk management program.

Further, the program must be the primary vehicle for the promulgation of all of the state's aviation security management programs. All other security programs will then be derived from the core principles of the risk management program.

Associated with, and an essential part of, the team is the creation of a formal section dedicated to the development and operation of the risk management program. The appointed head of the team must be a direct subordinate of a senior management official. An organizational chart should be developed in which responsibilities are clearly defined and have a dedicated point of contact. The specific procedures for the establishment of the organization can be left up to the individual states.

Each state that has air carriers operating in international airspace should cooperate with and assist those carriers in the development of their individual risk management/threat assessment programs so that the state's team can be complementary to the airlines/organizations.

An effective risk management program depends upon information, a lot of information, derived from state intelligence sources, Internet traffic, verbal tips, and a host of other sources that are needed in order to be able to properly identify and assess a potential threat. A particularly good example is the attack on the World Trade Center in New York on September 11, 2001. There was a wealth of intelligence indicating that a terrorist event was planned prior to the horrific events of that day, but it was not in the hands of a "threat assessment team" or an intelligence group in which all the bits of information could be examined in relation to the other parts. That being said, there was no "silver bullet" giving specific information as to what would be targeted or when or where the attacks would take place. Steps might have been taken by U.S. security organizations to alert airports, increase security measures, inspect incoming foreigners, and check those foreign individuals taking pilot training, had that information been made available to and properly assessed by a single intelligence group. Taking the appropriate steps might have delayed or even prevented the attacks.

A major problem that has been identified as a result of this incident is that the several security organizations in the U.S. did not, for whatever reason, share intelligence information. The sharing of pertinent intelligence information must be a vital part of any risk management program in every state. Information must be processed by one organization in the state dedicated to preventing unlawful interference with international civil aviation.

As part of the team there must be a threat assessment section, to analyze and assess unlawful interference with international civil aviation. The organization is responsible for threat assessment, and then for setting the state's threat level. Threat levels are established to assist security organizations to predict the general responses that are required at specific levels. The system is designed to be as efficient as possible. The threat level will dictate the general response from the state. The threat level also gives the international aviation community and the public information on the status of security in each particular state. The state may utilize the threat level to issue threat warnings or warnings of related incidents affecting civil aviation to many state organizations, departments, and agencies. The information can include in-depth reports on international incident trends, actual terrorist activities worldwide, or the capabilities of terrorist organizations. All the information will have been used to develop the threat level.

Some issues regarding the organization of the team need to be addressed. One of the most important of these is the fact that since the team will be, more than likely, an adjunct of ICAO, the staffing of the team will be controlled by the regulations that presently govern staffing matters in ICAO. This will present a problem. Since ICAO is made up of many sovereign states that must all receive the same consideration, it is possible that a state that actively sponsors international terrorism may wish to be part of the team and may have a qualified individual to present for a position. The requirement for equal treatment of states by ICAO and the existence of diplomatic immunity are ever present. The problems associated with this situation are clear. At present, there is no solution to this problem.

The team would be made up of professional security specialists selected by the Air Transport Bureau. It is recommended that the organization should be classified as staff members of the Air Transport Bureau (ATB) and report directly to the head of that organization. The ATB would give appropriate autonomy to the team and allow it to function independently of the Security and Facilitation Branch, while allowing it to have appropriate disciplines represented by adjunct members of the team. It is recommended that security qualified personnel from Air Transport, Rules of the Air and Search and Rescue, and Air Communications personnel be included as members. It is possible that a professional psychologist specializing in terrorist profiling techniques may be required or desirable. The specific organization of the team will be dictated by the contracting states and the Air Transport Bureau, in a conclave specifically convened for that purpose. Some responsibilities of the team are suggested here:

1. To review and recommend changes or alterations to all existing international civil aviation security-related documents;
2. To establish a threat assessment program for international civil aviation contracting states;
3. To review and recommend coordination requirements with all ICAO contracting states;
4. To establish a "gaming" program to examine existing procedures for weak and deficient areas;
5. To establish an after-the-fact investigative process with regard to every incident concerning international civil aviation, and provide appropriate recommendations to the Air Transport Bureau for changes, alterations, or supplements to existing regulations or procedures; and
6. To provide a formal, in-depth assessment of the incident, with recommendations, to the Air Transport Bureau.

The threat assessment section of the team will utilize risk management principles in its efforts to provide each contracting state with as much advance information on the possibility of an international incident as possible. Some of the principles of the risk management concept will include the following:

1. Identification of assets;
2. Identification of vulnerable areas of concern;
3. Identification of the threat;
4. Composition of threat scenarios;
5. Determination of whether the threat is credible;

6. Definition of countermeasures;

7. Calculation of the risk; and

8. Optimization of the countermeasures.

STEPS IN A THREAT ASSESSMENT

The first step of the team will be to identify the system's major assets. In the case of ICAO, the list would include all international civil aviation aircraft and ground support facilities. If possible, the team will provide the financial worth of the international civil aviation system if it or elements of it were destroyed or damaged. This initial function of the team is probably the most difficult of all. Each state could assist by preparing its own list of assets and reporting them to the team. The list and the financial aspect of the list will then be the basis for the structuring of the efforts made to prevent or minimize loss and will be used to prioritize potential threats.

The second step is to identify vulnerabilities and flaws in the contracting states' security regulations and procedures. It is possible to identify major areas of concern and optimize efforts to protect those areas. This is an iterative process and will be combined with the team's actual understanding of the threat. It will be necessary to prioritize vulnerable areas so as to be able to focus attention on the most valuable items.

The third step of the team will be to identify the threat. In order to accomplish this step, an assessment of current intelligence from a variety of sources is necessary, so that the team can evaluate the threat and determine what individual or organization constitutes the threat; also, can the organization or persons identified actually accomplish the potential terrorist incident?

The fourth step is to compose threat scenarios. In how many ways can the threat be actualized? When will the threat be accomplished? Where will it occur? How will it occur? What weapons will be used? Will it be directed against persons or facilities? Questions must be answered, as this process is vital to the determination of a threat level and an appropriate response.

The fifth step is to "game" the scenarios. This means introducing each scenario by computer and examining the actions and reactions of both sides of a potential incident, thereby preparing oneself to make decisions concerning threat level and appropriate responses. It is at this point that previous experience is utilized to compose the various scenarios, evaluate their feasibility, and the assess the probability of a particular scenario. This will enable the team to make appropriate suggestions to the various contracting states concerning security precautions they should prepare for. This step makes a final determination as to whether or not the threat is credible. Information gained from "gaming" the scenarios should give the team a realistic view of a credible event and will allow an appropriate response to be developed.

The sixth step is to define countermeasures. Upon "gaming" the scenarios and establishing that there is a credible threat, the team will determine what actions can be taken to prevent the incident or minimize the damage of a successful incident. This will include coordination with all affected states and their threat assessment teams.

The seventh step is to calculate the risk involved and determine the appropriate threat level. The threat level will have specific responses attached, and these will be implemented as soon as practicable.

The final step is to "fine tune" the countermeasures to ensure an appropriate response to a specified threat.

It is important to note that ICAO has no operational responsibility or authority to participate in any "action" pursuant to any given international incident. The team will be allowed only to seek and to question, to develop scenarios, to "game," and to discover and/or create innovative ways to meet a terrorist threat. A major advantage will be the opportunity to allow the team to critique all of the actions taken, in a live incident, by all concerned, and then to make recommendations to improve the management of aviation security. The team will be restricted to coordination functions during the actual occurrence of any incident involving a contracting state or its resources. With the use of such a team, ICAO can be an active participant in the development of better regulations, procedures, and programs to assist all contracting states in combating the current terrorist threat. The program will allow an ongoing evaluation and critique of the existing civil aviation security management system. The process would be in real time and on a continuing basis.

When there is no active threat, the team will be involved in developing various scenarios and "gaming" them in order to stay current on all potential threats. The system can be tested at any time for a specific scenario, and the team can accomplish what is known as a "command post exercise." Such an exercise essentially operates on the premise that a "fictional" incident is generated and all systems and organizations are tested to determine the strengths and weaknesses in the states' response. These exercises will be used to modify and modernize the system. As new technology is developed, it can be introduced into the system as a "gaming" item and be tested as if it were actually in place.

PROFESSIONAL TRAINING NEEDED FOR SECURITY SPECIALISTS

The final step in the process of revisiting the security management of international organizations is to address the training aspect. Since the events of September 11, 2001, it has been recognized by virtually all members of the international community that new, innovative technologies and procedures are in the process of being developed to counter the increasing terrorist threat.

It is obvious from some of the technology being currently developed that special training and education will be required in order to effectively utilize this new technology. It behooves the international aviation community to establish a formal training program for aviation security managers. In the following paragraphs, some of the technology that is now under development will be introduced.

The United States Department of Defense, Defense Advanced Research Projects Agency (DARPA), reported in 2002 that it had developed and was continuing to improve a program called War-Gaming the Asymmetric Environment (WAE).[14] WAE is a revolutionary approach to identifying predictive indicators of terrorist-specific attacks and behaviors by examining their behavior in the broader context of their cultural, political, and ideological environment. WAE has developed indication and warning models for select terrorist individuals and organizations. These models have been tested historically and, in some cases, operationally, to predict an active terrorist group's next action (attack/no attack, target characteristics, location characteristics, tactical characteristics, time frames, and motivating factors). The results have been statistically significant, and several models have been transitioned to Department of Defense and intelligence community partners. DARPA is extending its predictive technology research to model a larger set of terrorist groups and individuals, and these will further exploit predictive technologies to increase the level of detail for each predictive model. This technology needs to be included in the pantheon of tools to be used in the international community to combat terrorist activity.

The Defense Advanced Research Projects Agency (DARPA) has technology in the works that will provide a valuable tool in the identification of terrorists. It is called the Human Identification at a Distance (HumanID) Program, and it will use automated biometric identification technologies to detect, recognize, and identify humans at great distances.[15] A biometric technology approach is a method for identifying an individual from his/her face, or fingerprints, or the way he/she walks. These technologies will provide critical early warning support for force protection and homeland defense against terrorist, criminal, and other human-based threats. They will prevent or decrease the success rate of such attacks against operational facilities and installations. The HumanID Program will develop methods for fusing biometric technologies into advanced human identification systems to enable faster, more accurate, and unconstrained identification at great distances.

DARPA is also developing a device called the Handheld Isothermal Silver Standard Sensor (HISSS). This device is a biological sensor capable of laboratory quality detection of the full spectrum of biological threats—bacteria, viruses, and toxins.[16]

The operation of such a sophisticated piece of technology will require extensive specialized training/education, and so it is highly recommended that the international civil aviation community should establish a formal program to educate future aviation security managers/specialists.

SUMMARY

In order for the international civil aviation community to recognize the validity of the proposals in this chapter, it will be necessary to examine its members' current posture and determine whether the suggestions have merit.

If they are determined to have merit, and the community desires to implement these suggestions, a conference of all contracting states will be required. The conference would be convened to discuss the relative merits of the suggestions and decide on responsibilities, organization, and funding. It is strongly recommended, in any case, that the appropriate international aviation interests take positive steps to update and improve its system, and take aggressive action to provide a safer system for the international aviation community.

NOTES

1. William Gutteridge, Institute for the Study of Conflict, *The New Terrorism* (London: Mansell Publishing, 1996), 3.

2. International Civil Aviation Organization, Annex 17 to the Convention of Civil Aviation Security, *Safeguarding International Civil Aviation against Acts of Unlawful Interference* (Montreal: International Civil Aviation Organization, 2006) chapter 2, sub chapter 2.1.3b.

3. Ibid., Chapter 2., subchapter 2.4.

4. United States, Secretary of Transportation, *Anti-terrorist Act of 1996*, Title XIV, Code of Federal Regulations, section 129.25.

5. Hatch Amendment, http://900000_ASI_April_1996_hatch_amendment_USA_01, April 1999, 1–3.

6. Ibid., 6.

7. International Civil Aviation Organization, *Accomplishments under the ICAO Aviation Security Plan* (Air Transport Bureau), para. 3.9, sub para. 3.1.0.

8. International Civil Aviation Organization, *Aviation Security Plan of Action* (Security Training Programs), para. 3.8.

9. International Air Transport Association, *Security Management Systems for Air Transport Operators* (Executive Summary), September 2006.

10. Ibid.

11. Isaac Kfir, Institute for Counter Terrorism, *The United Nations Approach to International Terrorism Following 9/11* (Article, March 19, 2004), www.ict.org.il/apage/5522.php.

12. International Civil Aviation Organization, *Accomplishments under the ICAO Aviation Security Plan* (Air Transport Bureau), para. 3.9., sub para. 3.1.0.

13. International Civil Aviation Organization, Annex 17 to the Convention of Civil Aviation Security, *Safeguarding International Civil Aviation Against Acts of Unlawful Interference*, chapter 2, sub chapter 2.1.3b.

14. United States Department of Defense, Defense Advanced Research Projects Agency (DARPA) *A Compendium of DARPA Programs*, April 2002, 7–9, www.darpa.mil/body/news/2002/darpa-fact.html.

15. Ibid., 7–9.

16. Tony Tether, Director of the Defense Advanced Research Projects Agency (DARPA), *Report*, submitted to Sub-committee on Terrorism, Unconventional Threats and Capabilities of the House of Representatives Armed Services Committee, March 29, 2006, 25.

CHAPTER 3

Dealing with Human Vulnerability in Aviation Security: Effectiveness of SCAN Detecting "Compromise"

Anthony T. H. Chin

The aviation sector spends millions of dollars on sophisticated hardware in securing airports and airplanes. However, the weakest link, often overlooked, is that between security and airport or airline personnel. Lapses in security can be a result of graft, where an individual compromises security in exchange for payment. This is a criminal offense that can cost lives. Compromises in security or criminal behavior are perceived by many as decisions largely based on personality characteristics, moral values, socioeconomic conditions, or family background; factors that are seemingly beyond the study of economics. However, economists suggest that individuals make rational decisions as to whether to commit crimes. Armed with a robust economic theoretical framework, the economist seeks to show that increasing the probability of detection and the magnitude of punishment or penalties ought to deter a would-be criminal or compromiser of security. Such deterrence can perhaps be carried out in inexpensive and efficient ways through the use of forensic assessment tools. Simply increasing the probability of detection through effectively employing instruments such as the polygraph, verbal/behavioral analysis, and statement analysis can deter prospective security compromisers.

An experimental framework was thus set up to test the reliability of forensic tools as an instrument to increase the probability of detection. Scientific content analysis (SCAN), a technique that analyzes linguistic structure and content, was chosen as the object of interest. In the resulting analysis, various dominant strategies emerge for guilty as well as for innocent participants, which will provide a framework of applying SCAN to aviation security.

The results indicate that SCAN is most efficient if used together with other forensic tools. This is because it is weaker in detecting innocence in participants and hence would need to be employed jointly with other assessment tools in order to improve in this aspect. This study shows, however, that increasing probability of detection can be achieved through the use of forensic assessment tools such as SCAN, which is inexpensive to administer. Through the use of such tests, crime deterrence can now be efficiently achieved at a low cost by raising the probability of detection, which in turn results in an optimal equilibrium level of crime or deception.

INTRODUCTION

Prior to Becker's seminal study on the economics of crime and punishment, few economists looked at crime within an economic framework.[1] This was possibly due to the fact that crime is associated with immoral values and attitudes, which defy methodical economic investigation. In addition, crime seemed to be primarily influenced by socioeconomic factors, family background, personality, or even genetics, and thus was best left to psychology or sociology.[2] Moreover, crime was perceived as an irrational behavior resulting in an inefficient decision. This is because criminals having full knowledge of the penalties if arrested still choose to commit the crime. Crime was thus viewed as being incompatible with an economic framework, where rationality results in efficient decisions.[3]

However, an economic framework is possible if the act is viewed as part of an individual's choice set. Criminal activity seeks to maximize gains from crime, given the severity of punishment and the probability of apprehension. Viewed in this light, the decision to commit a crime is in fact an individual's rational choice maximization. Additionally, rational behavior entails an individual weighing the pros and cons of alternatives before choosing one that maximizes his utility. This is consistent with the criminal decision-making process, since individuals do consider the foregone opportunity costs of legal activities in deciding to commit a crime.[4]

From society's viewpoint, crime is inefficient because it generates negative externalities. Hence, deterrence is needed to inhibit criminal activity. The deterrence hypo-study states that the level of criminal activity responds to the costs and benefits of crime.[5] Since valuation of the benefits of crime is determined by individuals, law enforcers can only regulate crime through increasing its costs. This can be achieved by increasing the probability of arrest and/or the severity of punishment. Logically, it would seem that complete deterrence would be optimal for society since crime is something which society tries to avoid. This is incorrect and in actual fact inefficient, because deterrence comes at a cost. This cost includes expenditure on hiring law enforcement officers or installing anticriminal devices such as hidden cameras. Thus, the optimal level of deterrence is reached when the marginal cost of deterrence is equal to the marginal benefit of crime. This is contrary to popular wisdom in the economic analysis of crime, and if the larger deterrent effect is significant, it entails costly law expenditure.

This study seeks to examine whether the probability of detection can be increased indirectly through the use of affordable forensic assessment tools in criminal investigations. In particular, we are interested in examining the validity and time reliability of the forensic tool, scientific content analysis (SCAN). In addition, we examine how SCAN's validity is affected by gender and prior antideception training. Thus, this study endeavors to quantify SCAN assessment and determine how it affects the probability of detection as well.

The next section discusses the market for crime and the concept of optimal quantity of crime, followed by an analysis of how an individual optimizes his amount of crime based on expected payoffs and costs under norm-guided rational behavior. The third section introduces SCAN and explains how it detects deception by analyzing linguistic structures. The experimental framework, the objectives, and the way the experiment was conducted are covered in the fourth section. Results from the experiment are presented and analyzed, and the study concludes with a summary of the main findings from the experiment and the policy implications.

LITERATURE REVIEW

In the economic analysis of crime, individuals will only commit a crime when their expected marginal benefits exceed their expected marginal costs. This section looks at the macroeconomic market demand and supply of offenses, followed by the microeconomic behavior of individuals when deciding whether to commit a crime.

Supply and Demand for Offenses

The crime market is based on five key assumptions.[6] First, all participants in the market, buyers and sellers of illegal activities/goods and law enforcement officials, behave according to the rules of optimizing behavior. All agents seek to maximize personal utility subject to constraints. Second, certain expectations about legal and illegal activities payoff are formed based on the information that is available. This payoff is determined by the probability of detection and the severity of punishment. Third, there is a stable distribution of preference for crime as well as safety from crime. This translates into the derived demand for law enforcement. Fourth, law enforcement aims to maximize social welfare. Finally, the summation of all individuals' preferences in the market leads to an equilibrium level of crime (q^*), since this is where demand intersects with supply.

Supply of offenses

The supply of offenses is a function of why people choose to commit crime. With reference to the assumptions stated earlier, we can determine the profit function of crime. The profit function (π_c) varies positively with income from crime (w_c) and is negatively related to costs of crime (c_c),[7] wages forgone from legal activities (w_1), and the multiplication of probability of detection and severity of penalty ($p_c \cdot f$). Mathematically, this can be written as follows:

$$\pi_c = w_c - c_c - w_l - (p_c \cdot f) \tag{1}$$

Individuals are risk neutral and aversion to crime is a constant. This aversion to crime will affect an individual's decision to commit crime. To induce an individual to commit crime, the net expected benefits must exceed a certain level to compensate for his aversion. Thus, the resulting supply of offenses will be a function of an individual's private net expected benefit from crime.

Based on these assumptions, the supply of offenses is then the minimal level of benefit from illegal activities needed to induce crime. Conversely, it can be viewed as the summation of individuals' maximum threshold to crime aversion, since exceeding this level will entice one to crime. Assuming that the population's threshold for crime is normally distributed, the supply of offences will be upward sloping,[8] as depicted in Figure 3.1 (S). This means that crime (q_c) increases as the net benefits from crime rise.

Demand for offenses

The demand for crime is a derived demand because crime protection incurs costs. Since absolute protection from crime is costly, individuals need to live with an optimal amount of crime, which is the point where the marginal benefits of crime protection are equal to its marginal costs. Thus, demand for crime is derived from the optimal demand of crime protection.[9]

Figure 3.1
Regression Results of Detention Strategy

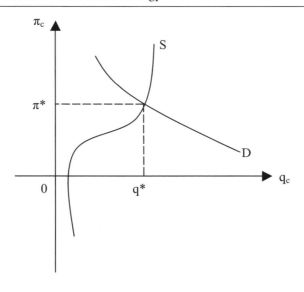

The demand for crime protection is derived from minimizing expected loss from crime. Optimal expenditure has a direct positive relationship with and is a function of the probability of being a crime victim and the expected loss from crime. Assuming rational expectations, every individual perceives his/her risk of being victimized as equal to the crime rate (q_c) in the population. Therefore, the demand for crime protection increases as the crime rate rises. With reference to Figure 3.1, the derived demand for crime is downward sloping (D). This is because with higher crime rates, individuals will spend more on crime protection (direct relationship between crime protection expenditure and crime rates), which in turn reduces the offender's benefit from crime. The benefits from crime are lowered as the offender has to spend more time and effort now to commit the crime (thereby raising his/her direct costs of crime, c_c), and his/her opportunity costs of losing wages from legal activities are higher (w_l). Thus, the expected net benefits from crime (see equation 1) are now reduced.

Extension of Rational Behavior with Norms

After establishing the market equilibrium for crime, we now turn our attention to how individuals rationally optimize their choice of criminal activity based on utility maximization. The rational criminal commits a crime only when his/her benefit from illegal activity is higher than that from legal alternatives. In contrast, sociologists, criminologists, and psychologists model crime based on social factors. Individual choice is not important and crime originates from biological, environmental, psychological, and socioeconomic factors. Norms[10] are therefore important in their analysis, since crime deviates from socially accepted behavior.

Empirical research thus far suggests that both approaches should be included in the analysis of crime and neither is superior to the other. To reconcile the two approaches, Eide suggests an extension of the traditional rational behavior model by including norms in the decision-making process.[11] This inclusion is important in the economic analysis of crime because norms do affect the desirability of outcomes. An individual has to consider monetary gains as well as society's disapproval and possible rejection when weighing the benefits and costs of crime. Figure 3.2 graphically delineates the extended rational decision-making process.

From Figure 3.2, it is clear that individual preferences affect the decision-making process with regard to the most desirable outcome. Preferences in the extended model include monetary benefits and norms like social acceptance and warmth. If we include norms as part of decision making, individuals may choose not to commit a crime even if the monetary benefits are higher than the costs. This is because if they value social acceptance highly, the costs of crime will be greater than its benefits, since they face possible rejection by society. In this extended model, then, norms guide the rational choice decision but are not pivotal in the final selection of outcome. Therefore, the individual still weighs the costs and benefits of each outcome before making an optimal choice.

Figure 3.2
Preferences and Decision-making Factors

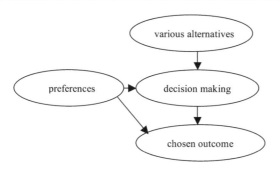

In a self-reported survey of 808 young males, more than 40 percent stated that personal restraints[12] would stop them from committing a crime, indicating that norms do play a significant role in the decision to commit crime.

The Individual's Risk Preference

To develop our understanding of an individual's decision-making process, it is important to know his/her risk preference under norm-guided rational behavior. This is attributable to microeconomic theory, where an individual's risk preference determines his/her behavior in a situation of uncertainty. A similar analysis is employed here because individuals do not know their true probability of detection, and risk preferences determine optimal law enforcement, which in turn affects criminal behavior. Risk neutral individuals will make a decision to commit crime by comparing the benefits and costs of crime. In contrast, risk averse individuals will only commit a crime when the marginal benefit of crime is greater than the marginal costs.

Compared to the case of a risk neutral population, the fine imposed for a risk adverse population will not be as large and the probability of apprehension will be higher. This is so because the benefits from lower law enforcement expenditure must be considered against the increased level of risk. Accordingly, the level of risk borne by risk averse individuals should be minimized. Thus, the optimal probability of apprehension and fine will be a calibration of how the probability of apprehension falls as law enforcement expenditure decreases and the degree of risk aversion in the population.

The Economic Theory of Crime

In the economic framework of crime, all offenders are assumed to have norm-guided rational behavior and they will choose criminal behavior only when the expected payoff is greater than the expected punishment. With reference to Figure 3.3, the x-axis is the seriousness of offence while the y-axis

Figure 3.3
Punishment, Seriousness of Offence, and Payoff

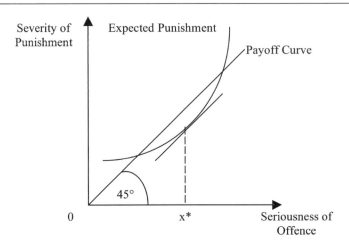

is the severity of punishment. In Figure 3.3, the severity of punishment is directly proportional to the seriousness of crime. This implies that that the expected gain is a function of crime. Thus, the expected payoff line has an angle of 45°, since x = y. The expected punishment curve is a function of the probability of apprehension (p_c) and the severity of punishment (f). Optimally, the rational criminal will choose to commit x* amount of crime since this is the point where marginal benefit from crime is equal to marginal cost. The expected punishment curve will shift when p_c or f changes. In reality, the probability of apprehension rises with the severity of the offense, since more serious crimes (e.g., murder) will produce greater enforcement effort. The severity of punishment is also positively related to the seriousness of the crime. In addition, the expected punishment is influenced by possible societal disapproval when norms are violated and by the shame felt by the offender.

It is clear that the optimal amount of crime is influenced by the probability of detection, severity of punishment, and degree of risk aversion. Since most individuals are assumed to be risk averse, it would be beneficial to modulate crime through increased probability of detection rather than by harsh penalties to reduce the risk premium. However, cost considerations come into play because of the direct relationship between higher detection rates and enforcement expenditure. It is plausible that forensic assessment techniques can contribute to aid detection since they are less costly to enforce. In particular, we employ scientific content analysis (SCAN).

SCIENTIFIC CONTENT ANALYSIS AND HYPO-STUDY

One way to increase the probability of detection of crime (p_c) is to increase the "amount" of law enforcement. This is so partly because the probability of detection can be increased indirectly through the use of forensic assessment interview tools such as the polygraph test, psychological profiling, and observation of body or verbal language and analysis of written statements.

Scientific Content Analysis (SCAN)

Scientific content analysis (SCAN) draws on many years of intensive research into verbal communication, specifically researching on linguistics in communication. The basic hypo-study postulates that most people do not want to lie and would rather give information freely, and that about 90 percent of all statements are truthful. However, if one tells lies, one prefers not to lie directly but to employ conversational tricks. Some of these tricks include the omitting facts, feigning forgetfulness, or pretending to be ignorant. A question is answered with a question, very brief in critical parts of stories. or narrative gaps are filled in with uninformative statements like "we talked" (about what topic?) or "afterward" (after what event?).

SCAN detects deception by analyzing the structure and content of the written statement through the use of speech patterns. The truth is simply hidden when people lie. Thus, through the analysis of written statements and the breaking of linguistic codes, linguistic inconsistencies are detected. SCAN testing also includes a section called View Guidebook, a series of structured questions based on the SCAN principles.[13] The linguistic structure of responses to these questions is also analyzed for deception. Statements are a form of alternate reality and are even more important than the person. "The person is dead, the statement is alive."[14]

Analysis of responses

The use of pronouns can indicate whether a person is being truthful.[15] Pronouns are significant in the analysis because one can never be confused by their use. A change in pronoun use thus suggests a shift in relationship. Inappropriate use of pronouns may also signal possible deception. To illustrate this, it is highly suggestive if a victim in a kidnapping case uses the pronoun "we" to refer to the kidnapper and himself. This is because "we" signifies compliance, teamwork, and partnership.

Hypo-study

Although SCAN has been proven useful in assisting law enforcement to determine a suspect's guilt, it is still far from an ideal system, because it is very subjective and does not have a formula for scoring. This is due to the fact that analysis is solely based on the evaluator's judgemnt upon reading the statements. This is a major point of contention and has led many people to doubt SCAN's validity. Further, there is a time lag between the crime and the interrogation. To be robust, SCAN should be able to accurately detect deception regardless of whether the suspect was tested one day after committing the crime or a few years later.

The Internet has created an awareness of forensic testing and of possible techniques to pass the examination. Rationally, both innocent and guilty suspects will seek this information and prepare themselves for an assessment. This is because the innocent are doubtful of the tool's accuracy and would want to avoid a false positive conclusion, so they learn these skills to prove their innocence. In contrast, the guilty would strive for a false negative outcome[16] and hope that learning such skills would enable them to beat the system.

Finally, in order for SCAN to be a valid testing tool for deception, its detection rates should be consistent across gender. If gender bias were present, this would render the test inefficient. This study seeks to examine whether SCAN is valid as a forensic assessment tool in an experimental setup. Its validity is ascertained by testing for accuracy, time consistency, and gender bias. In addition, we examine whether prior training to defeat forensic testing will affect SCAN's accuracy in detecting deception. By controlling for these factors that exist in reality, we gain more confidence in our resulting analysis, which has greater external validity.

As discussed earlier, deterrence has often been achieved by manipulating the severity of fine because it is the most cost efficient method. Unfortunately, this leads to a less than optimal amount of crime, because risk averse individuals are "over-deterred." If SCAN is determined to be valid as a tool in detecting deception, this means that it is able to significantly increase the probability of detection. Given that deterrence is a function of probability of detection and severity of fine, this translates into lower fines in law enforcement to achieve the same level of deterrence. Consequently, the risk premium of risk averse individuals can be lowered and an optimal level of crime will be achieved, because they will not be "over-deterred."

EXPERIMENTAL SETUP

Experimental Objectives

A crucial disadvantage of SCAN as a forensic assessment tool is its subjective scoring based on heuristics. Due to this, many have discredited its use because of the belief that this scoring method leads to biased judgments based on an evaluator's impression. In this experiment, we seek to test whether this censure is valid by having an evaluator assess SCAN using a scoring formula. Although this deviates from the usual heuristic assessment, the systematic evaluation technique is still founded on the principles of SCAN.

Due to investigative procedures, criminal suspects are often apprehended some time after committing the crime. The time lag varies from a day to a few years. Thus, this experiment attempts to find out if there is empirical support for SCAN's consistency as a forensic tool given a time difference between committing the crime and administering the test. This is achieved by assigning participants to be tested either one day (t+1) or three days (t+3) after the experiment (which is described below). A proportion of participants who have been assigned as guilty or innocent receive antideception training, that is, they are taught either mental or physical antipolygraph techniques. Although these skills are not specifically designed to deceive SCAN, it would be useful to see whether antideception training skills are transferable across forensic assessment tools.

As discussed in the hypo-study, both innocent and guilty suspects have an incentive to learn these techniques in order to appear innocent. This intrinsic motivation is replicated in the experiment by giving a larger monetary reward if participants are deemed to be innocent after testing, regardless of their true state. Through this monetary motivation, this study gains greater external validity as well, because participants will do all they can to appear innocent during testing, which is exactly what happens in real life. In addition, having the same payoff structure for both guilty and innocent participants ensures that their severity of punishment is kept constant. This means that their only variable in determining cost of crime is the probability of detection, which in this case is SCAN. Finally, an equal number of males and females were selected for this experiment to test for gender bias in SCAN.

Sample Population

From a pool of participants who responded to calls for participation in an experiment, a random sample of 72 males and 72 females were selected. All 144 participants were undergraduates from the National University of Singapore (NUS). In this 3 × 2 × 2 experimental design, an equal number of male and female participants were randomly assigned to each of the 12 experimental conditions. A graphical outline of the experimental design is given in Figure 3.4, while the distribution of participants from each gender in each of the 12 experimental conditions is shown in Table 3.1.

Figure 3.4
Sample Structure

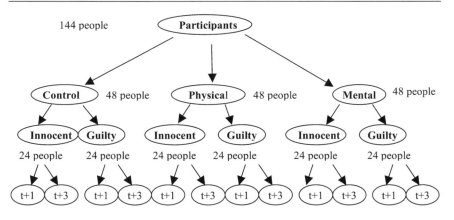

Table 3.1
Distribution of Participants Across Experimental Groups

Experimental group/ Gender	Number of Days	CG	CI	PG	PI	MG	MI
Male	t + 1	6	6	6	6	6	6
	t + 3	6	6	6	6	6	6
Female	t + 1	6	6	6	6	6	6
	t + 3	6	6	6	6	6	6
Total	–	24	24	24	24	24	24

CG = Control Guilty, CI = Control Innocent, PG = Physical Guilty, PI = Physical Innocent, MG = Mental Guilty, MI = Mental Innocent.

Experimental Groups

In this $3 \times 2 \times 2$ experimental design, there are three main treatment groups (control, physical, mental), two conditional groups within each treatment (innocent, guilty), and a further two conditional conditions within each group (t+1, t+3). Thus, there are in total 12 experimental conditions as depicted in Table 3.1, with 6 males and 6 females in each condition. Participants in the control group are not given antidetection training before testing. Therefore, they can be viewed as the baseline measurement for comparison with the other two experimental groups to observe the effects of training.

On the other hand, participants in the physical or mental treatment groups are taught techniques to pass the polygraph test. For example, participants in the physical treatment group are taught how to regulate or hasten their breathing rates when the control questions are asked, in order to corrupt the physiological readings. In contrast, participants in the mental treatment group are taught cognitive skills to defeat the polygraph. For example, they are taught how to count backwards when asked sensitive questions, in order to regulate their physiological responses.

In addition, participants who have been assigned to a guilty condition will have to simulate criminal behavior by accepting a bribe in the form of money from an individual in exchange for the security plans of an airport. In contrast, participants in the innocent conditions will have no knowledge except that a crime has been committed. Depending on whether they have been assigned to be tested either one (t+1) or three days (t+3) after the conduct of the experiment, all participants will report back to NUS for a SCAN test followed by a polygraph examination.

Conduct of the Experiment

The experiment was conducted in the grounds of the National University of Singapore (NUS). All participants were asked to report to a tutorial room where they were given instructions via a taped recording. Participants who were in any of the three guilty conditions[17] were given 15 minutes to complete the transaction, that is, commit the crime. Instructions were given for them to find their way with the aid of a map to a particular room where they would look for a black briefcase in which they were to put the security plans of an airport in exchange for a brown envelope marked "X" on both sides.[18] Before entering, they would have to knock on the door and check that no one was in the room. If no one answered, they would then proceed to let themselves into the room. They would then have to search the contents of the briefcase carefully to find a sealed envelope marked with an "X" on both sides. After locating the envelope, they would have to replace the contents and the plans in the briefcase as if it had not been tampered with. Participants were warned that should someone walk in at any time while they were committing the crime, they would have to think of an excuse and continue whatever they were doing.

This instruction was given to model the fear that criminals have when they are committing a crime in reality that someone might walk in on them. After committing the crime, the participants had a 20-minute break in which they were free to walk around the campus before reporting back to the experimenter with the envelope. Upon returning the envelope to the experimenter, they were asked to tear the envelope open and remove five 10-dollar notes from inside it. They would then return this money to the experimenter and sign their names on the stolen envelope. Instructions were also given to them not to discuss the experiment with anyone, to deny all involvement with the crime if asked, and always to appear truthful.

All participants would then return for testing either one or three days later, depending on their condition assignment. The only difference between the three guilty conditions would be that participants who had been assigned to be taught either mental or physical techniques would complete their training immediately after returning the money to the experimenter. Participants in the innocent conditions would listen to a taped recording as well. However, they would not be instructed to find the room with the black briefcase but instead be given a 15-minute leisure period in which they were free to do whatever they wanted. They did know that a crime was being committed during this time, but they had no details. After 15 minutes, they would report back to the experimenter and return for testing either one or three days later. As with the guilty participants, the only difference between the innocent treatment groups[19] was that participants in the physical or mental condition would have to receive their training immediately upon returning from their break.

All participants would first undergo the SCAN test and then a polygraph examination, regardless of whether they returned one or three days later. All participants had an incentive to prove themselves innocent in both tests. This was because they would receive a SG$50 token if they were declared innocent at the end of testing, regardless of whether they were truly innocent.[20] If the verdict was inconclusive or guilty, they would only receive a token of SG$30. Thus, all participants, including those who had been assigned to the innocent conditions, had a strong motivation to pass the detection tests and earn a higher token.

ANALYSIS AND DISCUSSION OF RESULTS

Evaluation of SCAN

The SCAN questionnaire consisted of eight pages on which suspects wrote their answers in full sentences. They were instructed to think of their answer carefully before writing, because they were not allowed to make corrections. All completed SCAN questionnaires were independently assessed by a certified forensic evaluator. As discussed earlier, the analysis of SCAN statements is very subjective because there is no precise numerical scoring technique. Therefore, evaluators make their judgment calls based on their experience and their impression of the narrative. We report the judgment calls from three experts based on the VIEW questionnaire[21] (based specifically on the eight questions; see Appendix).

The evaluator used an objective scoring system in which each question is given a possible rating of −2 to 2 (inclusive of zero). A rating of −2 or −1 means the evaluator feels that the suspect is lying or possibly lying, respectively. On the other hand, a score of 2 or 1 implies that the evaluator feels the suspect is truthful or possibly truthful. A score of 0 suggests that the evaluator cannot come to a conclusion about the statement.

Next, the rating of each question is added up and the final view call is based on the sum of the scores on the eight questions. The range of the sum of scores attainable is from −16 to 16. Based on these scores, participants are determined to be either problematic (i.e., guilty), leaning toward being problematic, leaning toward being cleared, or cleared (i.e., innocent). It must be noted that although this scoring scheme is markedly different from SCAN's standard assessment, it is based on the principles of SCAN. Figure 3.5 illustrates the assessment scheme.

Graphical Analysis of SCAN's Accuracy

One major obstacle to testing the accuracy of SCAN in detecting deception was that the true state of the suspect is not available in reality. This

Figure 3.5
Detecting Deception

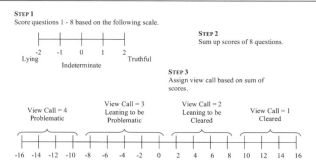

STEP 1
Score questions 1 - 8 based on the following scale.

$$-2 \quad -1 \quad 0 \quad 1 \quad 2$$
Lying   Indeterminate   Truthful

STEP 2
Sum up scores of 8 questions.

STEP 3
Assign view call based on sum of scores.

View Call = 4
Problematic

View Call = 3
Leaning to be
Problematic

View Call = 2
Leaning to be
Cleared

View Call = 1
Cleared

-16 -14 -12 -10 -8 -6 -4 -2 0 2 4 6 8 10 12 14 16

Figure 3.6
Gender Differences

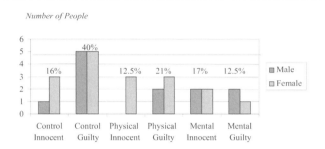

was overcome in the experimental framework because the true condition of each participant is known. With reference to the earlier discussion on SCAN evaluation, there are four view calls under which suspects fall. In this study, the accuracy of SCAN (the hit rate) is determined to be the correct fit between the true condition (guilty or innocent) and the view call (problematic or cleared). Participants who were classified as leaning toward being cleared or leaning toward being problematic are disregarded. Figure 3.6 illustrates the distribution of correct hits SCAN achieved between groups and within each gender.

The hit rate percentage from Figure 3.6 indicates that SCAN is reasonably accurate in detecting deception in all treatment groups, except when mental techniques are taught. This is reflected in the higher hit rates in the guilty condition compared to the hit rates in the innocent condition in both the physical and control groups, except in the mental group. It is most accurate in guilt detection in the control group, where there is a high hit rate of 40 percent.

However, SCAN is not very efficient in detecting innocence, because the innocence accuracy rates are lower than the guilty hit rates. It is higher only in the mental treatment group, but only at a marginal rate of 4.5 percent. This is in comparison with a difference of 24 percent in the control group and 8.5 percent in the physical group.

Gender Differences between Groups

Graphical analysis

One of the experimental objectives was to see if there is any gender bias in SCAN evaluation. As can be seen in Figures 3.7 and 3.8, which chart the mean score of females and males, respectively, across the groups, there is a clear difference between the scores of the control guilty and control innocent groups. In particular, the control innocent groups have positive scores while the control guilty groups' scores are negative. This trend supports SCAN's efficiency in detecting deception, because a clear disparity exists between the two groups.

Figure 3.7
Females

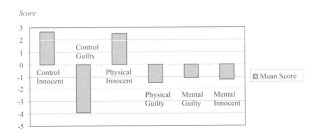

Figure 3.8
Males

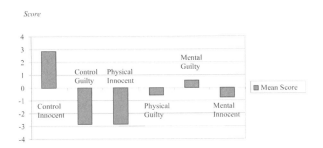

However, the mean scores for the remaining four treatment groups are skewed. To illustrate this, females' mean scores for mental innocent and males' mean score for physical innocent, mental guilty, and mental innocent all work against the theory of SCAN. This shows that SCAN is inefficient in detecting deception once participants have received any form of training. This result echoes the graphical analysis of SCAN's accuracy given in the previous section. Specifically, Figure 3.8 suggests that guilty males should employ mental techniques because they will be able to pass the test. In contrast, the negative score in the mental guilty condition in Figure 3.7 hints that the mental techniques are ineffective for females because the scores are negative. This is incorrect, however, because upon closer observation, we see that the score for mental guilty is higher than the score for physical guilty, which means that mental techniques are still more effective for females.

Innocent females should learn physical techniques because they will be able to ensure that their scores will be positive, matching their true state. This contrasts with innocent males, who should avoid physical techniques because their scores are negative. Thus, gender bias is suggested by the graphical analysis, as seen in the different mean scores obtained between groups and the conclusion that males and females should employ different techniques to achieve their goals of displaying innocence or hiding guilt.

F-Test of mean scores between groups for gender differences

F-tests were conducted to test if the gender difference in mean scores between groups is significant. The null hypo-study states that there is no significant difference in scores between males and females. If the null is not rejected, it shows that SCAN does not discriminate across gender when testing. The results are summarized in Table 3.2 below. At the 10 percent significance level, all p-values are greater than 0.1, which means that the test fails to reject the null, except for the physical innocent group. Therefore, there is a gender bias in the SCAN test in this treatment group. This statistical result concurs with the graphical analysis shown earlier, where there were differences across gender mean scores in the physical innocent group.

F-tests were also carried out to test the mean scores of the six groups within each gender. The results are summarized in Table 3.3. The F-statistic obtained for males was 1.632 (p > .1), which means that scores are not significant between groups for males. Simply, the different treatment groups had no effect on males' SCAN scores. However, the F-statistic obtained for females was 2.672 (p < .1), which rejects the null. Thus, we can conclude that after controlling the gender variable, the mean scores differ significantly between groups for female participants at 10 percent significance level.

Time Consistency of SCAN

Graphical analysis

Participants underwent SCAN testing either one or three days later after being taught antipolygraph techniques. This experimental variable sought to test if SCAN gives the same consistent result regardless of when the test is administered after the crime is committed (i.e., time effect). If SCAN is a consistent tool, there should be no divergence in scores whether participants are tested one day or three days after committing the crime. This is to say

Table 3.2
Results of F-Test for Gender Differences Between Groups

Experimental Group	CG	CI	PG	P I	MG	MI
F-statistic	1.2169	0.1709	5.5162	0.1321	0.3447	0.0492
df	(1, 22)	(1, 22)	(1, 22)	(1, 22)	(1, 22)	(1, 22)
Probability	0.2819	0.6833	0.0282	0.7198	0.5631	0.8265
CATEGORY statistics						
Female mean	0.33333	−3.9166	2.5000	−1.5000	−1.0833	−1.2500
Male mean	−2.3333	−2.8333	5.6219	−0.5833	0.5833	−0.7500

CG = Control Guilty, CI = Control Innocent, PG = Physical Guilty.

Table 3.3
Results of F-Test for Mean Score Differences Between Male and Female

Gender	Male	Female
F-statistic	1.631533	2.672493
df	(5, 66)	(5, 66)
Probability	0.1639	0.0293
CATEGORY statistics—Mean scores		
Control Guilty	−2.833333	−3.916667
Control Innocent	2.833333	2.666667
Mental Guilty	−0.750000	−1.250000
Mental Innocent	0.583333	−1.083333
Physical Guilty	−0.583333	−1.500000
Physical Innocent	−2.833333	2.500000

Figure 3.9
Breakdown by Groups

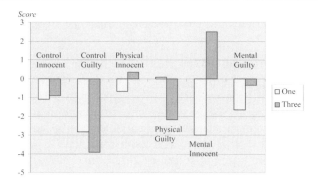

that all guilty participants and innocent participants should always have negative and positive scores, respectively. Figure 3.9 illustrates the distribution of mean scores between the six groups, with a breakdown of the mean score for participants who were tested one day or three days after training.

As seen in Figure 3.9, the mean scores are unambiguously negative for the control group, regardless of whether participants are guilty or innocent. The only observable difference is that the scores for the guilty are higher on the negative scale in comparison to the scores for the innocent. This is consistent with the analysis provided above, showing that SCAN detects guilty suspects more efficiently. A time effect is observed in the physical treatment group, because there is a divergence of scores in both the guilty and innocent conditions. The distribution of mean scores reveals that the innocent obtain negative scores when testing is performed one day later and positive scores when it is performed three days later. Guilty participants, on the other hand, obtain negative scores when tested three days later and positive scores when tested a day later.

Like the physical innocent, mental innocent participants have a disparity in mean scores between testing after one or three days. This leads us to the same conclusion that we came to earlier: that innocent participants should not learn any form of techniques to pass forensic tests because their scores will be biased in the wrong direction. There is also a wider difference in scores in the mental innocent condition compared to the scores in the physical innocent condition. This means that the mental innocent have a higher probability of being incorrectly deemed guilty after learning mental techniques. Figure 3.9 also shows that no time effects exist for guilty participants, because their scores are negative regardless of the time they are tested after committing the crime.

F-Test of mean scores between groups for time differences

The preceding graphical analysis indicates that time inconsistency exists in the SCAN results, so an F-test was conducted to test for mean score differences between participants who took the test one day after training and those who took it three days after training. The null hypo-study states that the number of days (t+1 or t+3) after which SCAN is administered following the crime does not significantly affect the mean scores between the two groups. The F-statistic obtained was 0.582 (p > .1) with degrees of freedom (1, 142). Therefore, we fail to reject the null at 10 percent significance level and conclude that the SCAN results are consistent between participants who take the test either one day or three days after committing the crime.

Further F-tests were performed within each condition to check if mean score differences exist due to time differences. The results are summarized in Table 3.4, and we fail to reject the null hypo-study across all the groups, except in the mental innocent condition where p-value is less than 0.1. Thus, we can infer that time differences do not exist within each group except within the mental innocent treatment group. The significant result obtained in the mental innocent condition supports our previous argument that innocent participants should avoid learning mental techniques to prove their innocence, because of the great difference in scores in the wrong direction.

Regression of Scores against Gender, Experiment Groups, and Test Effects

The analysis thus far suggests that the SCAN score is a function of experimental groups, gender, and the number of days after the crime that the test is given. This is represented by equation 2.

$$Score = Constant + Gender + Experimental\ Group + Time\ Effects \qquad (2)$$

An ordinary least squares (OLS) regression analysis was performed to test the function with score as the regressand, and gender, experimental

Table 3.4
Results of F-Test for Time Effects Within Groups

Experimental Group	CG	CI	PG	P I	MG	MI
F-statistic	0.0045	0.1708	0.1562	0.8203	4.44416	0.3548
df	(1, 22)	(1, 22)	(1, 22)	(1, 22)	(1, 22)	(1, 22)
Probability	0.9471	0.6833	0.6965	0.3749	0.0467	0.5575
CATEGORY statistics—Mean scores						
One Day	–1.0833	–2.8333	–0.6666	0.0833	–3.0000	–1.6666
Three Days	–0.9166	–3.9166	0.3333	–2.1666	2.5000	–0.3333

CG = Control Guilty, CI = Control Innocent, PG = Physical Guilty, PI = Physical Innocent, MG = Mental Guilty, MI = Mental Innocent.

groups, and number of days testing took place after the crime as the regressors. Since all explanatory variables are binary, the regression model has seven dummies. For example, the independent variable CNTRL_INNOC is the dummy that takes the value of 1 for the control innocent participants and 0 for all other participants. The variables GENDER takes on a value of 1 for males and 0 for females. TIME measures the time consistency of SCAN and takes on a value of 1 when testing takes place one day after the crime and 0 if testing takes place three days after the crime. The base group for this regression is the group in the mental guilty condition, whose effects are captured by the intercept, C. Table 3.5 shows the results of the regression analysis where all coefficients are statistically insignificant at 10 percent significance level and R-squared is 0.0373. This means that the model has low explanatory power since the independent variables account for only 3.73 percent of the variation in scores. The F-statistic for the model is 0.7533 (p > .1), which implies that the regression is statistically insignificant.

Although the coefficients are statistically insignificant in this regression model, they do have a practical significance in explaining how scores are related to gender, experimental groups, and number of days testing took place after the crime. From Table 3.5, it can be seen that all guilty experimental groups have a negative partial effect on scores when all other variables are fixed, with the control guilty affecting scores greatest by reducing scores by 2.375.

The physical guilty condition negatively affects scores the least, by 0.0417.

Innocent experimental groups have a positive partial effect on scores with the exception of the control group. This is similar to earlier graphical analysis, in which SCAN does not detect innocent suspects efficiently in the control group. SCAN has a mild gender bias as well, because being male reduces scores by 0.639. This is congruent with earlier analysis in which guilty males are more likely to be detected by SCAN.

Table 3.5
Regression Results of Score Against Gender, Experimental Groups and Time Effects

Variable	Coefficient	Standard error	t-Statistic	Probability
C	–0.291667	1.449017	–0.201286	0.8408
Gender	–0.638889	1.024610	–0.623544	0.5340
Control Innocent	–2.48E-16	1.774676	–1.40E-16	1.0000
Control Guilty	–2.375000	1.774676	–1.338272	0.1830
Physical Innocent	0.833333	1.774676	0.469569	0.6394
Physical Guilty	–0.041667	1.774676	–0.023478	0.9813
Mental Innocent	0.750000	1.774676	0.422612	0.6732
Time	–0.777778	1.024610	–0.759097	0.4491
R-squared	0.037323	Mean dependent variable		–1.138889
Adjusted R-squared	–0.012226	S.D. dependent variable		6.110419
S.E. of regression	6.147659	Akaike info criterion		6.523972
Sum squared resid	5139.944	Schwarz criterion		6.688962
Log likelihood	–461.7260	F-statistic		0.753254
Durbin-Watson stat	1.843377	Prob(F-statistic)		0.627366

Testing one day after the crime negatively affects scores by 0.778. *Ceteris paribus*, this shows that the scores for all suspects, regardless of their true state, will be lower. However, since the coefficient is statistically insignificant at 10 percent significance level, we conclude that SCAN does give a consistent result when tested across time.

Discussion of Results

Accuracy of SCAN

SCAN has a satisfactory accuracy rate of at least 12.5 percent across all treatment groups. It is most accurate in detecting deception in the control guilty group, with a 40 percent hit rate. Comparing between gender, SCAN is able to better detect male guilt in comparison with females in the control group. Gender-biased anti-detection strategies also emerge from our graphical analysis. Table 3.6 shows what techniques each gender should employ to maximize their payoff (i.e., being deemed innocent if they are innocent or being deemed innocent if they are guilty). Table 3.6 reveals a dichotomy in the strategies that each gender should employ. The dominant strategy for guilty females would be to employ mental techniques to avoid detection, while guilty males show no difference between physical or mental techniques. This is consistent with reality, as females have been found to be superior in cognitive processes; therefore they are more adept at deciphering patterns. Thus they will be better able to avoid detection by employing mental techniques.

The graphical analysis thus brings us to the following conclusions:

1. *Ceteris paribus*, mental techniques are superior to physical training in antidetection.
2. SCAN is effective in detecting guilt in the control groups.
3. Gender bias is present in SCAN because guilty males have a higher hit rate than females in the control groups.

Gender differences between groups

The result of analyzing gender differences in mean scores strengthen the conclusion that SCAN is effective in detecting deception in the control groups. This is evident in the positive scores both genders obtain when in the control innocent group and the negative scores in the control guilty group. However, once participants receive training, SCAN becomes inefficient in detecting guilt because the scores are now skewed in the wrong direction.

Referring to Table 3.6, which depicts the various optimal strategies each gender should employ, the analysis of gender differences between groups lends support to the contention that guilty females should use mental techniques to evade detection while innocent females should use physical techniques. In Table 3.6, guilty males are indifferent between physical or mental techniques because the detection rates were the same. In this analysis, the dominant strategy for guilty males is distilled; they should choose mental techniques because the scores are positive compared to when physical techniques are used.

A significant result was obtained for females when an F-test was conducted to test for mean differences between groups within each gender. This shows that the different treatment conditions had an effect on females' mean score. This in turn, leads to the conclusion that learning antidetection training has an effect on females' SCAN scores but not on males' scores.

Time consistency of SCAN

The argument that SCAN can accurately detect deception in the control group is further reinforced when time effects are analyzed between groups. This conclusion is evident in the higher negative scores that participants obtain in the control guilty group compared to the control innocent participants.

Table 3.6
Antidetection Strategies that Maximize Each Gender's Payoffs

Techniques	Physical	Mental
Guilty Females	×	✓
Innocent Females	–	×
Guilty Males	–	–
Innocent Males	×	✓

The fact that scores for the control innocent are negative corresponds to the analysis in section on the accuracy of SCAN, which concludes that SCAN is relatively inefficient in detecting innocence.

Graphically, time effects exist for both physical and mental treatment conditions. Most striking in the analysis is the fact that there is a great divergence in scores for the mental innocent condition in the wrong direction when testing is done one day after committing the crime. Thus, mental techniques affect the scores of innocent participants negatively. This analysis illuminates the earlier conclusion that any form of training improves an innocent participant's probability of being deemed innocent. The introduction of time effects changes the conclusions completely. Specifically, the innocent should avoid learning any form of training because their scores will be negatively affected and they will receive a wrong judgment call.

Regression analysis

The coefficients obtained in the regression analysis strengthen the assertion that SCAN is most effective in detecting guilt in the control guilty group. It is relatively less efficient in determining innocence, a conclusion that was reached above and supported by the negative coefficient in the regression model. The gender bias toward males is also substantiated by the regression analysis, where males are more likely to have negative scores. SCAN gives time consistent results because the coefficient of TIME is insignificant.

Contradictions between Graphical and Statistical Analysis

One recurring feature of the analysis is the contradiction between graphical and statistical analysis. The graphical analysis indicates differences between groups but these observed differences are mostly not supported by statistical testing. One possible reason for this discrepancy would be the small sample size of 12 in each condition. With a sample size of less than 30, the population does not follow a normal distribution and hence nonsignificant results are observed.

There is also a restriction in the range of scores observed, as most of the participants are classified as leaning toward being problematic. Therefore, insignificant results are obtained because the differences between scores are too small. However, these slight differences are magnified in a graphical analysis, which allows us to detect trends between groups.

Implications of Results

Clearly, the results show that SCAN is accurate in detecting deception in the control group. This result holds even after accounting for gender and time effects. However, SCAN is relatively inefficient in detecting innocent suspects as innocent. This does not jeopardize the use of SCAN as a forensic assessment tool because in reality, suspects are evaluated using various tools and innocent suspects will be cleared in subsequent testing. Therefore, SCAN is still very useful as a screening tool in the early stages of investigation to assess guilt. Most importantly, it is easier and more convenient to administer than polygraph testing. This is especially so when a criminal case involves a large number of suspects and an easy and effective screening tool is needed.

With the advent of Internet technology, information can be shared freely across national borders at any time. This means that criminals are now more informed on the forensic assessment tools that they might face if they are brought in for investigation. Thus, they can now prepare themselves to increase their probability of being detected as innocent during assessment. Since the most commonly known tool is the polygraph machine and antipolygraph techniques are easily available online, criminals can be rationally expected to acquire this knowledge and lower their probability of being apprehended.

Although the techniques learnt are not designed specifically to pass a SCAN test, the results show that these mental or physical forms of training do have an effect on SCAN results. Explicitly, we observe the dominant strategies that emerge for each gender to maximize their payoff to crime after controlling for the true state of the suspect, gender effects, and time effects. In particular, we note that innocent suspects should avoid learning any form of techniques to ensure that they will be correctly assessed, because the training backfires and will make them look guilty instead.

Gender bias is present in SCAN testing, as guilty males have a higher probability of detection compared to females. Although this seems to reduce the validity of SCAN as an assessment tool, we have to bear in mind that the gender differences observed may not stem from flaws in SCAN. Specifically, the gender bias in SCAN may be a result of fundamental differences in each gender's cognitive workings. As mentioned earlier, females are better at detecting patterns, and hence they are able to escape from detection because they can predict the questions and answer accordingly.

A significant result from the analysis was that the accuracy rate of SCAN declines once participants have learnt antipolygraph techniques. This implies that once suspects have received antideception training, SCAN will not be able to detect their true state accurately. Since criminals are rationally expected to train themselves, criminal investigations in the real world call for a "multiple hurdles" approach to assessing a suspect. This implies that SCAN should be used as one of many assessment tools to gauge a suspect's true condition.

Future Research Possibilities

The results of SCAN are based on analyzing the difference in linguistic structure between a guilty and an innocent suspect. This suggests that an incorrect conclusion may be reached due to differences in the suspect's educational background or geographical difference in language. In this experiment, the assessment criteria have been modified to suit the local language structure. In future research, it would be intriguing to employ SCAN in languages other than English and observe its validity in assessment.

The overall nonsignificant F-statistic obtained and the low R-squared from the regression model suggest that the choice of explanatory variables may be incorrect. In later research, other variables such as a person's number of years of education, family background, or intelligence quotient (IQ) scores may be tested to see if they affect the mean scores in SCAN testing.

Gender bias can also be examined across the different forms of forensic assessment techniques in future research. If gender bias is present in other forensic tools as well, then an alternative form of assessment has to be invented or an existing form modified for females so that they can be accurately detected.

Finally, if SCAN is to be part of a multitude of assessment tools used to assess deception, it is worth researching what would be the optimal basket of forensic tests that SCAN should be used with. This is because deception can be expressed in varied forms, and different forensic tools measure the concept on diverse scales. Determining the optimal number and type of tools that appraise guilt differently will lower enforcement costs without compromising the probability of detection. This will provide insights into the multifaceted façade of deception and the ways in which people express it.

CONCLUSION

The economic framework in the analysis of deception or crime assesses an effective level of deterrence that can be achieved by adjusting the probability of detection or the severity of punishment. Economic analysis prescribes that efficiency should be achieved at the lowest possible cost. In the context of law enforcement, this would mean higher fines and lowered probability of detection. However, higher fines would mean additional risks undertaken by risk averse individuals. As a result, they will be "over-deterred" and the equilibrium level of crime will be below the optimal amount. Therefore, it would be best to seek a solution in which probability of detection can be increased in other ways besides hiring more law enforcers. This study identifies SCAN as a possible remedy and seeks to test if it is reliable and efficient in increasing the probability of detection.

Results from the experimental framework indicate that although SCAN is useful in detecting deception, it is still far from ideal. This is because it can correctly assess guilt in the control groups but this accuracy rate declines once participants have been trained in antideception. Thus, it is best to employ a broader bundle of assessment tools to increase the probability of detection.

Besides being able to accurately detect guilt, a reliable assessment tool should be able to determine innocence as well. The findings show that innocent suspects should refrain from learning antideception techniques, to ensure that they will be judged correctly. This is because such training will make them appear guilty. This is important because it means that the probability of detection in innocent suspects who have undergone training is lowered. Assuming that the severity of punishment is kept constant, innocent suspects will now have a greater incentive to commit crime because their expected cost is lowered.

Since the results show that SCAN is not superior to other assessment techniques in detecting deception, it would be best employed together with other techniques such as polygraph testing and verbal/behavioral analysis to increase the probability of detection. This will ensure that the probability of detection will be higher across both guilty and innocent suspects. Consequently, an optimal level of deterrence will be achieved through higher probabilities of detection and lowered penalties.

Through the experiments, this study has illustrated that the probability of detection can be increased without great addition to cost in terms of hiring more law enforcers, especially for white collar crime. Given this insight, the equilibrium level of crime can now be achieved through lower costs with a higher probability of detection rather than through harsher punishments. This lowers the risk premium of risk averse individuals, resulting in an optimal level of crime.

NOTES

1. Gary S. Becker, "Crime and Punishment: An Economic Approach," *Journal of Political Economy* 76, no. 2 (1968): 169–217.

2. Cesare Lombroso, *L'Uomo delinquente: The Criminal Man* (Milan: Hoepli, 1876).

3. Robert Cooter and Thomas Ulen, *Law and Economics* (Glenview, IL: Scott, Foresman and Company, 1988).

4. Erling Eide, *Economics of Crime: Deterrence and the Rational Offender* (Amsterdam: North Holland, 1994).

5. Cooter and Ulen, *Law and Economics*.

6. Eide, *Economics of Crime: Deterrence and the Rational Offender*.

7. These costs include self-protection costs incurred in order to avoid detection.

8. This is because crime (q_c) is a function of πc and the second derivative is greater than or equal to zero. Mathematically, $q_c = S(\pi_c)$ and $S'(\pi_c) \geq 0$.

9. Protection from crime may range from buying insurance, locks, and burglar alarm systems to paying higher rents to live in a safer neighborhood and hiring bodyguards. See Issaac Ehrlich and Gary Becker, "Market Insurance, Self Insurance, and Self Protection," *Journal of Political Economy* 80, no. 4 (1972): 386–402.

10. Norms are defined as specific rules for behavior in particular situations. See Craig Calhoun, Donald Light, and Suzanne Keller, *Sociology* (New York: McGraw-Hill, 1997). These rules are imposed by society, and deviation from these socially accepted behaviors may result in society's rejection or disapproval.

11. Eide, *Economics of Crime: Deterrence and the Rational Offender*.

12. Personal restraints include reasons of conscience after violating norms and consideration for the injured party. They exclude physical inability to commit crime.

13. See the appendix to this chapter.

14. Avinoam Sapir, *The View Guidebook: Verbal Inquiry—The Effective Witness* (Phoenix, AZ: Laboratory of Scientific Interrogation, 1995).

15. For example, pronouns like "I," "you," "he," and "she" indicate partnership. Pronouns like "we," "you," "they," "my," "your," "his," "her," and "our" indicate possession.

16. A negative outcome is one in which the suspect is determined to be innocent. Thus, guilty suspects will strive to achieve a false negative judgment.

17. These three treatment conditions would be control guilty, physical guilty, and mental guilty.

18. Participants were given the security plan of an airport and briefed on it.

19. These treatment groups would be control innocent, physical innocent, and mental innocent.

20. At the time of the experiment US$1 = SGD1.70.

21. See Sapir, *The View Guidebook*, for a detailed description of the VIEW questionnaire. When this questionnaire is used to obtain information, it is employed for the purposes of identifying the truth, rather than identifying instances of deception.

Appendix

VIEW Questionnaire

1. How do you feel now that you have completed this form?
2. Should we believe your answers to the questions?
3. If your answer to the last question was yes, give us one reason why.
4. What would you say if it was later determined that you lied on this form?
5. While filling out this form what were your emotions?
6. Were you afraid while completing this form?
7. Did you ever discuss the possibility and reasons for this investigation with anyone? If yes, with whom?
8. If you are asked to compensate for the missing money, how much are you willing to pay?

CHAPTER 4

Emotive Profiling

Terry A. Sheridan

Airline passenger profiling in the past has been based on behavioral observation (for example, excessive sweating or rapid breathing), or purely on the race of known terrorists.[1] Well-known signs of short-term acute stress have been used app ropriately to pick up passengers showing distress. And, in today's context of terrorism, any Middle Eastern Muslims are regarded with suspicion. However, in many cases they prove to be false positives, and much time and effort is wasted in this regard.[2]

Most passengers are fairly accepting of the methods used, but there have been accusations that profiling, as it is implemented today, is racially oriented, which leads to confrontation on very shaky grounds.[3] This chapter contends that looking for acute stress symptoms may not reveal potential suicide bombers. Neither will racial profiling, as the terrorist strategists will respond with the use of different and unexpected racial types for their horrific task.

Not all suicide bombers who want to die for their cause would show stress, as the desire to be a martyr would override their fear of imminent death.[4] Hostages who saw suicidal terrorists at first hand in the Chechen rebels' seizure of a Moscow theater in 2002 were quoted as saying, "They were calm about it. Death was not something that they were afraid of."[5] Suicidal terrorists would have been practicing, imagining the moment of their death and immediate salvation, hundreds if not thousands of times. Also the physicians attending the hostages in the Moscow theater reportedly noted that most of the terrorists were euphoric and some were in a trance-like state. None were showing signs of depression, hopelessness, or despair—states of mind traditionally associated with impending suicide.[6] Nevertheless, the potential suicide bombers would have shown signs of deep long-term stress, noticeable to the informed outsider. Death is what martyrs want above all else, however bizarre and contrary it is to our thinking. Most people want to live a normal lifespan. And some cohorts in society, like teenage males, feel invincible and think they will live forever. In our society, it is not normal to think constantly about your own death, or to take actions to induce your death, as most Western people fear dying and take few risks that might lead to an early death. Many give up smoking to avoid an early death.

LIVING WITH THE NOTION OF DEATH

Let me share with you a personal event, so that you may understand the death wish more. I am an adoptee, and for years I suffered from long-term stress brought about by being separated from my mother as a baby. Recent research is demonstrating that such separation is traumatizing for the infant, and I lived under this cloud for nearly five decades.[7] The infant conceptualizes upon birth that it is still part of the mother, and when the mother disappears, usually forever for an orphan or adoptee, the infant feels the death of a part of him- or herself. This is a real death to the infant, but the problem is that the infant continues to live. Therefore he or she has to accommodate to a perpetual dying in "normal" life.[8]

The way I processed this notion of continually dying was to experience the event in dreams or in daytime fears. For most of my adult life I would think about dying before I went to sleep. I would experience the moment of death over and over in my mind. I would imagine what it would feel like—the possible pain and the release when my soul left my dead body. Repeatedly, I have gone through the final moments of my life. So, in some sense, I have felt what the suicide bomber goes through in coming to terms with his or her final action. However, in my case, it would be resolved through dealing with my feelings about my first "death," in the form of my mother leaving me.

For the suicide bomber, it is only resolved through the completion of their last act on this earth to overcome evil and enshrine themselves as martyrs to the cause. I feel sure that imagining death before the event is an experience also shared by prisoners on death row, as well as people who contemplate suicide for a long time. There has been some research on suicidal individuals who have survived, who have talked about seeking relief through death, as they see it as their only solution to the crisis at hand.[9] However, I went through this for a much longer time than most others. And for me, it wasn't a matter of release. Like the death row prisoners, I knew that it would happen sooner or later, that it would hurt and be painful, that I would have to put up with it, and that my soul would live on in an eternal abyss.

As I was brought up as a Catholic, a sense of "soul" was instilled in me. I have often wondered if people without a religious belief in a soul would have the same death experience, as all death would be for them merely an end to sensation. However, suicide bombers, as they present themselves today, also believe in the concept of a soul, and this feeling of release would be in their minds too. To me, death was a pathway into darkness, but death to a martyr is a pathway to eternal bliss. So how can security pick out passengers who are actually happy as they are about to die for their cause, and therefore typically do not show signs of acute stress? No one ever picked me out from a passenger line, yet I travel frequently on aircraft. I am not a terrorist, but I knew what it would be like if the airplane crashed, or if it were bombed, or just fell out of the sky, as I lived those moments over and over again. I did not suffer from sweaty hands or go weak at the knees, but I knew in every intimate detail what death of this type would be like.

The Chechen women terrorists, who had bombs strapped on them, were very calm about it; they just sat there waiting for death. So how would an airport security officer pick me out if I were a terrorist? They would not. I look too ordinary, despite my alliance with death. Clearly, different approaches are needed and have been called for by others.[10] The answer that came to me in my research effort was another, entirely different approach, called emotive profiling.

Emotive profiling is based on an emerging theory of emotional energy, which has been developing in a variety of fields over the last 17 years.[11] Recently it has reached a wider audience and acceptance through the concept of emotional intelligence.[12] This concept is now taught in management schools in many countries, essentially using awareness of emotions as a management tool. I have developed this concept further to assist with screening in recruitment, as well as helping hundreds of candidates understand their behavior and create pathways for change.

Having a very different background than most airline security investigators, being a career-development specialist for managers and executives, I have faced the problem of screening, but in a totally different environment. My problem is how to sort out the good managers from the bad. Which ones pose the risk? They all look fine at interview, yet some will wreak havoc in their new positions. Similarly, airline passengers have to be screened, and the same question has to be asked: which ones pose a risk? For airline security personnel, it is about saving an aircraft and its passengers; for me it is about saving companies and their personnel (and their emotional fallout) from potential fraudsters and corporate psychopaths. I found that normal screening wasn't adequate to assess these risky candidates. No matter how confident they were at interview, my intuition told me to be wary, but it was unfair to deny them opportunities purely on a gut feeling. This led me to initiate an investigation of existing screening techniques.

Modern, advanced techniques of psychometric testing and behavioral-based interviewing have not made any impact on executive fraud. When I talked to experienced recruiters about this problem, they informed me that this is due to the age-old problem of "impression management." That is, people like to make a good impression on others, and sometimes they will exaggerate claims in order to do so. It is virtually certain that potential fraudsters will do this, covering up their deceitful and harmful purposes. Similarly, terrorists seeking to board an aircraft will use impression management so that they behave and look like ordinary passengers to airline security. Furthermore, they will likely not show signs of acute stress at being about to blow themselves up, as ordinary people would.

EMOTIONAL ENERGY MODEL

It struck me from the psychological literature that as emotions rule our thoughts and behaviors, this just might be the means by which potentially damaging behavior may be uncovered. After considerable investigation and research with various groups and individuals, I constructed a model representing emotional energy. There are three dimensions to this energy (see Figure 4.1).

The first dimension is all about connection. Connection refers to all the emotions that one feels connecting to another in a relationship, whether it is a casual, single meeting or a fullblown, lifelong relationship. The positive emotion that is experienced in this dimension is love or respect; the negative emotion at the other end of the spectrum is anger.

Initially, this may be a little puzzling, with two diverse emotions of love and anger. In what way could anger be in the same dimension of connection as love? Consider the example of two warring individuals engaged in contentious litigation following some bad behavior on one side or the other. If you walked up to them on the steps of the court and told them that they each have the same amount of connection as the day they released the great news of their initial partnership, the two parties would give vehement responses to the contrary. They would express in simple terms that they hated each other. However, if there is no connection, there is no emotion. The hostile parties are very much connected, but the connection is strongly negative, hence the legal battle. Connection is the fundamental emotion in any human relationship. It ranges from loving to liking, to thinking they are okay, to finding them irritating, and to finally hating them.

Hatred is the overt expression of extreme negative human connection. Terrorist-martyrs believe they are dying for love of their religion, political party, or nation, because they have hatred in their hearts for the dominating faction. These people are just as connected to you and me as we are to ourselves, but the connection is in a highly negative form. The fact of the matter

Figure 4.1
CAT Model

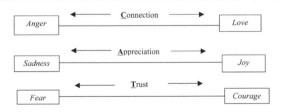

is that connection is a very strong emotion that will drive them to conceive and implement many actions that will connect them with the "other side—and the more it hurts the better. Westerners and nonextremists will likely retaliate, because the provocateurs have inflicted great pain. The strike back usually results in many lives lost (on both sides), to "teach them a lesson." This strike–counter strike *danse macabre* proves the power of connection. This negative form of emotional energy is so powerful that it drives wars and large-scale threats to society.

The second dimension is that of appreciation. On one side there is the positive emotion of joy; on the other side is sadness. Again, there is a whole range of feelings between being appreciated and not being valued by others. Joy is the expression of the positive side of being appreciated, and sadness is all about loss. Sadness brings about terrible emotions of feeling subjugated, not having what others have, envy, greed, and miserliness, and it also fuels depression in people over time.

The third dimension is that of trust. At the positive end of the continuum there is the emotion of courage or confidence; at the negative end lies fear. As we all know, fear is the basis of phobias and anxiety states. Insecure people commit troublesome acts as they have low self-esteem and in reality, low confidence in their abilities. What they have learned to do for years is to bury these inner feelings completely, even to themselves.

Once the emotional model (which is referred to as the CAT model, short for connection, appreciation, and trust model) is understood, it is clear that people can be fairly easily measured on the three dimensions. For instance, if people are feeling very upset and angry, they will be at the low, or negative end, of their emotional energy in that dimension, maybe at around 10 percent. If they are just feeling mildly irritated with life, perhaps the measure would be more like 40 percent. If they are feeling "on top of the world" and gain valid respect from those around them, then the measure may be 80 percent or even 90 percent. People can easily find words that describe their feelings and they can place themselves on the scale without too much trouble.

Now, so far so good, but what about the potential martyrs who are reading this, too? Regardless of their knowledge base, they will want to represent themselves as being in the 70–85 percent range, to impress security as they line up at the X-ray machines and passport control. In reality, they are feeling about 5 percent or lower, and are just waiting for the moment to achieve the disaster/holy release that they have been dreaming of. And this is the nub of their problem; they cannot hide their emotional energy from people. It's just that those around them don't understand the small emotional signs underpinning the terrorists' highly destructive negative behavior.

One of the rules of recruitment is that "like seeks like," and the negative energy–based terrorist will surround him- or herself with other negative energy individuals. A negative energy mastermind will choose fearful incompetents, who make you look good but are prone to make mistakes, so they are given basic tasks or will be blackmailed or brainwashed into actions they would not ordinarily perform. Not many people will go against their desire to live; they have to be in an extremely negative state of emotion to allow the ending of their life. The masterminds choose their candidates very well: the sad and the fearful and those who hate society.[13]

Notice that the perpetrator does not get on the plane him- or herself; it is always others who commit these acts. Moreover, the martyr candidates are not necessarily illiterate peasants. Recently the West was shocked to learn that professional doctors blew themselves up in a terrorist attempt on Glasgow Airport.[14] The emotional energy or CAT model predicts that any people—no matter who they are, whatever their class, education, or bank balance—can perform such destructive acts if they are in a state of sufficient negative energy. Therefore, detecting abnormal emotional energy levels is vital and possibly more important than focusing on racial characteristics and acute stress symptoms. Not all terrorists will have dark skin and look devious. The masterminds will choose other candidates, with different skin color, race, and socioeconomic background, to throw the behavioralist-trained security staff off the scent.

Negative energy passengers will include nonterrorists. It requires a skillful interrogation to weed out the final group of terrorist suspects from among the negative energy passengers (see Figure 4.2).

INTERRELATION OF THE EMOTIONAL ENERGY DIMENSIONS

One of the characteristics of the emotional energy dimensions is that they work in conjunction with each other. If Person A is feeling high self-esteem (this excludes narcissism and egocentric behavior), he or she will generally have a good outlook on life (which will be measured as courage, say, 80 percent), value the job and family (joy, 80 percent), and have self-respect (love, 80 percent). In other words, the score on connection will be roughly the same as for the dimensions of appreciation and trust on the CAT model. Figure 4.3 shows what the 80 person for Person A would look like on the model.

Similarly, when Person B is in negative energy, he will record a low score on the connection dimension if he is admitting to much frustration in his life

Figure 4.2
The Energy Look

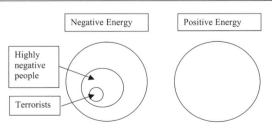

Figure 4.3
The 80/20 Rule

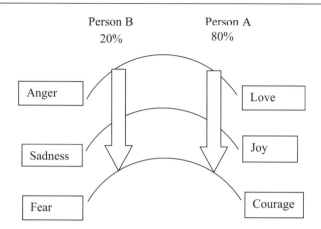

(anger measured at perhaps 20 percent). It would also be expected that he is feeling fairly low (sadness, 20 percent) and anxious (fear, 20 percent) as well.

What about people who have contradictory scores? Here a rather facetious example will be used: a passenger with expensive luggage demonstrates that she has self-respect (say, 70 percent), and she is showing nonchalance, perhaps even a smile as she lines up to board a plane (courage, 70 percent), but she smells badly from several days' accumulation of body odor (indicating a severe lack of self-worth, say, 10 percent). This should be investigated as it is incongruous on the emotional energy model. There are no incongruities in the CAT model. The truth is that the woman is operating at the lowest denominator of 10 percent; the rest is show or impression management, as the bad odor would not be tolerated by any self-respecting person in the 70 percent range. With this clue, security personnel would interview the woman and ask her questions about where she has been to get such a body odor (ruling out cultural nuances regarding differences in body odor, or the possibility that the odor came about, for example, due to delays caused by canceled flights.

Innocuous tests could easily be carried out to check the traveler's ability to smell, for instance, acknowledging and getting the traveler to talk about the duty-free fragrance in her bag (ruling out a physical cause). If no satisfactory explanation (e.g., delays are confirmed, olfactory malfunction is present, or there is verification by passport that she is from a culture that tolerates body odor) is found, further, serious questioning should take place. Figure 4.4 demonstrates the appearance of the inconsistent scores if represented on the CAT model.

EMOTIONS DETERMINE BEHAVIOR

The CAT model demonstrates the dimensions of the range of emotions. We do know that emotions determine our behavior, even such a simple

Figure 4.4
The 70/10 Rule

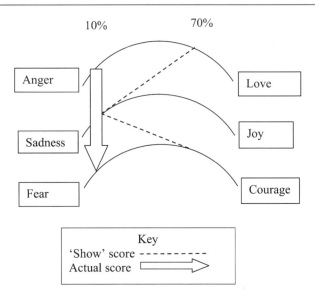

emotion as embarrassment.[15] Taking the CAT model as the foundation, it can be seen that that emotional energy determines emotions and the depth of what is felt, which determine thoughts, which in turn determine behavior. If assumptions are made about behavior, that is, about the underlying emotional base, then misleading conclusions are drawn. There is a masking or a deliberate attempt to disguise the feelings underneath, where there is negative emotional energy. Positive energy is never disguised or withheld; only negative emotional energy is camouflaged to deceive (see Figure 4.5).

The terrorist will mask her own negative behavior as much as she can, in order to act within culturally allowable limits of acceptable behavior, but she cannot do it on all dimensions all the time.

EMOTIONAL ENERGY AND STRESS

The theory of emotional energy is linked with stress. The more stress in a person's life, the more likely that the emotional energy will be negative. It is assumed that babies are born on the positive side of the equation, confident of their mother's love and nurturing, which develops their self-esteem and self-worth. But babies grow up and eventually go to school, college, and work; then they get married and have their own kids. Each step along the life cycle creates stress to some degree in an individual, and it is this stress that pushes the person into negative emotional energy. The bigger the stress, the more quickly and deeply the individual's emotional energy becomes negative.

Figure 4.5
Value Chains

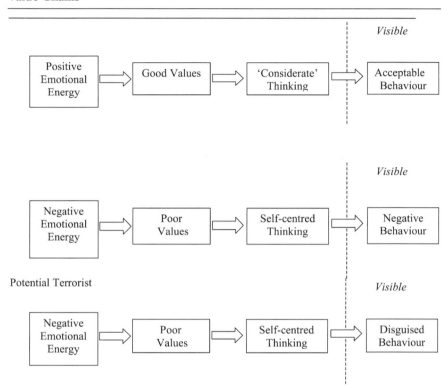

Some individuals get pushed more quickly than others, due to life's lottery, for example, being born to a depressed mother who is unable to care emotionally for her child, a bullying episode at school, marrying the wrong person, the death of a beloved partner, and other reasons. However, for many, there is a process of adjustment and acceptance of what has happened, thus relieving the impact of the stress (without the person concerned or others being harmed) and permitting a return to the positive side of the model.

For the ones who experience setbacks in life at a very early age, it is very likely that they will be more stressed and will exhibit negative behavior for a longer time than a resilient adult. It has long been observed that orphans growing up in orphanages and refugee children exhibit different, sometimes bizarre behavior.[16]

Traumatic events occur inside and outside the family unit, and may be caused by societal or environmental events, but most commonly they are caused by car accidents, fires, abductions, poor sanitation and disease control, and war.

Finally there are natural disasters—earthquakes, cyclones, and hurricanes, tsunamis, electrical storms, tornadoes, and others. Being in the wrong place at the wrong time has an enormous impact on many people's lives. Events that can cause negative energy are listed in Table 4.1.

Table 4.1
Categories of Traumatic Attachment Levels and Examples of Events

Category of attachment level	Examples of events
Maternal Attachment: loss of, or disorder.	Orphans, those not living with their families, adoptees, children with mothers who were "emotionally absent" through disease, disability, or mental illness, particularly in the first 2 years of life.
Familial attachment—fathers, siblings, close relatives, close friends of family that take on parenting roles.	Fatherless children, absence of major family figures, parents and siblings who have died or become severely affected through disease, etc. Sibling rivalry. Abuse by family figures, or friends of the family, or step-parents, etc.
Secondary attachment—school, work, university, college, hobby groups, church.	Bullying, violence, tyrannical behavior by supervisors, bosses, alienation, apathy.
Community attachment—income maintenance systems, education, penal systems, religion, public sanitation and disease control.	Low-level or nonexistent social involvement, which causes a class of people to live in disease and permanent poverty.
Social attachment—disasters caused by humans.	War, drug trade, terrorism, car accidents, industrial accidents, etc.
Random events—no attachment, disasters caused by nature.	Earthquakes, tornadoes, tsunamis, cyclones and hurricanes, landslides, floods, and fires.

It is suspected that those who endure random natural disasters wars and come through relatively unscathed have had a good attachment or bonding with their mother, but there has been little research in this area, most of it from studies of animal behavior.[17] The security of initial attachment enables the individual to face each event with a degree of strength. It is as if there is an understanding, a basic optimism, in the individual, who is confident that somehow she or he will survive.[18] Optimism is an inner belief built into the child that he or she has a right to live fairly and decently and to be respected. Those who have not had that luxury grow up to believe that bad things will continually happen to them (pessimism), events that are equal to or worse than the event that originally caused their pessimism. Adults that have been caught up in terrible situations for the first time in their lives have a resilience, but those affected earlier, children and babies, have far less resilience and are likely to develop problematic behaviors.[19]

War zones result in stressed-out dysfunctional families and societies that are, in turn, breeding grounds for negative energy.[20] Furthermore, children grow up ignorant of the positive ends of the dimensions and without experiencing real love, real joy, and real confidence. The paradox is that they probably think that they do experience happiness, but when a further in-depth look is taken, the reality will be seen in unhappy, dysfunctional relationships, fear, depression, and feelings of inadequacy and insecurity. Early childhood stress sets a person on a negative pathway for years. And there lies another problem: the person may be blind to his own behavior, as the negativity has been an ongoing theme throughout life and is perceived as normal, cloaked by an outer layer of impression management. The length of time for which a person experiences problems is always a clue to that person's emotional energy level. The more ingrained the negativity is, the more self-destructive it will be.

"BLINDNESS"

It has been found that apart from conscious behavior, the individual is blind to underlying negative behavior, sometimes referred to as our shadow self.[21] Blind behavior is similar to habits that we all have and don't realize that we have, such as scratching ourselves or picking our teeth. It takes an outsider to tell us at times when we are doing these things, as we are unaware of them. Similarly, there may be emotional indicators below the conscious radar.

Table 4.2 provides a list of some of the behaviors indicating negativity, many of which will be exhibited unconsciously by negative energy individuals. The Chechen rebels in the Moscow theater, as described by Speckhard and associates, recounted their emotions, and one to which the terrorists themselves would have been blind was a degree of laziness, particularly in the latter part of the siege.[22] No earnest martyrs would want it to be known that they were lazy! Yet laziness is a strong negative emotion that is found on the connection dimension—see Table 4.2—and people trained in emotive profiling could expect this to appear, despite the terrorists' unawareness.

Because one negative condition indicates that a person will show the same degree of negativity on the other emotional dimensions, similar negativity will be exhibited in the negative sets of anger, fear, or sadness. Questioning in the other dimensions will bring the other negative areas to light in an intensive interview. The answers have to be immediately tested, to avoid unwarranted detention.

It is my contention that "blindness" creates terrorism and other extreme social behavior. Damage early in childhood creates the parameters for later life. The more negative the emotional energy is, the more self-harm occurs. This self-destruction can be long-term, as in alcoholism or drug dependency, or it can be short-term, as in suicide. In addition, self-destructive people always exhibit a notable lack of concern about the effects of their self-harm on others. When corporate psychopaths and fraudsters are looked at in some depth, they share a similar lack of empathy.[23] They also share the same inflated sense of self (narcissism)—which derives from the negative side of the CAT model.

The brains behind airplane sabotage are usually extremely narcissistic and strategically cunning, pushed on by their success with their own groups.[24] These leaders are perceived as demonstrating their power and strategic ability

Table 4.2
Negative Emotions Generate Negative Behaviors

Dimension	Negative emotion	Negative behaviors
Connection	*Anger*	Lying, cheating, overt aggression, passive aggression, showing no respect for others, killing, harassing, domineering. Self abuse and harm. Suicide talk or actual attempts. Short fuse. Hatred, despising others and/or self. Racism. Criticism. Putting down others. Being hateful, spiteful, or malicious. Getting back at others. Revenge. Holding secrets. Laziness. Physical, sexual, and emotional abuse. Sabotaging behavior. Gossip.
Appreciation	*Sadness*	Depression. Tiredness. narcissism, kleptomania, envy, greed, stealing, "keeping up with the Joneses," consumption beyond income, status symbols, traveling as a "been there, done that" exercise. Excessive collection of artifacts, excessive hoarding. Home is cluttered, untidy. Maximizing profits to excess, at other people's expense. Miserliness. Lack of generosity. Jealousy. Taking credit where one does not deserve it. Nit-picking, taunting, teasing. Withholding love and kindness. Isolating others. Being excessively untidy, dirty, smelly, having an unkempt appearance. Arrogance.
Trust	*Fear*	Difficulties in relating directly to people. Isolating oneself from normal social activities. No close adult partner for a few years. No one to confide to. Excessive worry or anxiety. Phobias—anxiety fixated on certain things or conditions, e.g., agoraphobia. Free-floating anxiety—worrying about anything or anyone. Predicting doom and gloom—the world is coming to an end. Pessimism. Insecurity. Uncertain future, can't decide. Procrastination. Being in a rut, never moving out of it. Excessively codependent relationships. Double checking oneself. Constant reminders of previous failures. Overcontrolling. Overprotective. Micromanaging, excessive supervision. Bullying others.

to push their agenda, and many have inflated egos as well. Ordinary members of the groups are attracted to or put up with negative emotional energy, as they rally around the cause that the mastermind has skilfully articulated as the objective. Followers become spellbound or are coerced to bear extreme negativity in order for the oppressed group to benefit from the organizer's strategies.[25] Similarly, if the terrorists are operating in a group, there will be a leader who will exhibit negative emotional energy in dealing with his subordinates, and if dealing with a group of suspects at an airport, it would be wise to watch for negative behavior by the group leader.

Quite frequently, the investigator may be the only one who is suspicious of a passenger, a lonely voice crying in the wilderness. Tapping into the suspect's emotional energy will increase the confidence of the examiner, as it will give an understanding of the suspect's capability for terrorism and reinforce the examiner's intuition regarding the intended wrongdoing. Sometimes investigators give up the trail as it becomes politically unwise to continue (for example, taking a Muslim clergyman into questioning), and therefore emotional energy assessments of travelers will provide a far better assessment of potential harm than a gut feeling. Every terrorist sabotage attempt can be discovered before the event; it is purely a matter of resources.

Emotional energy assessments should be used as an additional layer added to existing protocols for passenger traffic, not on their own. The other proviso is that the facts need to be tested before a final judgment is made to allow a person onto a plane. Perhaps only one lie needs to be revealed, and it must not be ignored. Even if it is a tiny detail, it could well be the crack in the mask that warrants further investigation.

The other use for emotive profiling is for screening airport personnel themselves. Terrorists are increasingly infiltrating airlines and baggage handling and catering companies, in order to get past the passenger security line. It is imperative that emotional energy assessments should be made at all personnel levels, just as executives are screened to guard against fraud and other negative and destructive behavior in companies.

While only an outline of emotive profiling has been provided in this chapter, more detailed and intensive work has been undertaken that would prove useful for the security front line at airports as well as for other uses. Emotional energy is a new tool, which, with correct training, can be very useful in screening passengers with harmful objectives. It takes us far beyond watching for certain racial characteristics or acute stress symptoms in passenger line-ups, instead concentrating on observations of emotional functioning, which in many ways is far more revealing of a passenger's true intentions.

NOTES

1. Peter Robinson, *Israeli Style Air Security, Costly, and Intrusive, May Head West*, 2006, http://www.bloomberg.com/apps/news?pid=20601109&sid=aFyfihM1e3G4& refer=news; John Horgan, *Why We'll Never Construct a Single Profile for Terrorists*, November 2007, news.scotsman.com.

2. Pat O'Malley, "Risks, Ethics and Airport Security," *Canadian Journal of Criminology and Criminal Justice* 48, no. 3 (2006).

3. Ihekwoaba D Onwudiwe, "Defining Terrorism, Racial Profiling and the Demonisation of Arabs and Muslims in the USA," *Community Safety Journal* 4, no. 2 (2005).

4. Anne Speckhard et al., "Research Note: Observations of Suicidal Terrorists in Action," *Terrorism and Political Violence* 16, no. 2 (2004).

5. Ibid., 319.

6. Anthony Spirito and Christianne Esposito-Smythers, "Attempted and Completed Suicide in Adolescence," *Annual Review of Clinical Psychology* 2 (2006).

7. Cynthia M. Kuhn and Saul M. Schanberg, "Responses to Maternal Separation: Mechanisms and Mediators," *International Journal of Developmental Neuroscience* 16, nos. 3–4 (1998).

8. Norma Tracey, "From Oblivion to Being: Faith and Catastrophe," *Psychoanalytic Review* 94, no. 2 (2007).

9. Spirito and Esposito-Smythers, "Attempted and Completed Suicide in Adolescence."

10. Michael P. Arena and Bruce A. Arrigo, "Social Psychology, Terrorism, and Identity: A Preliminary Re-Examination of Theory, Culture, Self, and Society," *Behavioural Sciences and the Law* 23, no. 4 (2005).

11. William A. Kahn, "Psychological Conditions of Personal Engagement and Disengagement at Work," *Academy of Management Journal* 33, no. 4 (1990); Michael Schwalbe, "Emile Durkheim and Erving Goffman Meet Dr. Magneto," *Contemporary Sociology* 36, no. 3 (2007); Peter A C Smith and Meenakshi Sharma, "Rationalizing the Promotion of Non-Rational Behaviors in Organizations," *The Learning Organisation* 9, no. 5 (2002); Philip Vassallo, "Turning Emotional Energy into Purposeful Writing," *et Cetera* 61, no. 1 (2004).

12. Reuven Bar-On and James D A Parker, eds., *The Handbook of Emotional Intelligence: Theory, Development, Assessment, and Application at Home, School and in the Workplace* (San Francisco: Jossey-Bass, 2000); Daniel Goleman, *Emotional Intelligence: Why It Can Matter More Than IQ* (New York: Bantam Books, 1995).

13. Laurence Miller, "The Terrorist Mind," *International Journal of Offender Therapy and Comparative Criminology* 50, no. 2 (2006).

14. Horgan, *Why We'll Never Construct a Single Profile for Terrorists.*

15. Christine R Harris, "Embarrassment: A Form of Social Pain," *American Scientist* 94, no. 6 (2006).

16. Julie B. Kaplow et al., "The Long-Term Consequences of Early Childhood Trauma: A Case Study and Discussion," *Psychiatry* 69, no. 4 (2006).

17. Kuhn and Schanberg, "Responses to Maternal Separation: Mechanisms and Mediators."

18. Beverly H Brummett et al., "Prediction of All-Cause Mortality by the Minnesota Multiphasic Personality Inventory Optimism-Pessimism Scale Scores: Study of a College Sample During a 40-Year Follow-up Period," *Mayo Clinic Proceedings* 81, no. 12 (2006).

19. Elizabeth M. Hill et al., "Family History of Alcoholism and Childhood Adversity: Joint Effects on Alcohol Consumption and Dependence," *Alcoholism: Clinical and Experimental Research* 18, no. 5 (1994).

20. Patricia B. Sutker et al., "Exposure to War Trauma, War-Related PTSD, and Psychological Impact of Subsequent Hurricane," *Journal of Psychopathology and Behavioral Assessment* 24, no. 1 (2002).

21. Kenneth Reeves, "Racism and Projection of the Shadow," *Psychotherapy: Theory, Research, Practice, Training* 37, no. 1 (2000).

22. Speckhard et al., "Research Note: Observations of Suicidal Terrorists in Action."

23. James Blair, Derek Mitchell, and Karina Blair, *The Psychopath: Emotion and the Brain* (Malden, MA: Blackwell Publishing, 2005).

24. Ian Palmer, "Terrorism, Suicide Bombing, Fear and Mental Health," *International Review of Psychiatry* 19, no. 3 (2007).

25. Miller, "The Terrorist Mind."

CHAPTER 5

Principles and Requirements for Assessing X-Ray Image Interpretation Competency of Aviation Security Screeners

Adrian Schwaninger, Saskia M. Koller, and Anton Bolfing

COMPETENCY ASSESSMENT IN AIRPORT SECURITY SCREENING

In response to the increased risk of terrorist attacks, large investments in aviation security technology have been made in recent years. However, the best equipment is of limited value if the people who operate it are not selected and trained appropriately to perform their tasks effectively and accurately. In recent years, the relevance of human factors has increasingly been recognized. One important aspect of the human factors is the competency of the aviation security screeners and its assessment.

Competency assessment maintains the workforce certification process. The main aim of certification procedures is to ensure that adequate standards in aviation security are consistently and reliably achieved. Certification of aviation security screeners can be considered as providing quality control over the screening process. Using certification tests, important information on strengths and weaknesses in aviation security procedures in general as well as on each individual screener can be obtained. As a consequence, certification can also be a valuable basis for qualifying personnel, measuring training effectiveness, improving training procedures, and increasing motivation. In short, certification and competency assessment can be very important instruments to improve aviation security.

The implementation of competency assessment procedures presents several challenges. First, what should be assessed has to be identified. Then, there should be consideration of how procedures for the certification of different competencies can be implemented. Another important challenge is international standardization, since several countries, organizations, and even companies are developing their own certification or quality control systems.

The following international documents refer to the certification and competency assessment of aviation security staff:

- EU Regulation 2320/2002
- ICAO Annex 17, 3.4.3[1]
- ICAO-Manual on Human Factors in Civil Aviation Security Operations (Doc. 9808)[2]
- ICAO Human Factors Training Manual (Doc. 9683), Part 1, Chapter 4, and Appendix 6, Appendix 32[3]
- ICAO Security Manual for Safeguarding Civil Aviation against Acts of Unlawful Interference, Doc. 8973, Chapter 4, I-4-45[4]
- ECAC Doc. 30, Chapter 12, and Annex IV-12A[5]
- ECAC Doc. 30 of the European Civil Aviation Conference specifies three elements for *initial* certification of airport security screeners:
  - an X-ray image interpretation exam
  - a theoretical exam
  - a practical exam

The *periodical* certification should contain a theoretical exam and an X-ray image interpretation exam. Practical exams can be conducted if considered necessary.

This section covers the first element, that is, how to examine X-ray image interpretation competency. Guidance material on the two other elements (theoretical exam and practical exam) already exists in the above-mentioned documents.

First, human factors best practice guidance for assessing the X-ray image interpretation competency of aviation security screeners is provided. Three different possibilities are mentioned, which can serve to measure X-ray image interpretation competency: covert testing, threat image projection (TIP), and computer-based image tests. Second, on-the-job assessment of the screener competency using TIP is discussed. Third, an example of a reliable, valid, and standardized computer-based test is presented: this test is used at more than 100 airports worldwide to measure X-ray image interpretation competency and also for certification purposes. Fourth, the application of this test in an EU-funded project (the VIA Project) including several European airports is presented.

Requirements for Assessing Competency

One of the most important tasks of an aviation security screener is the interpretation of X-ray images of passenger bags and the identification of prohibited items within these bags. Hit rates, false alarm rates, and the time used to visually inspect an X-ray image of a passenger bag are important measures that can be used to assess the effectiveness of screeners at this task. A hit is a correctly detected prohibited item within a passenger bag. The hit rate refers to the percentage of all bags containing a prohibited item that are correctly judged as being NOT OK. If a prohibited item is reported in a bag that does not contain one, this counts as a false alarm. The false alarm rate consequently is the percentage of all harmless bags (i.e., bags not containing any prohibited items) that is judged by a screener as containing a prohibited item. The time taken to process each bag is also important, as it helps in determining throughput rates and can indicate response confidence.

The results of an X-ray image interpretation test provide very important information for civil aviation authorities, aviation security institutions, and companies. Moreover, failing a test can have serious consequences, depending on the regulations of the appropriate authority. Therefore, it is essential that a test should be fair, reliable, valid, and standardized. In the last 50 years, scientific criteria have been developed that are widely used in psychological testing and psychometrics. These criteria are essential for the development of tests for measuring human performance. A summary of the three most important concepts, namely reliability, validity, and standardization, is now presented.[6]

Reliability

Reliability in the sense of the quality of measurement refers to the "consistency" or "repeatability" of measurements. It is the extent to which the measurements of a test remain consistent over repeated tests of the same participant under identical conditions. If a test yields consistent results for the same measure, it is reliable. If the repeated measurements produce different results, the test is not reliable. If, for example, an IQ test yields a score of 90 for an individual today and 125 a week later, it is not reliable. The concept of reliability is illustrated in Figure 5.1. Each point represents an individual. The x-axis represents the test results in the first measurement and the y-axis represents the scores of the second measurement with the same test. Figure 5.1 represents tests of different reliability. The test on the left in Figure 5.1 is not reliable. The score a participant achieved in the first measurement does not correspond at all with the test score in the second measurement.

The reliability coefficient can be calculated by the correlation between the two measurements. In Figure 5.1 left, the correlation is near zero, that is, $r = 0.05$ (the theoretical maximum is 1). The test in the center of Figure 5.1 is somewhat more reliable. The correlation between the two measurements is 0.50. Figure 5.1 right shows a highly reliable test with a correlation of 0.95.

The reliability of a test may be estimated by a variety of methods. When the same test is repeated (usually after a time interval during which job performance is assumed not to have changed), the correlation between the scores achieved on the two measurement dates can be calculated. This measure is called *test-retest reliability*. A more common method is to calculate the *split-half reliability*. In this method, the test is divided into two halves. The whole test

Figure 5.1
Reliability Correlations

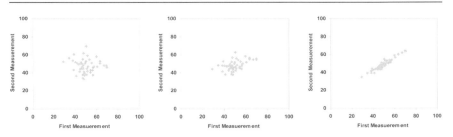

is administered to a sample of participants and the total score for each half of the test is calculated. The split-half reliability is the correlation between the test scores obtained in each half. In the alternate forms method, two tests are created that are equivalent in terms of content, response processes, and statistical characteristics. Using this method, participants take both tests and the correlation between the two scores is calculated (*alternate forms reliability*). Reliability can also be a measure of a test's internal consistency. Using this method, the reliability of the test is judged by estimating how well the items that reflect the same construct or ability yield similar results. The most common index for estimating the internal reliability is Cronbach's alpha. Cronbach's alpha is often interpreted as the mean of all possible split-half estimates. Another internal consistency measure is KR 20 (for details see the documents mentioned above).

Acceptable tests usually have reliability coefficients between 0.7 and 1.0. Correlations exceeding 0.9 are not often achieved. For individual performance to be measured reliably, correlation coefficients of at least 0.75 and Cronbach's alpha of at least 0.85 are recommended. These numbers represent the minimum values. In the scientific literature, the suggested values are often higher.

Validity

Validity indicates whether a test is able to measure what it is intended to measure. For example, hit rate alone is not a valid measure of detection performance in terms of discriminability (or sensitivity), because a high hit rate can also be achieved by judging most bags as containing prohibited items. In order to measure detection performance in terms of discriminability (or sensitivity), the false alarm rate must be considered, too.[7]

As for reliability, there are also different types of validity. The term *face validity* refers to whether a test appears to measure what it claims to measure. A test should reflect the relevant operational conditions. For example if a test for measuring X-ray image interpretation competency contains X-ray images and screeners have to decide whether the depicted bags contain a prohibited item, it is *face valid*. *Concurrent validity* refers to whether a test can distinguish between groups that it should be able to distinguish between (e.g., between trained and untrained screeners). In order to establish *convergent validity*, it has to be shown that measures that should be related are indeed related. If, for example, threat image projection (TIP, i.e., the insertion of fictional threat items into X-ray images of passenger bags) measures the same competencies as a computer-based offline test, one would expect a high correlation between TIP performance data and the computer-based test scores. Another validity measure is called predictive validity. In *predictive validity*, the test's ability to predict something it should be able to predict is assessed. For example, a good test for preemployment assessment would be able to predict on-the-job X-ray screening detection performance. *Content validity* refers to whether the content of a test is representative of the content of the relevant task. For example, a test for assessing whether screeners have acquired the competency to detect different threat items in X-ray images of passenger bags should contain X-ray images of bags with different categories of prohibited items according to an internationally accepted prohibited items list.

Standardization/developing population norms

The third important aspect of judging the quality of a test is standardization. This involves administering the test to a representative group of people in order to establish norms (a normative group). When an individual takes the test, it can then be determined how far above or below the average her or his score is, relative to the normative group. It is important to know how the normative group was selected, though. For instance, for the standardization of a test used to evaluate the detection performance of screeners, a meaningful normative group of a large and representative sample of screeners (at least 200 males and 200 females) should be tested.

In summary, competency assessment of X-ray image interpretation needs to be based on tests that are reliable, valid, and standardized. However, it is also important to consider test difficulty, particularly if results from different tests are compared to each other. Although two tests can have similar properties in terms of reliability, an easy test may not adequately assess the *level* of competency needed for the X-ray screening job.

Competency Assessment of X-ray Image Interpretation

Currently, there are several methods used to assess X-ray image interpretation competency: Covert testing (infiltration testing), threat image projection (TIP), and computer-based image tests.

Covert testing

Covert testing as the exclusive basis for individual competency assessment of X-ray image interpretation is only acceptable if the requirements of reliability, validity, and standardization are fulfilled. For covert testing to achieve these requirements, a significant number of tests of the same screener is necessary in order to assess competency reliably. Note that this section does not apply to principles and requirements for covert testing used to verify compliance with regulatory requirements.

Threat image projection (TIP)

Screener competency can also be assessed using TIP data. TIP is the projection of fictional threat items into X-ray images of passenger bags during the routine baggage screening operation. In this way the detection performance of a screener can be measured under operational conditions. However, using *raw* TIP data alone does not provide a reliable measure of individual screener detection performance For example, data need to be *aggregated* over time in order to have a large enough sample upon which to perform meaningful analysis. In order to achieve reliable, valid, and standardized measurements, several other aspects need to be taken into account as well when analyzing TIP data. One requirement is to use an appropriate TIP library. It should contain a large number of threat items, which represent the prohibited items that need to be detected and which feature a reasonable difficulty level. See the section on reliable measurement of performance using TIP for more information on how to use TIP data for measuring X-ray detection performance of screeners.

Computer-based X-ray image interpretation tests

Computer-based X-ray image interpretation tests constitute a valuable tool for standardized measurements of X-ray image interpretation competency. These tests should consist of X-ray images of passenger bags containing different prohibited objects. The categories of threat items should reflect the prohibited items list and requirements of the appropriate authority, and it should be ensured that the test content remains up to date. The test should also contain clean bag images, that is, images of bags that do not contain a prohibited object. For each image, the screeners should indicate whether or not a prohibited object is present. Additionally, the screeners can be requested to identify the prohibited item(s). Image display duration should be comparable to operational conditions.

Test conditions should be standardized and comparable for all participants. For example, the brightness and contrast on the monitor should be calibrated and similar for all participants. This applies equally to other monitor settings that could influence detection performance (e.g., the refresh rate). In order to achieve a valid measure of detection performance, not only hit rates but also false alarm rates should be taken into account. An additional or alternative measure would be to count the number of correctly identified prohibited items (in this case, candidates have to indicate where exactly in the bag the threat is located).

The test should be reliable, valid, and standardized. Reliability should be documented by scientifically accepted reliability estimates (see above). If possible, validity measures should also be provided (see above). Individual scores should be compared to a norm that is based on a large and representative sample of screeners (see above).

The probability of detecting a threat item depends on the knowledge of a screener as well as on the general difficulty of the threat item. Image-based factors such as the rotation in which a threat item is depicted in the bag (view difficulty), the degree by which other objects are superimposed on a threat object (superimposition), and the number and type of other objects within the bag (bag complexity) influence detection performance substantially.[8] Tests should take these effects into account.

One of the skills that experienced screeners acquire is the ability to distinguish threat from non-threat objects and to have stored representations of what non-threat items look like within an X-ray image. Although the main task of an aviation security screener is the detection of threat items, an additional option could be the inclusion of non-threat objects in the test, which the test candidates are required to identify.

The section below on the X-Ray CAT describes a computer-based X-ray image interpretation test that is used at more than 100 airports worldwide for measuring screener competency and for certification purposes.

Certification of X-Ray Image Interpretation Competency

As indicated above and as specified in ICAO Annex 17, 3.4.3, individuals carrying out screening operations should be certified initially and periodically. Certification can not only be considered as providing quality control over the screening process; it is also a valuable basis for qualifying personnel, measuring training effectiveness, improving training procedures, and increasing motivation. Certification data provide important information on strengths and weaknesses in aviation security procedures in general as well as on individual screeners. Furthermore, standardized certification can help in achieving an international standardization in aviation security. However, this is very challenging, since many countries, organizations, and companies develop their own certification and quality control systems. The present section gives a brief overview of how a certification system can be implemented.

As mentioned above, certification of screeners should contain a theoretical exam and an X-ray image interpretation exam. For periodical certification, practical exams can be conducted if considered necessary, unlike the initial certification, where practical exams are required. The exams should meet the requirements of high reliability and validity and standardization (see above).

The theoretical exam should inquire into the content of the regulations on aviation security screening. Apart from national rules and specifications, individual airports may enunciate questions covering special conditions. The questionnaire should feature an acceptable reliability. It stands to reason that the questionnaire should be developed as a multiple choice exam. Good questions with qualitatively high answer possibilities (including distractor answers) are the basis for a good questionnaire, which differentiates between knowledgeable screeners and those who do not know the regulations very well.

The X-ray image interpretation exam can be adapted to the domain in which a screener is employed, that is, cabin baggage screening, hold baggage screening, or both. Since not every threat object always constitutes a threat during the flight, depending on where aboard the aircraft it is transported, screeners should be certified according to their domain. The certification of cabin baggage screeners should be based on cabin baggage images that contain all kinds of threat objects that are prohibited from being carried on in cabin baggage (e.g., guns, knives, improvised explosive devices, etc.). Objects that are prohibited from being transported in the cabin of an aircraft do not necessarily pose a threat when transported in the hold. Furthermore, different types of bags are transported in the cabin and the hold, respectively. Usually, small suitcases or bags serve as hand baggage, whereas big suitcases and traveling bags are transported in the hold of the aircraft. The certification of hold baggage screeners should be done using images of hold baggage. Hold baggage screeners only have to detect threat objects that are prohibited from being carried in the hold of an aircraft, like explosive materials. Persons working in both domains should be certified with both versions.

Screeners should be kept up to date regarding new and emerging threats. In order to verify whether this is consistently achieved, it is recommended that a recurrent certification should be conducted every year. The minimum threshold that should be achieved in the tests in order to pass certification should be defined by the national air transportation authority and should be based on a large and representative sample (see also the subsection below on standardization for more information on this topic).

RELIABLE MEASUREMENT OF PERFORMANCE ON THE JOB USING THREAT IMAGE PROJECTION (TIP)

Threat image projection (TIP) is a function of state-of-the-art X-ray machines that allows the exposure of aviation security screeners to artificial but realistic X-ray images during the process of the routine X-ray screening operation at the security checkpoint. For cabin baggage screening (CBS), fictional threat items (FTIs) are digitally projected in random positions into X-ray images of real passenger bags. In hold baggage screening (HBS), combined threat images (CTIs) are displayed on the monitor. In this case, not only the threat item is projected but also an image of a whole bag that may or may not contain a threat item. This is possible if the screeners visually inspecting the hold baggage are physically separated from the passengers and their baggage. If a screener responds correctly by pressing a designated key on the keyboard (the "TIP key") it counts as a hit, which is indicated by a feedback message. If a screener fails to respond to a projected threat within a specified amount of time, a feedback message appears indicating that a projected image was missed. This would count as a miss. Feedback messages also appear if a screener reports a threat although there was no projection of a threat or a CTI. In this case, it could be a real threat. Projecting whole bags in HBS provides not only the opportunity to project threat images (i.e., bags containing a threat item) but also non-threat images (i.e., bags not containing any threat item). This also allows the recording of false true alarms (namely, if a non-threat image was judged as containing a threat) and correct rejections (namely, if a non-threat image was judged as being harmless).

TIP data are an interesting source for various purposes like quality control, risk analysis, and assessment of individual screener performance. Unlike the situation in a test setting, the individual screener performance can be assessed on the job when using TIP data. However, if used for the measurement of individual screener X-ray detection performance, international standards of testing have to be met, that is, the method needs to be reliable, valid, and standardized (see above). In a study of CBS and HBS TIP, it was found that there were very low reliability values for CBS TIP data when a small TIP image library of a few hundred FTIs was used.[9] Good reliabilities were found for HBS TIP data when a large TIP image library was available. It is suggested that a large image library containing a representative sample of items of varying difficulty should be used when TIP is used for individual performance assessment. Also viewpoint difficulty, superimposition, and bag complexity may need to be considered. Finally, the data need to be aggregated over time in order to have a large enough sample upon which to perform meaningful analyses.

In addition to providing measures of operational performance, TIP is also a useful tool for increasing the motivation and attention of screeners. Screeners have to be continuously alert to avoid missing a TIP image. Finally, TIP allows the exposure of screeners to threat items they would usually not encounter (e.g., improvised explosive devices).

X-RAY COMPETENCY ASSESSMENT TEST (X-RAY CAT)

This section introduces the X-Ray Competency Assessment Test (CAT) as an example of a computer-based test that can be used for assessing X-ray image interpretation competency. The CAT has been developed based on scientific findings regarding threat detection in X-ray images of passenger bags.[10] How well screeners can detect prohibited objects in passenger bags is influenced in two ways. First, it depends on the screener's knowledge of what objects are prohibited and what they look like in X-ray images. This knowledge is an attribute of the individual screener and can be enhanced by specific training. Second, the probability of detecting a prohibited item in an X-ray image of a passenger bag also depends on image-based factors. These are the rotation of the prohibited item within the bag (view difficulty), the degree by which other objects are superimposed over an object in the bag (superposition), and the number and type of other objects within the bag (bag complexity). Systematic variation or control of the image-based factors is a fundamental property of the test and has to be incorporated in the test development. In this test, the effects of viewpoint are controlled by using two standardized rotation angles in easy and difficult view for each forbidden object. Superposition is controlled in the sense that it is held constant over the two views and as far as possible over all objects. With regard to bag complexity, the bags are chosen in such a way that they are visually comparable in terms of the form and number of objects with which they are packed.

The test contains two sets of objects in which object pairs are similar in shape. This construction not only allows the measurement of any effect of training, that is, if detection performance can be increased by training, but also possible transfer effects. The threat objects of one set are included in the training. By measuring detection performance after training using both sets of the test, it can be ascertained whether training also helped in improving the detection of the objects that did not appear during training. Should this be the case, it indicates a transfer of the knowledge gained about the visual appearance of objects used in training to similar-looking objects.

Materials

Stimuli were created from Smiths-Heimann Hi-Scan 6040i color X-ray images of prohibited items and passenger bags (Figure 5.2 displays an example of the stimuli).

Based on the categorization of current threat image projection systems (Doc. 30 of the European Civil Aviation Conference, ECAC), four categories of prohibited items were chosen to be included in the test: guns, improvised explosive devices (IEDs), knives, and other prohibited items (e.g., gas, chemicals, grenades, etc.). The prohibited items were selected and prepared in collaboration with experts from the Zurich State Police, Airport Division, to be representative and realistic. Sixteen exemplars are used of each category (eight pairs). Each pair consists of two prohibited items of the same kind that are similar in shape.

Figure 5.2
Prohibitive Item Identification

Figure 5.3
Prohibitive Item Screen Projection

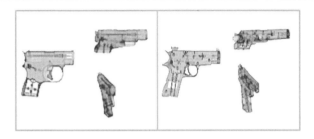

The pairs were divided into two sets, set A and set B. Furthermore, each object within both sets is used in two standardized viewpoints (see Figure 5.3).

The easy viewpoint shows the object in canonical (easily recognizable) per-spective,[11] the difficult viewpoint shows it with an 85 degree horizontal rotation or an 85 degree vertical rotation. In each threat category, half of the prohibited items of the difficult viewpoint are rotated vertically and the other half horizon-tally. The corresponding object of the other set is rotated around the same axis.

In order to compare the detection performance of an object to the detection performance of its counterpart in the other set, the two items (i.e., the bag images containing the threat objects) should not be different except for the object they contain. This means that the two objects should be comparable in regard to the rotation of the objects and their superimposition. Furthermore, the superposition should also be the same for both viewpoints of an object. This was achieved using an image-processing tool to combine the threat ob-jects with passenger bags, controlling for superposition. This tool calculates the difference in brightness between the pixels of the two superimposed im-ages (threat object and bag) using the following formula for superimposition:

$$SP = \frac{\sqrt{\Sigma[I_{SN}(x,y) - I_N(x,y)]^2}}{ObjectSize}$$

SP = Superimposition; I_{SN} = Grayscale intensity of the S_N (Signal plus Noise) image (contains a prohibited item); I_N = Grayscale intensity of the N (Noise) image (con-tains no prohibited item); Object Size: Number of pixels of the prohibited item where R, G, and B are < 253

This equation calculates the superposition value of an object independent of its size. This value can be held constant for the two views of an object and the two objects of a pair, independent of the bag complexity, when combining the bag image and the prohibited item. To ensure that the bag images do not contain any other prohibited item, they were checked by at least two highly experienced aviation security instructors.

Clean bag images were assigned to the four categories and the two viewpoints of the prohibited items such that their image difficulty was balanced across all groups. This was achieved using the false alarm rate as the difficulty indicator for each bag image based on a pilot study with 192 screeners. In the test each bag appears twice, once containing a prohibited item (threat image) and once not containing a prohibited item (non-threat image). Combined with all prohibited items this adds up to a total of 256 test trials: 4 threat categories (guns, IEDs, knives, other) * 8 (exemplars) * 2 (sets) * 2 (views) * 2 (threat images v. non-threat images).

The task is to visually inspect the test images and to judge whether they are OK (contain no prohibited item) or NOT OK (contain a prohibited item). Usually the images disappear after 10 seconds. In addition to the OK/NOT OK response, screeners have to indicate the perceived difficulty of each image in a 100-point scale (difficulty rating: 1 = easy, 100 = difficult). All responses can be made by clicking buttons on the screen. The X-Ray CAT takes about 30–40 minutes to complete.

Assessing Detection Performance

The detection performance of screeners can be assessed by their judgments of X-ray images. It should be stressed that not only is the hit rate (i.e., the proportion of correctly detected prohibited items in the threat images) an important value but so is the false alarm rate (i.e., the proportion of non-threat images that were judged as being NOT OK, that is, as containing a prohibited item). This incorporates the definition of detection performance as the ability not only to detect prohibited items but also to discriminate between prohibited items and harmless objects (that is, to recognize harmless objects as harmless). Therefore, in order to evaluate the detection performance of a screener, his or her hit rate in the test has to be considered as well as his or her false alarm rate.[12] There are different measures of detection performance that set the hit rate against the false alarm rate, for example d' or A'. These measures are explained in more detail below.

Reliability of the X-Ray CAT

As elaborated earlier in this chapter, the reliability of a test stands for its consistency. As a measure of the X-Ray CAT's quality, the internal reliability index Cronbach's alpha and the Guttman split-half reliability were computed. The calculations are based on the results of a study at several airports throughout Europe (see below for the details and further results of the study) including the data on 2265 screeners who completed the X-Ray CAT. The reliability measures were calculated based on correct answers, that is, hits for threat images and correct rejections (CR) for non-threat images (# correct rejections = # non-threat items—# false alarms). The analyses were made separately for threat images and for non-threat images. Table 5.1 shows the reliability coefficients.

Table 5.1
Reliability

Reliability analysis			
Reliability coefficients		Hit	CR
X-Ray CAT	Alpha	.98	.99
	Split-half	.97	.99

As stated above, an acceptable test should reach reliability values of at least .85 (Cronbach's alpha). Bearing this in mind, the reliability coefficients listed in Table 5.1 show that the X-Ray CAT is very reliable and therefore a useful tool for measuring the detection performance of aviation security screeners.

Validity of the X-Ray Cat

Regarding the different types of validity as described above, the face validity and the content validity can be confirmed instantly. In terms of face validity, the X-Ray CAT is valid as it appears to measure what it claims to measure and it reflects the relevant operational conditions. In terms of content validity, the X-Ray CAT is valid as its content is representative of the content of the relevant task. The test includes prohibited items from different categories based on the definition in Doc. 30 of the European Civil Aviation Conference (ECAC) that have to be detected by the aviation security screeners. Regarding the convergent validity of the CAT, it can be compared to another test that measures the same abilities. An example of such a test that is also widely used at different airports is the Prohibited Items Test.[13] To assess convergent validity, the correlation between the scores on the X-Ray CAT and the scores on the PIT of a sample that conducted both tests is calculated. This precise procedure was applied to a sample of 473 airport security screeners. The result can be seen in Figure 5.4 (r = .791).

Since correlation coefficients range from 0 (no correlation) to 1 (perfect correlation) (see also above), the convergent validity can be classified as quite high. This means that the X-Ray CAT and the PIT measure the same X-ray image interpretation competency. Other studies have also confirmed the concurrent validity, that is, the ability of a test to discriminate, for example, between trained and untrained screeners.[14] Figure 5.5 shows the results of the study. It can be seen that the detection performance increases for the trained screeners but not for the untrained screeners. This means that the test is able to discriminate between screeners who received training with the computer-based training system X-Ray Tutor and those who did not receive training with X-Ray Tutor.[15] Therefore, the concurrent validity of the X-Ray CAT can be confirmed.

Figure 5.4
CAT and PIT Detection Performance

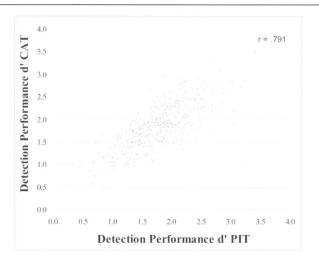

Figure 5.5
Detection Performance of Groups

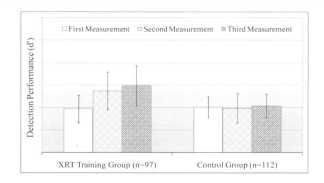

Standardization

The X-Ray CAT was standardized in regard to its development. The revisions of the test were based on data from representative samples (N > 94) of airport security screeners (more details on the revisions can be found in the following subsection). In the study described in the section on real world application, involving a large and representative sample of airport security screeners (N = 2265), a mean detection performance A' of 0.8 (SD = 0.08) was achieved. There are different approaches to the definition of pass marks. The normative approach defines a pass mark as the threshold at which a certain proportion of screeners fails the test (e.g., not more than 10 percent), based on a test measurement. That is, a screener is rated in relation to all other screeners. The criterion-referenced approach sets the pass mark according to a defined criterion. For instance, the results could be compared to the test results obtained in other countries when the test was conducted the first time or by having a group of experts (e.g., using the Angoff method)[16] rate the difficulty of the test items (in this case the difficulty of the images) and the minimum standard of performance. These approaches can of course be combined. Furthermore, the standard might be adjusted by taking into account the reliability of the test, the confidence intervals, and the standard error of measurement.

According to the Measurement Research Associates, the level of performance required for passing a credentialing test should depend on the knowledge and skills necessary for acceptable performance in the occupation and should not be adjusted to regulate the number or proportion of persons passing the test.[17] The pass point should be determined by careful analysis and judgment of acceptable performance. The Angoff method is probably the most basic form of criterion-based standard setting, due to the relatively simple process of determining the pass points.[18] In this method, judges are expected to review each test item and a passing score is computed from an estimate of the probability of a minimally acceptable candidate answering each item correctly. As a first step, the judges discuss and define the characteristics of a minimally acceptable candidate. Then, each judge makes an independent assessment of the probability for each item that this previously defined minimally acceptable candidate will answer the item correctly. To determine the probability of a correct response for each item, that is, the passing score, the judges' assessments of the items are averaged. Then, these probabilities for all items of the test are averaged to obtain the pass point for the test.[19] The Angoff method features several advantages: it is easy to implement, understand, and compute.[20] However, the Angoff method also has disadvantages. First, it assumes that the judges have a good understanding of the statistical concepts. Second, the panelists may lose sight of the candidates' overall performance on the assessment due to the focus on individual items, as this method uses an item-based procedure.[21] Moreover, the continuum of item probabilities tends to result in considerable variability among the judges. Many judges have difficulties defining candidates who are minimally competent.[22] In the case of aviation security screeners, judges would have to focus on a person who would be just sufficiently capable of doing the job.

Revision

The development of a scientifically approved test is a complex procedure. Here, the development of the X-Ray CAT is explained in order to provide an example. The first step in a test's development is the definition of what should be measured and how. It was planned that a test should be developed for the purpose of measuring the X-ray image interpretation competency of airport security screeners when they search X-ray images of passenger bags for prohibited objects. In order for the test to be face valid (see above), the nature of the items to be chosen was obvious. They should be X-ray images of passenger bags where some of these images contain a prohibited item and some do not. Careful thought should be invested in the design of the test. In this case, since it is known that several factors can influence the detection performance of an aviation security screener, the items should be constructed considering these factors. That is, the items should be constructed by controlling for the image-based factors view difficulty, superposition, and bag complexity. Furthermore, the effects that should or could be measured with the test should be considered. Depending on the initial point and the aims, the items can be developed quite differently. The X-Ray CAT is composed of two similar sets and contains prohibited items of different categories, each one in two different viewpoints. The set construction serves the purpose of measuring the transfer effects. Transfer effect means the transfer of knowledge about threat objects that is gained during training to threat objects that were not included in training but are similar to objects that were included. The X-Ray CAT can measure several effects: the effect of viewpoint, threat category, training, and transfer (see above for a more detailed description).

After the first version of the test had been constructed, it was administered to a large and representative sample in a pilot study ($N = 354$ airport security screeners). Based on the results of this pilot study, the first revision took place. First of all, a reliability analysis gave information on the quality of the test and each item (item difficulty and item-to-total correlation). Those items with a difficulty below the range of acceptable difficulty had to be revised. The range of acceptable item difficulty depends on the answer type. In this case, an item can be correct or incorrect, that is having a 50 percent chance probability. The range of acceptable difficulty was defined between 0.6 and 0.9. Furthermore, the items should possess as high an item-to-total correlation as possible. In this case, all items with a negative or very small item-to-total correlation were corrected. In order to measure any effect of threat category on the detection performance, the detection performance of a threat object should depend only on the threat object itself and not on the difficulty of the bag it is placed in. To this end, the difficulty of the bags should be balanced across all categories, across both viewpoints of the test, and also across the two sets. As a measure of difficulty for the bag images, the false alarm rate was consulted (i.e., how many times a bag was judged as containing a threat item although there was none). Then, the bags were assigned to the four categories in such a way that their mean difficulty was not statistically different. The threat objects were built into the new bags if necessary, again considering superposition. At last, the items were shifted between the two sets (always incorporating the twin structure) in order to equalize the difficulty of the sets. The revised test was administered to another sample ($N = 95$ airport security screeners), repeating the revision steps as necessary. After a third ($N = 359$ airport security screeners) and a fourth ($N = 222$ airport security screeners) revision, the X-Ray CAT was acceptable in terms of stable reliability, item difficulty, and item-to-total correlation.

In summary, the test was revised according to the image difficulty, the item-to-total correlation, and the balancing of the difficulty of the clean bag images. The aim is a high reliability with items featuring high item-to-total correlations and acceptable item difficulty. The difficulty of a threat image (a bag containing a prohibited object) should depend only on the object itself and not on the difficulty of the bag. Otherwise, a comparison between the detection performance for the different threat categories could be biased.

REAL WORLD APPLICATION OF THE X-RAY COMPETENCY ASSESSMENT TEST (X-RAY CAT)

X-Ray CAT was used in several studies and in a series of international airports in order to measure the X-ray image interpretation competencies of screening officers. In this section, the application of X-Ray CAT is presented along with discussions and results obtained by means of the EU-funded VIA Project.

The VIA Project

The VIA Project evolved from the tender call in 2005 of the European Commission's Leonardo da Vinci program on vocational education and training. The project's full title is "Development of a Reference Levels Framework for A'VIA'tion Security Screeners." The aim of the project is to develop appropriate competence and qualification assessment tools and to propose a reference levels framework (RLF) for aviation security screeners at national and cross-sectoral levels.

To date, 11 airports in six European countries are involved in the project. Most of these airports are going through the same procedure of recurrent tests and training phases. This makes it possible to scientifically investigate the effect of recurrent weekly computer-based training and knowledge transfer and subsequently to develop a reference levels framework based on these outcomes. The tools used for testing in the VIA project are the computer-based training (CBT) program, X-Ray Tutor,[23] and the X-Ray CAT. Subsequently, the results of the computer-based test measurements included as part of the VIA project procedure are reported in detail.

VIA Computer-Based Test Measurement Results

As explained earlier, the X-Ray Competency Assessment Test (CAT) contains 256 X-ray images of passenger bags, half of which contain a prohibited item. This leads to four possible outcomes for a trial: a "hit" (a correctly identified threat object), a "miss" (a missed threat object), a "correct rejection" (a harmless bag correctly judged as being OK), and a "false alarm" (an incorrectly reported threat object).

In terms of sensitivity, the hit rate alone is not a valid measure to assess X-ray image interpretation competency. It is easy to imagine that a hit rate of 100 percent can be achieved by simply judging every X-ray image as containing a prohibited item. In this case, the entire set of non-threat items is completely neglected by this measure (the false alarm rate would also be 100 percent). In contrast, Green and Swets in 1966 developed a signal detection performance measure d' (say, d prime), taking into account hit rates as well as false alarm rates.[24] Often, d' is referred to as sensitivity, emphasizing the fact that it measures the ability to distinguish between noise (in our case an X-ray image of a bag without a threat) and signal plus noise (in our case an X-ray image containing a prohibited item).

D' is calculated using the formula d' = z(H)—z(F), where H is the hit rate, F the false alarm rate, and z the z-transformation. For the application of d', the data have to fulfill certain criteria (noise and signal plus noise must be normally distributed and have the same variance). If these requirements are not fulfilled, another established, "non-parametric" measure is often used: A' (say, A prime). The measure also meets the requirement of setting the hit rate against the false alarm rate in order to achieve a reliable and valid measure of image interpretation competency. A' was the measure of choice for the current analyses because its non-parametric character allows its use independently from the underlying measurements distributions. A' can be calculated as follows, where H represents the hit rate of a test candidate or group and F represents its false alarm rate: A' = 0.5 + [(H—F)(1 + H—F)] / [4H(1—F). If the false alarm rate is greater than the hit rate, the equation must be modified:[25] A' = 0.5—[(F—H)(1 + F—H)] / [4F(1—H)].[26]

The reported results provide graphical displays of the relative detection performance measures A' at the nine European airports that participated in the present study by the VIA Project, as well as another graph showing the effect of the two viewpoints on the different threat categories as explained earlier. In order to provide statistical corroboration of these results, an analysis of variance (ANOVA) on the two within-participants factors, view difficulty and threat category (guns, IEDs, knives and other items), and the between-participants airport factor is reported as well. As part of the ANOVA, only the significant interaction effects are reported and considered to be noteworthy in the context.

Detection performance comparison between airports

Figure 5.6 shows the comparison of the detection performance achieved at eight European airports that participated in the VIA project. First, the detection performance was calculated for each screener individually. Then, the data were averaged across screeners for each airport; this is shown in Figure 5.6. Thin bars represent the standard deviation (a measure of variability) across screeners.. Due to its security sensitivity and for data protection reasons, the individual airports' names are not indicated and no numerical data are given here.

Although no numerical data is displayed in the graph, we can discern substantial differences between the airports in terms of mean detection performance and standard deviation. As described above, all VIA airports go through a similar procedure of alternation of test phases and training phases. Nevertheless, there are considerable differences between them. There were large differences

Figure 5.6
Detection Performance of Airports

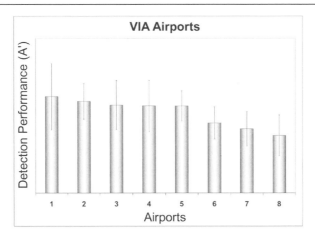

in the initial positions when the project was started, and the baseline assessment test, which is reported here, was conducted at different times at different airports. The differences can be put down to differences in the amount of training that was accomplished prior to this baseline testing as well as to differences in the personnel selection assessment. Some of the reported airports were already coached prior to the VIA project, though with diverse intensity and duration. Taking these differences into account, the reported results correspond fairly well with our expectations based on earlier studies of training effects.

Detection performance comparison between threat categories regarding view difficulty

Figure 5.7 shows again the detection performance measure A', but with a different focus. The data are averaged across the airports shown in figure 5.6, but analyzed by view difficulty within threat categories. There is a striking effect on detection performance deriving from view difficulty. Performance is significantly higher for threat objects depicted in easy views than for threat objects depicted in difficult views (canonical views rotated by 85 degrees).

Although this effect can be found in every one of the four threat categories, there are significant differences between them regarding general differences between the mean detection performances and also between the effect sizes of view difficulty that are unequal between threat categories. Knives and IEDs, for example, differ very much in view difficulty effect size but not so much in average detection performance. As can be seen in Figure 5.8, the reason is quite simple: IEDs consist of several parts and not all parts are depicted in easy or in difficult view at the same time. Some parts are always depicted in easy view when others are difficult, and vice versa. Knives have very characteristic shapes. They look consistently longish when seen perpendicular to their

Figure 5.7
Airport Detection of Prohibitive Items

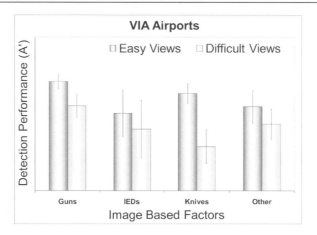

Figure 5.8
Views of Prohibitive Items

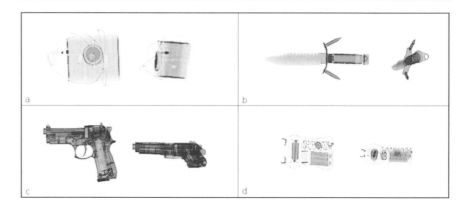

cutting edge but very small and thin when seen in parallel to their cutting edge. This interaction effect between threat item category and view difficulty can easily be observed in Figure 5.7, where the difference between easy and difficult views is much larger in knives than in IEDs. Furthermore, based on earlier studies of training effects, it is important to mention here that this pattern shown in Figure 5.7 is also highly dependent on training (interaction effects [category * airport and view difficulty * airport]).[27] Figure 5.8 illustrates two separate views of four prohibitive items.

Analysis of Variance (ANOVA)

The following statistics provide quantitative values for what has been reported graphically. This allows us to compare the effects of the different factors. We applied a three-way ANOVA to the two within-subjects factors, category and view difficulty, and one between-subjects airport factor on the detection performance measure A'.

The analysis revealed highly significant main effects on threat category (guns, IEDs, knives, and other items) with an effect size of $\eta^2 = .131$, $F(3, 5602.584) = 339.834$, $MSE = 2.057$, $p < .001$, on view difficulty (easy view v. difficult/rotated view) with an effect size of $\eta^2 = .47$, $F(1, 2257) = 2009.772$, $MSE = 9.031$, $p < .001$, and also on the between-subjects airport factor with an $\eta^2 = .080$, $F(1, 2257) = 28.128$, $MSE = 1.415$, $p < .001$. The following two-way interactions were also highly significant: threat category * view difficulty: $\eta^2 = .094$, $F(3, 6542.213) = 233.969$, $MSE = .931$, $p < .001$, threat category * airport $\eta^2 = .068$, $F(3, 5602.584) = 23.411$, $MSE = .142$, $p < .001$, and view difficulty * airport $\eta^2 = .159$, $F(1, 2257) = 60.953$, $MSE = .274$, $p < .001$. These results indicate different detection performance for different threat categories and higher detection performance for prohibited items in easy view than for rotated threat items (the effect of viewpoint).[28] This is consistent with results reported in the view-based object recognition literature (for reviews see, for example, two works by Tarr and Bülthoff.[29] The effect sizes were very large according to Cohen's conventions.[30]

Discussion

Although the reported real world application consists of baseline measurement data only, some important features of the X-Ray CAT could be illustrated well. X-Ray CAT allows us to measure and to evaluate the effects of view difficulty and threat objects practically independently of each other. Furthermore, the X-Ray CAT can be used as very reliable tool to compare the X-ray image interpretation competency of security staff at different airports and other types of infrastructure using X-ray technology for security control procedures.

SUMMARY AND CONCLUSIONS

The competency of a screener to detect prohibited items in X-ray images quickly and reliably is important for any airport security system. Computer-based tests, TIP, and to a limited extent covert tests can be used to assess individual competency in X-ray image interpretation. However, to achieve reliable, valid, and standardized measurements, it is essential that the requirements and principles detailed in this chapter are followed by those who produce, procure, or evaluate the competency assessment of the X-ray image interpretation tests of individual screeners.

This chapter introduced the competency assessment in airport security screening. In order to achieve a meaningful result the assessment has to meet the criteria of reliability and validity. Furthermore, the assessment has to be standardized to allow the evaluation of screeners' performance in relation to the population norm. There are three means for assessing X-ray image interpretation competency: covert testing, threat image projection (TIP), and computer-based image testing. Another important feature of maintaining the high level of X-ray baggage screening within aviation security is the initial and recurrent certification of screening personnel.

Threat image projection (TIP) as a means to assess X-ray image interpretation competency was illustrated in detail, as well as the conditions that have to be fulfilled in order for TIP to be a reliable and valid instrument.

This chapter also focused on the computer-based X-Ray Competency Assessment Test (X-Ray CAT). It features very high reliability scores and its design allows us to measure the X-ray image interpretation competency of aviation security screeners with regard to different aspects of their ability and knowledge. The X-Ray CAT is widely used at many different airports throughout the world, for competency assessment and certification purposes as well as in studies assessing the fundamentals of the demands required for the job of the aviation security screener.

This chapter continued by showing how a reliable, valid, and standardized test can be used to compare X-ray image interpretation competency across different airports and countries. The results of an EU-funded project (the VIA Project) showed remarkable differences in mean detection performance across nine European airports. All these countries conduct now weekly recurrent computer-based training. Since the X-Ray CAT will be conducted again in the first quarter of 2008, the VIA Project will also provide important insights on the benefits of computer-based training for increasing security and efficiency in X-ray screening.

NOTES

1. ICAO Annex 17, 3.4.3 ("Each Contracting State shall ensure that the persons carrying out screening operations are certified according to the requirements of the national civil aviation security programme").

2. ICAO Manual on Human Factors in Civil Aviation Security Operations, Doc. 9808.

3. ICAO Human Factors Training Manual, Doc. 9683, part 1, chapter 4, and in Appendix 6—"Guidance on Recruitment, Selection, Training, and Certification of Aviation Security Staff"—and Appendix 32—"Guidance on the Use of Threat Image Projection."

4. ICAO Security Manual for Safeguarding Civil Aviation against Acts of Unlawful Interference, Doc. 8973, chapter 4, I-4–45 ("Recruitment, Selection, Training, and Certification of Security Staff").

5. ECAC Doc. 30, Annex IV-12A, "Certification Criteria for Screeners," and ECAC Doc. 30, chapter 12, 12.2.3, "Certification of Security Staff," 1.1.10.3.

6. Joshua A. Fishman and Tomas Galguera, *Introduction to Test Construction in the Social and Behavioural Sciences. A Practical Guide* (Oxford: Rowman & Littlefield, 2003); Paul Kline, *Handbook of Psychological Testing* (London: Routledge, 2000); Kevin R. Murphy and Charles O. Davidshofer, *Psychological Testing* (Upper Saddle River, NJ: Prentice Hall, 2001).

7. Neil A. MacMillan and C. Douglas Creelman, *Detection Theory: A User's Guide* (New York: Cambridge University Press, 1991); Franziska Hofer and Adrian Schwaninger, "Reliable and Valid Measures of Threat Detection Performance in X-ray Screening," *IEEE ICCST Proceedings* 38 (2004): 303–8.

8. Adrian Schwaninger, Diana Hardmeier, and Franziska Hofer, "Measuring Visual Abilities and Visual Knowledge of Aviation Security Screeners," *IEEE ICCST Proceedings* 38 (2004): 258–64; Adrian Schwaninger, "Evaluation and Selection of Airport Security Screeners," *AIRPORT* 2 (2003): 14–15.

9. Franziska Hofer and Adrian Schwaninger, "Using Threat Image Projection Data for Assessing Individual Screener Performance," *WIT Transactions on the Built Environment* 82 (2005): 417–26.

10. Schwaninger, Hardmeier, and Hofer, "Measuring Visual Abilities and Visual Knowledge of Aviation Security Screeners"; Schwaninger, "Evaluation and Selection of Airport Security Screeners."

11. Stephen E. Palmer, Eleanor Rosch, and Paul Chase, "Canonical Perspective and the Perception of Objects," in *Attention and Performance IX*, ed. John Long and Alan Baddeley, 135–52 (Hillsdale, NJ: Erlbaum, 1981).

12. David M. Green and John A. Swets, *Signal Detection Theory and Psychophysics* (New York: Wiley, 1966); Neil A. MacMillan and C. Douglas Creelman, *Detection Theory: A User's Guide* (New York: Cambridge University Press, 1991); Hofer and Schwaninger, "Reliable and Valid Measures of Threat Detection Performance in X-Ray Screening"; Hofer and Schwaninger, "Using Threat Image Projection Data for Assessing Individual Screener Performance."

13. Diana Hardmeier, Franziska Hofer, and Adrian Schwaninger, "Increased Detection Performance in Airport Security Screening Using the X-Ray ORT as Pre-employment Assessment Tool," *Proceedings of the 2nd International Conference on Research in Air Transportation*, ICRAT 2006, Belgrade, Serbia and Montenegro, June 24–28, (Belgrade, Serbia: ICRAT, 2006), 393–97.

14. Saskia M. Koller et al., "Investigating Training, Transfer and Viewpoint Effects Resulting from Recurrent CBT of X-Ray Image Interpretation," *Journal of Transportation Security* 1, no. 2 (2008).

15. Adrian Schwaninger, "Computer-Based Training: A Powerful Tool for the Enhancement of Human Factors," *Aviation Security International* 10 (2004): 31–36; Adrian Schwaninger, "Increasing Efficiency in Airport Security Screening," *WIT Transactions on the Built Environment* 82 (2005): 405–16.

16. William Herbert Angoff, "Norms, Scales, and Equivalent Scores," in *Educational Measurement* (2nd ed.), ed. Robert L. Thorndike, 508–600 (Washington, DC: American Council on Education, 1971).

17. Measurement Research Associates, *Criterion Referenced Performance Standard Setting*, 2004, http://www.measurementresearch.com/wwa/default.shtml.

18. Muhammad Naveed Khalid and Muhammad Saeed, "Criterion Referenced Setting Performance Standards with an Emphasis on Angoff Method," *Journal of Research and Reflections in Education* 1 (2007): 66–87.

19. Angoff, "Norms, Scales, and Equivalent Scores."

20. Ronald A. Berk, "A Consumer's Guide to Setting Performance Standards on Criterion-Referenced Tests," *Review of Educational Research* 56 (1986): 137–72.

21. Measurement Research Associates, *Criterion Referenced Performance Standard Setting*.

22. Angoff, "Norms, Scales, and Equivalent Scores."

23. Ibid.

24. David Green and John Swets, "Signal Detection Theory and Psychopsychies," in *Detection Theory: A User's Guide*, ed. Neil MacMillan (London: Earlbaum, 1966).

25. Doris Aaronson and Brian Watts, "Extensions of Grier's Computational Formulas for A' and B" to Below-Chance Performance," *Psychological Bulletin* 102 (1987): 439–42.

26. Harold Stanislaw and Natasha Todorov, "Calculation of Signal Detection Theory Measures," *Behavior Research Methods, Instruments, and Computers* 31, no. 1 (1999): 137–49; Green and Swets, *Signal Detection Theory and Psychophysics;* Irwin Pollack and Donald A. Norman, "A non-parametric Analysis of Recognition Experiments," *Psychonomic Science* 1 (1964): 125–26; J. Brown Grier, "Nonparametric Indexes for Sensitivity and Bias: Computing Formulas," *Psychological Bulletin* 75 (1971): 424–29; ICAO Security Manual for Safeguarding Civil Aviation against Acts of Unlawful Interference, Doc. 8973, chapter 4, I-4-45 ("Recruitment, Selection, Training and Certification of Security Staff").

27. Ibid.

28. Paul Kline, *Handbook of Psychological Testing* (London: Routledge, 2000).

29. Michael J. Tarr and Heinrich H. Bülthoff, "Is Human Object Recognition Better Described by Geon Structural Descriptions or by Multiple Views? Comment on Biederman and Gerhardstein (1993)," *Journal of Experimental Psychology: Human Perception and Performance* 21 (1995): 1494–1505; Michael J. Tarr and Heinrich H. Bülthoff, "Image-Based Object Recognition in Man, Monkey and Machine," in *Object Recognition in Man, Monkey and Machine*, ed. Michael J. Tarr and Heinrich H. Bülthoff, 1–20 (Cambridge, MA: MIT Press, 1998).

30. Jacob Cohen, *Statistical Power Analysis for the Behavioral Sciences* (New York: Erlbaum, Hillsdale, 1988).

CHAPTER 6

Constructing a Comprehensive Aviation Security Management Model (ASMM)

Chien-tsung Lu

In 1999, the Federal Aviation Administration (FAA) began to promote a new scientific and systemic troubleshooting procedure for aviation security and safety, derived from the FAA's Office of System Safety. Yet by the year 2007, most U.S. air carriers, manufacturers, and airports had not implemented the processes recommended in the *System Safety Handbook* and elsewhere. In addition to the absence of regulations, the lack of implementation results primarily from the fact that the value of system safety is unclear. While the concept of system safety is viewed with skepticism by the aviation industry, academia possesses an opportunity to help explain that it is essential and useful.

This chapter uses a case study with philosophy and documentary analysis to accomplish research objectives, which include the following: (1) reviewing the FAA's voluntary safety programs and revealing operational difficulty; and (2) proposing and demonstrating the process of a comprehensive aviation security management model.

Safety is the mission priority and universal norm for the worldwide aviation industry including airlines, airports, traffic control, fixed-base operators, and related sectors. The September 11 terrorist attacks in 2001 provided the impetus for further air transportation security measures. Airport security is of the utmost importance and, to a great extent, has triggered numerous studies and research projects involving operational performance. In the official report of the 9/11 Commission, a multilayer redundant system is recommended to effectively secure the needed safety quality and security levels.[1] According to the report,

The FAA set and enforced aviation security rules, which airlines and airports were required to implement. The rules were supposed to produce a "layered" system of defense. This means that the failure of any one layer of security would not be fatal, because additional layers would provide backup security.[2]

SAFETY MANAGEMENT PROGRAM

In fact, system safety's philosophy of "redundancy" or the "safety net" inspired the U.S. government to generate a better aviation safety program beginning in 1996. Originally, the Office of System Safety was empowered to lead aviation system safety research, promote findings, and apply the findings. As described in the FAA's Order 8040–4,

This order establishes the safety risk management policy and prescribes procedures for implementing safety risk management as a decision-making tool within the Federal Aviation Administration (FAA).[3]

FAA Administrative Order 8040–4 requires the Office of System Safety (1) to incorporate a risk management process for all high-consequence decisions including those involving airlines and airports, and (2) to provide a handbook/manual of system risk management and recommend system safety tools to all U.S.-based airlines.[4] To accomplish the appointed tasks and promote risk management within the industry, the Office of System Safety began sponsoring an annual system safety conference and workshop for airline and airport managers in 1999. Research efforts of the FAA, project contractors, and conference participants were exchanged and ideas were discussed during each workshop. Despite the fact that the *System Safety Handbook* contains safety theories, the current system safety studies coming from the industry are limited to engineering/hardware design such as that of navigation systems, weather and turbulence forecasts, global positioning systems, runway incursions, and airport operational procedures. Although an error management model has been disseminated by the FAA, a comprehensive procedure of application for nonengineering disciplines is nonexistent.

In 2006, Lu, Wetmore, and Przetak further conducted a content analysis study of the annual system safety conference.[5] They discovered that the FAA's advocate was mostly concerned with the conceptual nature of risk management, rather than with an in-depth demonstration of safety analysis techniques (see Table 6.1). As a result, most airlines (flag or nonflag), airports, and flight based operations (FBOs) did not incorporate nonmandatory system safety management procedures into their operation unless a voluntary engagement had been initiated.[6] In addition, the use of system safety concepts has primarily been tied to risk management using a basic descriptive trend study, however, most of the results are not accessible to the public. Examples of such voluntary programs include the FAA's Runway Incursion Information (RII), the Air Transportation Oversight System (ATOS) or Advanced Quality Program (AQP), the Safety Reporting System and Database (SRSD), Flight Operational Quality Assurance (FOQA), the Air Carrier Operations System

Table 6.1
System Safety Workshops And Conferences—Content Analysis

	2001	2002	2003	2004
System Safety Management	X	X	X	X
Aviation System Safety Program (AvSP)	X	X	X	X
FAA-Airlines Collaboration	X	X	X	X
Data Collection & Risk Analysis	X	X	X	X
System Risk Management (SRM) & Safety Culture		X	X	X
Flight crews-centered	X	X		X
Non-flight crews-centered	X	X	X	X
All aviation workers	X			
Air Carrier Operations System Model (ACOSM)	X			
Aviation Safety Action Program (ASAP)	X	X		X
Flight Operational Quality Assurance (FOQA)	X	X		X
Advanced Quality Program (AQP)	X			
Aviation Safety Reporting System (ASRS)	X			X
Continuous Analysis and Surveillance Systems (CASS)	X			
Maintenance Resource Management (MRM) training	X	X		
Human Factor CRM training	X	X	X	X
Case-based training/Naturalistic Decision-making	X	X	X	X
Regulations	X	X	X	
Cost-benefit and Safety Investment	X	X	X	X
Failure Mode and Effective Analysis (FMEA) Concept		X		
Failure Mode and Effective Analysis (FMEA) Application				
Fault Tree Analysis (FTA) Concept		X		
Fault Tree Analysis (FTA) Application				
Risk Control Management (RCA)				X
Hybrid Causal Modeling			X	X

Note: The origin of this Content Analysis Table was statistically extracted from the research projects and papers presented at the FAA System Safety workshops and conferences between 2000 and 2004. As shown in the above table, most researches either focused on the advocate of using System Safety concepts or risk analysis covering trend study. Researchers did not apply tools (i.e, FTA or FMEA) to their studies for a demonstration. Especially, there were only two papers explained FMEA and FTA techniques over the past four years. Yet no further application was found.

Model (ACOSM), the Aviation Safety Action Program (ASAP), and NASA's Aviation Safety Reporting System (ASRS).

All the aforementioned programs are checklisted trend studies centered around hazard identification, but they are segregated instead of integrated into one system. More critically, despite the Air Cargo Program, the Alien Flight Student Program, HAZMAT programs, passenger screening, and other modern security-related programs coming from the Transportation Security Administration (TSA) that focus on the philosophy of "layers of security," there is no internal error reporting system or real-time alert program in place at U.S. airports. This situation has increased the government's workload simply because information about possible hazards and threats is not compiled into prioritized data banks up front by airports. Likewise, airport workers and passengers can not benefit from a risk-free environment without the implementation of an early warning mechanism, which system safety management is encouraging. In some cases, although airports might have had a security system, the functionality and benefits of the threat reporting system were not explained well enough to employees, and this resulted in incomplete information collection and system inaccuracy. These details reveal an opportunity for improvement and suggest a more comprehensive, user-friendly, and dynamic airport security management model.

FAA AC 120–92 and AC 107–1

In 1972, the FAA published its *Advisory Circular (AC) 107–1 Aviation Security—Airport.* This circular recommends that airports comply with FAA Federal Aviation Regulation (FAR) 107 security requirements with regard to personnel, identifications, authority, signs, trainings, audit, security areas, and so on. The purpose of AC 107–1 is to provide guidelines for an airport security program and to "describe minimum acceptable standards for: (a) preparation of a master security plan, (b) establishing and maintaining a suitable authorized persons identification program, and (c) establishing and maintaining an adequate identification system for certain ground vehicles."[7] However, there is no detailed procedure for filing a threat report; and therefore no proactive airport threat analysis program could be set up.

In 2006, in view of the increasingly recognized merits of using system safety management in aviation safety, the FAA published its *Advisory Circular (AC 120–92) Introduction to Safety Management Systems for Air Operators* to meet two goals: (1) introducing the concept of a safety management system (SMS) to air transportation service providers, and (2) providing air carriers and airports with a guideline for an SMS. The purposes of this advisory circular focus on (1) safety management (risk management and safety assurance using quality management techniques, and a systemic approach to safety management), and (2) safety culture (the human-centered psychological, behavioral, and organizational elements).[8] Using safety risk management and safety assurance to manage safety in this publication is sound and plausible. However, the model embracing the risk matrix given by the FAA lacks specific details: first, the report's format is not user-friendly, which creates confusion about the proposed error management model; second, system safety tools like fault tree analysis (FTA) and operations and support hazard analysis (O&SHA)

should have been included in this guideline so that aviation industry could have a better picture of a true, proactive SMS.

MIL-STD 882

To detect potential hazards, the FAA and TSA currently recommend risk management programs, which shed light on the applicability of a system safety concept. The original *Standard Practice for System Safety* (MIL-STD-882A, published in 1969) helps aircraft and aerospace engineers to better design products without utilizing the expensive fly-fix-fly doctrine embraced by the U.S. military, especially in the early project teams of X-planes before the end of World War II. After 1969, the U.S. Air Force and NASA both realized that MIL-STD-882 was extremely helpful in reducing a hardware system's causal failures, both active and latent.[9]

Safety Theories

The security net for the air transportation system is rarely breached by a singular hazardous factor or an isolated risk.[10] When an aircraft hijacking occurs, it reveals the total failure of the layered security system. This can be examined by traditional safety models such as 5-M factors, the Swiss Cheese model, the Domino effect, the SHELL model, chain of events, and related safety analysis devices. Therefore, the concept of multifactor *causes event* $(X_s Y)$, where multiple causes contribute to the accident, is not a contentious issue. The cause, X, could be identified as a violation, distraction, complacency, carelessness, recklessness, fatigue, poor situational awareness, and other mechanical or human deficiencies. Although each is considered to be one security element/layer, there are some precursors to the so-called single element failure. For instance, the cause of the accident involving Comair Flight 5191 (initiating takeoff on the wrong runway) could be categorized as human error but may include miscommunication, situational awareness, crew resource management, flight training, ATC's complacency, or other latent preconditions. Nevertheless, the most reasonable question is: Why did human error (error involving pilots or the air traffic controller) occur in the first place? Was it due to a lack of training, personal problems, health, shortage of staff, sociopsychological status, or carelessness, or was it simply an intentional act?

Organizational Factor

Problems with airport management can also endanger security. In 1997, James Reason published *Managing the Risk of Organizational Accidents*, showing that people make mistakes no matter what their intentions are. Reason categorized human behavior into three subgroups: (1) skill-based behavior (SB), (2) rule-based behavior (RB), and (3) knowledge-based behavior (KB). To identify potential errors hidden in the dark corners of a given management

Figure 6.1
The Correlation Among 3Ps

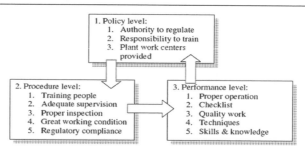

system, Reason suggested the examination of salient problems using three dimensions: (1) personnel: a worker is an agent of a system; (2) engineering: statistical prediction; and (3) organizational: various management segments of an organization are responsible for safety.[11] These three dimensions intertwine; for example, the organizational model controls the personnel and engineering models. Thus, understanding an organizational accident is critical in ensuring security performance. For instance, a security problem could occur when there is a breakdown within a hierarchical management system, in particular, when a safety management structure is ill-formed and allows threats to penetrate.[12]

Policy, Procedure, and Performance

In his book, *Safety and Health: Management Planning*, and his paper, "Three Ps in Safety: Policies, Procedures, and Performance," Ted Ferry emphasized how essential it is to set up a policy so that procedure is created and performance is measured.[13] Moreover, the 3Ps concept is not a linear process but a recursive and cyclic activity linking policies, procedures, and performance into one frame (see Figure 6.1). If any segment of a management system is lacking, the entire safety/security loop will collapse and the program will fail. Clearly, setting policy is urgent and should first be done by the government. This concept has been echoed by Wells, who states that "Policy is usually referenced in the early part of all plans."[14] However, in today's aviation industry, establishing a new policy is not only unwelcome but it could also be extremely time consuming without knowledge of immediate or known threats.[15] With this in mind, an alternative policy should be introduced. An effective and efficient threat-prevention model is most cost effective when aviation workers can easily go through its guidelines, provide comments, gain recognition, be protected, and ultimately make aviation security flawless.

DEFINITIONS OF SYSTEM SAFETY TECHNIQUES

To proactively identify potential threats leading to security breakdown, MIL-STD-882D suggests several techniques that security experts can apply.

Although this study demonstrates the basic application of only two tools, FTA and O&SHA, experts could expand their skills by applying other techniques that are recommended below. The system safety techniques described here are those most commonly used by system safety engineers.

Job safety analysis (JSA). "A generalized examination of the tasks associated with the performance of a given job and an evaluation of the hazards associated with those tasks and the controls used to prevent or reduce exposure to those hazards. Usually performed by the responsible supervisor for that job and used primarily to train and orient new employees."[16]

Operating and support hazard analysis (O&SHA). "Performed to identify and evaluate operational-type hazards. It is based upon detailed design information and is an evaluation of operational tasks and procedures. It considers human system integration factors such as human error, human task overload, cognitive misconception, [and] the effect on humans of hardware failure."[17]

Fault tree analysis (FTA). "Systems analysis technique used to determine the root causes and probability of occurrence of a specified undesired event. A fault tree analysis is a model that logically and graphically represents the various combinations of possible events, faulty and normal, occurring in a system that lead to a previously identified hazard or undesired event."[18]

Failure mode and effective criticality analysis (FMECA). "Tool for evaluating the effect(s) of potential failure modes of subsystems, assemblies, components or functions. It is primarily a reliability tool to identify failure modes that would adversely affect overall system reliability. FMECA has the capability to include failure rates for each failure mode in order to achieve a quantitative probabilistic analysis."[19]

Management oversight and risk tree (MORT). "MORT is an analytical technique for identifying safety-related oversights, errors, and/or omissions that lead to the occurrence of a mishap."[20] Regardless of the informed system risks, the focus of this model is on management's omissions or less than adequate (LTA) performance.

RECENT STUDIES APPLYING SYSTEM SAFETY MANAGEMENT

In addition to aerospace engineering, applications of system safety techniques and concepts have been useful in the field of medicine. For instance, in the medical engineering industry, Robert L. Helmreich, an aviation safety legend now dedicated to the medical field, advocated the use of system safety's error management concept in medical practice.[21] In 1999, another medical device assessment was carried out by Manon Croheecke and his research associates, advocating FMEA.[22] William Hyman utilized the leading tool of system safety, the FTA, in evaluating potential hazards associated with newly developed medical equipment before moving toward the production-manufacturing phase in the device's life cycle.[23]

In aviation safety, the U.S. Air Force launched risk management and causal study to improve pilot training procedures. Diehl's cross-referenced analysis of 208 military accidents discovered the breakdown of the cockpit communication and team performance known as crew coordination.[24] This communication breakdown led to military aircraft mishaps. Diehl's study applied an ergonomic human-face interface (an O&SHA concept) and suggested a modification of the cockpit layout of the Cessna Citation used by U.S. Air Force officers. This study linked accident investigation, hazard identification, and basic descriptive analysis to human factor and crew resource management (CRM) training and later provided an exemplary study to academia. Lu, Przetak, and Wetmore conducted a similar causal study using statistical analysis to discover the causes of nonflight accidents for FAR Part 121, on U.S.-based carriers yielding another view to measure aviation safety.[25]

A study by Thom and Clariett, published in *Collegiate Aviation Review* (*CAR*), focused on an essential section of system safety, the applicability of job safety analysis (JSA) and task analysis.[26] In their study, JSA was closely interpreted and the layout of the human-machine interface was emphasized. Using the risk homeostasis theory (RHT) of human dynamic behavior to study risk taking, Thom and Clariett helped identify potential hazards involving hangar, factory, or student workers, both within and outside the aviation industry. This study was of great interest to a safer aviation community.

Luis Bastos presented a risk management model based on feedback from 14 Code of Federal Regulations (14CFR) Part 135 pilots as well as the National Transportation Safety Board's (NTSB) accident data.[27] Bastos discovered that accidents are usually caused by multiple safety factors, which agrees with Reason's theory of organizational accidents. Since potential risk exists, reducing risk probability (Rp) and risk severity (Rs) upstream is essentially targeted. Bastos also proposed a risk management model similar to MIL-STD-882D Risk Matrix model (see Table 6.2).

Lu, Wetmore, and Przetak demonstrated the application of FTA in promoting safety performance.[28] Their analysis indicated that FTA, based on a risk tree analysis and a statistical forecast, can help proactively prevent undesired events or stop events from occurring. According to their study, FTA helps organizations such as the government or airlines to effectively and promptly identify accident postulates and to trigger the implementation of strategic safety prevention programs from the bottom up (upstream) (see Figure 6.2). Based on the FTA hierarchical block-diagram associated with the use of Boolean gates, any of the root factors on the bottom level can form a cut-set or a failure-chain contributing to an accident or system failure (a top event). Hence, compressing or eliminating the failure probability of root factors from the lowest level of the risk tree also identifies a training priority. A statistical simulation based on the required risk calculation concerning hazard probability and severity is shown in Figure 6.3. With the computerized-system design, a real-time, dynamic system safety model is possible.

Although the FAA realized the value of collecting data and monitoring trends, the FTA model provides a dynamic system with which to identify

Table 6.2
Risk Matrix, Severity & Probability

Risk Matrix* *Frequency*	*Catastrophic (I)*	*Critical (II)*	*Marginal (III)*	*Negligible (IV)*
Frequent (A)	1A	2A	3A	4A
Probable (B)	1B	2B	*3B*	*4B*
Occasional (C)	1C	*2C*	*3C*	4C
Remote (D)	*1D*	2D	3D	4D
Impossible (E)	1E	2E	3E	4E

* A "Risk" falling into this category [1A, 2A, 3A, 4A, 1B, 2B, 1C] is "Unacceptable"
A "Risk" falling into this category [1D, 2C, 3B, 3C, 4B] is "Undesirable"
A "Risk" falling into this category [1E, 2D, 2E, 3D, 4C] is "Acceptable With Review"
A "Risk" falling into this category [3E, 4D, 4E] is "Acceptable Without Review"
The determination of "Unacceptable," "Undesirable," "Acceptable With Review," or "Acceptable without Review" is based on a System Safety analyst's subjective decision-making based on the onsite situation from case to case.

Risk Severity (S) and Probability (P) are defined as:

Risk Severity (S) *Description*	*Category*	*Mishap Definition*
Catastrophic	I	Death or system loss/failure
Critical	II	Severity injury, occupational illness, or system damage
Marginal	III	Minor injury, occupational illness, or system damage
Negligible	IV	Other

Risk Probability (P) *Description*	*Level*	*Mishap Definition*
Frequent	A	Likely to occur frequently
Probable	B	Will occur several times during the life of an item
Occasional	C	Likely to occur sometimes in the life of an item
Remote	D	Unlikely, but may possibly occur in life of an item
Impossible	E	So unlikely, assumed that hazard will not occur at all

Source: DOD MIL-STD-882B System Safety Program Requirements (1984)

hazards and to assign risk values using Bayesian analysis. Bayesian inference provides a quantitative framework for the iterative process of integrating information into useful models. It is the essence of predicting and therefore preventing accidents. The model is the keystone of safety management but has apparently been overlooked by the FAA.

Captain Luis Lupolis of the Brazilian Air Force achieved the application of organizational accident theory in July 2006.[29] His research hypothesized that

Figure 6.2
Simulating the Probability of the Top-Level Event

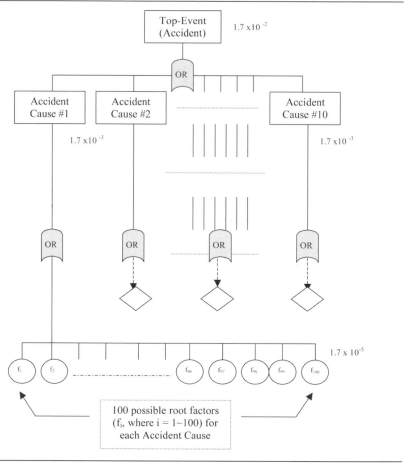

Source: Chien-sung Lu, Michael Wetmore & Robert Przetak. Another approach to enhance airline safety: Using System Safety techniques. *Journal of Air Transportation* 11, no. 2 (2006): 113–139.

deficient decision-making processes and poor organizational management by top-ranking officers could result in aircraft mishaps. Lupolis revealed, via self-administered surveys, that Brazilian Air Force squadron commanders have a limited knowledge of advanced safety theories like organizational accident theory, but they are all committed to operational safety. Thus, a more advanced safety education for top management is needed. Furthermore, although the top-ranking officers are aware of their lack of knowledge of a reliable decision-making process, they still use empirical means to make safety decisions. Capt. Lupolis recommends further research on the rationale these officers use to make safety decisions.

Figure 6.3
Managing a Security Event

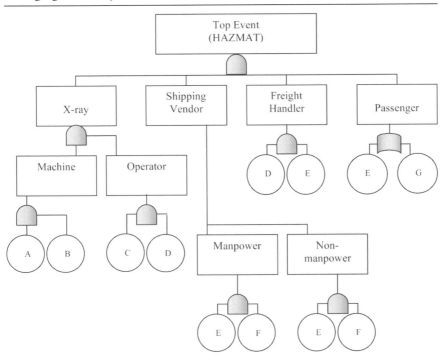

RESEARCH FOCUS

Apparently, utilizing system safety in relation to flight safety has been recognized as useful. Yet in aviation security, it is new, innovative, and challenging. Therefore a well-designed aviation security management model prepared for airport security would be beneficial. The proposed security model meets the following criteria: (1) it is administratively practical; (2) its basis of measurement is quantifiable for qualitative analysis; (3) a valid measurement presents what it is supposed to represent; (4) the system safety tools utilized are understandable, user-friendly, and sensitive to situational change; (5) the security data is presented in a real-time reflection/alert fashion; and (6) the results are distributable and disseminated.[30]

PROPOSED AVIATION SECURITY MANAGEMENT MODEL (ASMM)

The proposed aviation security management model (ASMM) contains nine major steps: (1) data collection, (2) threat identification, (3) data analysis, (4) threat matrix calculation and response, (5) system safety tools implementation and regulatory compliance, (6) reports and feedback, (7) result

Figure 6.4
The Risk Analysis Process

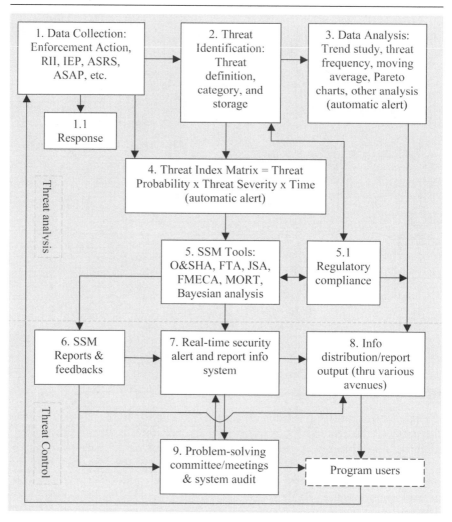

monitoring, (8) information distribution, and (9) problem-solving meetings (see Figure 6.4).

Data collection. Hazardous data can be retrieved from the current ongoing threat/hazard reporting programs such as the airport Enforcement Action database, TSA incident reports, runway incursion incidents (RII), the Aviation Safety Action Program (ASAP), the airport Internal Evaluation Program (IEP), the Aviation Safety Reporting System (ASRS), and others. The data on potential threats can be (1) reported by employees, (2) downloaded from self-maintained databases, or (3) obtained from government's documentary reviews. A suggestion with regard to this data collection phase is that the data reporting mechanism should be ready for and open to all workers, allowing security project managers to receive genuine information from field specialists or anyone who would like to contribute. This collection must meet several requirements in order to encourage contributions: it must be (1) penalty-free, (2) anonymous, (3) confidential, (4) easy to report, (5) open-door in nature, and (6) useful for feedback and solutions.

Threat identification. The purpose of threat identification is twofold: threat definition and categorization. The criticality of threat identification focuses on the review of reports from frontline experts to see if it is a reportable threat (not blackmail or the like) and if it requires prompt internal analysis. In addition, collected data should be categorized and prepared for an immediate analysis and threat study.

Data analysis. This is the first analytical output of a review focused on identifying and reporting threat prioritization associated with a quick solution or immediate automatic security alert. Data analysis should contain, but not be limited to, some basic hazardous information, such as a trend study, hazard ranking, and preliminary reports provided during a specific time. Regulatory compliance must be reviewed, and this part of the information can be distributed to employees for self-alert and as weekly safety/security brief/ educational materials.

Threat matrix calculation and response. During this phase of ASMM, the formation of a threat index matrix (TIX) can be generated. An example provided (see Table 6.3) suggests that the TIX uses addition instead of multiplication in order to provide an easier means of threat calculation and interpretation using figures ranging between 2 and 10, the higher number being better.

Meanwhile, a color-coded numerical index matrix indicates the risk level of a situation reported by employees. In this proposed model, the risk index 1 to approximately 4 is qualitatively defined as an "Emergency" threat that needs response or solution quickly. The risk index 6~12 indicates a "Cautious" situation needing a fast review and resolution, for which more information and analysis may be needed to determine the level of risk over the entire security system. Finally, the risk index 15~24 represents a "Supervisory" case and the

Table 6.3
Threat Index Matrix (TIX)

	Threat Probability					
Threat severity	*Impossible* 6	*Improbable* 5	*Remote* 4	*Occasional* 3	*Probable* 2	*Frequent* 1
Negligible 4	24	20	16	12	8	4
Marginal 3	18	15	12	9	6	3
Critical 2	12	10	8	6	4	2
Catastrophic 1	6	5	4	3	2	1

* Index note: 1 ~ 4 Emergency   6 ~ 12 Cautious   15 ~ 24 Supervisory

reported threat needs continuous measurement in the future. In the matrix for the airport industry, although the threat probability is extremely low ("Impossible" = 6), any possible fatality ("Catastrophe" = 1) is unacceptable, thus it is also categorized as "Cautious" instead of "Supervisory." Meanwhile, a "Frequent" rating (1) of threat probability with a "Negligible" (4) threat severity is also unacceptable because the threat could immediately be mitigated at a very low cost (i.e., a passenger's nonintentional violation of or carelessness with regard to a security procedure). Otherwise, threat accumulation (i.e., overlook) may lead to a larger scale of damage (i.e., from an intentional act, a lack of required HAZMAT training, or security breach to worker injury or facility damage). Equally important, the threat probability levels should be manipulated based on an individual airport's operational nature.

System safety tools implementation and regulatory compliance. This phase processes the information/reports and receives the hazard probability from the previous processing stage. The exemplary reporting forms using FTA and O&SHA (see Table 6.4) provide a conceptual demonstration. The real value of this phase is the application of system safety tools to conduct a detailed threat-incident-accident analysis and suggest countermeasures for new employee orientations, routine safety education, recurrent training, and an accident-prevention course based on regulatory requirements and identified safety gaps within the operational system.

Reports and feedback. The purpose of the investigation is to identify the problems, provide safety measures, and prevent similar problems from happening again. With this in mind, the analytical reports will be sent to a safety committee for review if the calculation of the threat index indicates a need. Also, the result and resolution need to be distributed to the submitters, if known. Otherwise, it should be posted on a security bulletin board or to a monitoring system for public review. A threat tracking system is equally important for two reasons: (1) it will help the safety manager identify the status of a threat report, and (2) it will show threat submitters the importance of their input and further motivate their participation.

Real-time security alert. The qualitative threat alert index of this proposed ASMM provides a visible image to safety managers or system users who need up-to-date information for prompt understanding. The author suggests a color-coded (at least three colors: red, yellow, and green, or more) system design for threat alert and identification. To accomplish this goal, sufficient digital databases and computerized systems are both critical.

Information distribution. This process should inform all employees about the status of the security level, as well as about cases identified by employees, peer airports, trade associations, or governments, since a threat to security at one airport would quickly raise concerns for other airports. Information distribution is accomplished by utilizing several formats such as e-mail, auto-voicemail, internal circulation, flight crew briefings, ground crew discussions, maintenance safety notices, recurrent/routine training, or airport notice to airmen (NOTAMs).

Table 6.4
Conceptual O&SHA Analysis

Item	Procedural tasks	Hazard condition	Cause	Effect	Risk level, criti-cality index	Assessment	Recommendation
1	Luggage Ninspection	HAZMAT	Lack of training	Fire alert on board	4(Emergency)	Inspector error	Reassurance and training
2	Luggage inspection	HAZMAT	Carelessness	Onboard fire	3 (Emergency)	Inspector error	Reassurance and training
3	Luggage inspection	HAZMAT	Complacency	Freight dam-age	7 (Supervisory)	Handler error	Reassurance and training
4	Luggage handling	HAZMAT	Carelessness	Toxic fumes	2 (Emergency)	Handler error	Special tag, reassur-ance and special HAZMAT training
5	Luggage handling	HAZMAT	Ignorance	Dangerous weapon	2 (Emergency)	Passenger error	Prohibited items reminder, X-ray, and reassurance
6	Luggage handling	Animal (such as iguana, dart frog, etc.)	Lack of knowl-edge	Worker injury	5 (Cautious)	Handler error	Reassurance and training

Note: Items are based on specific situations and can be expanded. O&SHA focuses on the problems of operator and operational interface. The threat index 2~4 means it is an "Emergency" case and needs an immediate response or solution. The threat index 5 ~7 indicates a "Cautious" situation that needs a fast review and resolution; more information and analysis may be needed to determine the level of threat eroding the entire operational system. The threat index 8 ~10 represents a "Supervisory" case and the reported hazard needs continuous measurement in the future.

Problem-solving meeting and system audit. Members of the safety committee should receive routinely, at least daily, a risk analysis and have the opportunity to provide comments and recommendations to upper management for further decision-making reviews (action or nonaction), if necessary. The safety committee generates solutions and mitigates potential hazards based on the magnitude of a risk. Frontline managers, employees, or union representatives should be invited to safety meetings, focus group discussions, and system audits periodically and be allowed to suggest training or resolutions because of their involvement in daily activities, their observations, and their career specialty.

CONCLUSION: THE UPCOMING CHALLENGE

Although we "cannot protect every person against every risk at every moment in every place . . . in order to protect our country and defend our freedoms, we must continue to focus resources on the areas that pose the greatest risk."[31] We have recognized the value of the system safety concept to airport security (in terms of threat report, identification, risk analysis, risk matrix calculation, system safety analysis, safety countermeasures, performance assessments, and documentation). An airport security program could be more proactive and effective if risk analysis techniques such as O&SHA, FTA, FMECA, JSA, and MORT are used.

Over the last seven years, the Government Accountability Office (GAO)[32] has reported that using system safety would be beneficial to the aviation industry including airlines, airports, and FBOs. Most importantly, the airline industry and the FAA have both remarked that a sufficient database is critical to a mature threat prediction, mishap mitigation, passenger protection, and national security. With this in mind, the reluctance to use new analytical techniques by the aviation industry is dangerous to its loyal customers. The ASMM specifically follows a systemic and scientific way to troubleshoot a given system by identifying potential risks that endanger the whole air transportation system within the error-latent environment.

This study provides a comprehensive safety management model, namely ASMM, which combines error management, system safety techniques and MIL-STD-882D to form a streamlined risk analysis and risk control program for easier use and safety reporting. An exemplary format of FTA and O&SHA was applied to demonstrate the fundamental application of this proposed model. Because this is a conceptual safety management model, enthusiasts can freely and flexibly revise this model using different system safety techniques that are based on the characteristics of a unique hazardous environment such as those involving maintenance safety, flight safety, cabin safety, ground operations safety, air traffic control, and others. Launching an internal hazard reporting system is the key to a successful safety program and a vital safety culture.

FUTURE STUDIES

Using computers to quickly solve problems is the future. Advocating a follow-up study implementing FTA, FMECA, or MORT by designing computerized statistical analysis and risk prioritization will improve the discipline of threat prediction and generate an automatic auditing or alert model for a system's real-time operational safety. Another follow-up study should focus on the performance and usefulness of the proposed ASMM as tested by airports, airlines and FBOs.

NOTES

1. National Commission on Terrorist Attacks, *The 9/11 Commission Report: Final Report of the National Commission on Terrorist Attacks Upon the United States*, authorized ed. (New York: W.W. Norton, July 2004).

2. National Commission on Terrorist Attacks Upon the United States (New York: W.W. Norton, 2006).

3. FAA, *FAA Order 8040–4 Safety Risk Management* (Washington, DC: FAA, 1996).

4. Ibid.

5. Chien-tsung Lu, Michael Wetmore, and Robert Przetak, "Another approach to enhance airline safety: Using System Safety Techniques," *Journal of Air Transportation* 11, no. 2 (2006): 113–39.

6. Chien-tsung Lu, Robert Przetak, and Michael Wetmore, "Discovering the Non-flight Hazards and Suggesting a Safety Training Model," *International Journal of Applied Aviation Science* 5, no .1 (June 2005): 135–52.

7. FAA, *Advisory Circular (AC) 107–1 Aviation Security—Airport* (Washington, DC: FAA, 1972).

8. FAA, *AC 120–92 Introduction to Safety Management Systems for Air Operators* (Washington, DC: FAA, 2006).

9. Department of Defense (DoD), *MIL-STD-882D: Standard Practice for System Safety* (Washington, DC: FAA, 2000).

10. Dan Petersen, *Safety Management: A Human Approach*, 2nd ed. (Goshen, NY: Aloray, 1988); Alexander Wells and Clarence Rodrigues, *Commercial Aviation Safety*, 4th ed. (New York: McGraw Hill, 2004); Richard H. Wood, *Aviation Safety Programs: A Management Handbook*, 3rd ed. (Englewood, CO: Jeppesen, 2003).

11. James Reason, *Managing the Risks of Organizational Accidents* (Burlington, VT: Ashgate, 1997).

12. Ibid.

13. Terry S. Ferry, *Safety and Health: Management Planning* (New York: Van Nostrand Reinhold, 1990); Terry S. Ferry, "Three Ps in Safety: Policy, Procedures, and Performance," *Professional Safety* 51, no. 6 (2006): 48–52.

14. Alexander. T. Wells, *Commercial Aviation Safety*, 3rd ed. (New York: McGraw Hill, 2002), 234.

15. Chien-tsung Lu, "Discovering the Regulatory Considerations of the Federal Aviation Administration: Interviewing the Aviation Rulemaking Advisory Committee," *Journal of Air Transportation*, 10, no. 3 (2005): 32–48.

16. Jeffrey W. Vincoli, *Basic Guide to System Safety*, 2nd ed. (Hoboken, NJ: Wiley & Sons, 2006), 206.

17. Cliffton A. Ericson, III, *Hazard Analysis Techniques for System Safety* (Hoboken, NJ: Wiley & Sons, 2005), 476.

18. Ibid., 472.

19. Ibid., 471.

20. Ibid., 423.

21. Robert L. Helmreich, "On Error Management: Lessons from Aviation," *British Medical Journal* 320, no. 7237 (2000): 781–85.

22. Manon Croheecke, Rachel Mak, and Mas B.A.J. de Mol, "Failure Mode and Effect Analysis and Fault Tree Analysis in the Use of the CoaguChek® Prothrombin Time System," *International Journal of Risk in Medicine* 12, (1999): 173–79.

23. William A. Hyman, "Generic Fault Tree for Medical Device Error," *Journal of Clinic Engineering* 27, no. 1 (2002): 134–40.

24. Alan E. Diehl, "Human Performance and Systems Safety Considerations in Aviation Mishaps," *International Journal of Aviation Psychology* 1, no. 2 (1991): 97–106.

25. James Thom and D. R. Clariett, "A Structured Methodology for Adjusting Perceived Risk," *Collegiate Aviation Review* 22, no. 1 (2004): 97–121.

26. Luis Lupolis and M. Bastos, "Risk Management Model for On-Demand Part 135 (Air Taxi) Operator" (master's thesis, University of Central Missouri, 2005).

27. Luis C. Lupolis, "Discovering the Brazilian Air Force Squadron Commanders' Perceptions Regarding Organizational Accidents" (master's thesis, University of Central Missouri, 2006).

28. U.S. Army, *Safety Program* (Washington, DC: Department of the Army, 1972).

29. Ibid.

30. Michael Chertoff, "There Is No Perfect Security," *Wall Street Security—Eastern Edition* 247 (2006): 22A.

31. USGAO, *System Safety Approach Needs Further Integration into the FAA's Oversight of Airlines* (Washington, DC: USGAO, 2005).

32. USGAO, *FAA's Safety Oversight System Is Effective but Could Benefit from Better Evaluation of Its Programs' Performance* (Washington, DC: USGAO, 2005).

CHAPTER 7

Growing Pains at the Transportation Security Administration

Jeffrey Ian Ross

Since September 11, 2001, the United States has significantly revamped the ways and means used to provide and ensure national security against terrorist attacks. Key legislation included the PATRIOT Act (signed October 2001) and its revision, the USA PATRIOT Improvement and Reauthorization Act of 2005 (passed March 2006), which created new rules on domestic surveillance and detention; the Homeland Security Act (signed November 2002), which established the Department of Homeland Security (DHS); and the Aviation and Transportation Security Act (passed November 2001), which created the Transportation Security Administration (TSA).[1]

Given the nature of the September 11 attacks, coupled with the failure of the then current safety measures to detect and/or deter the 19 al Qaeda terrorists, it seems logical that there would be increased demands for changes in the way the United States' transportation industry conducts its business. Congress has given the TSA responsibility for supervising all modes of travel in the United States. The TSA is, further, charged with implementing relevant security changes. In general, "The primary goals of the new TSA were to increase the effectiveness and efficiency of (1) identifying passengers who were potential threats and (2) screening passengers and luggage for potential weapons and explosives."[2]

Unless they work for the federal government agencies and/or as a first responder for either state or local government, most Americans are probably not directly or physically affected by the PATRIOT and Homeland Security acts. On the other hand, the average person traveling on a commercial airliner will be directly affected by changes brought about because of the establishment of the TSA.

Special thanks to Richard Hogan and Dawn L. Rothe for comments.

The TSA has been singled out for intense scrutiny, in large measure because of the inconveniences passengers must now endure when boarding, deplaning, and traveling on commercial airlines inside, and to and from, the United States. In addition to the restrictions and other measures air passengers encounter, there have been increased citizen criticisms surrounding the privacy rights that are curtailed every time they take a plane trip. These difficulties are not felt just by consumers but also by airline personnel and TSA workers who have also expressed their discontent. Consequently, the TSA has been singled out for intense scrutiny. However, it is not my intent to gauge how widespread these criticisms are, nor to undervalue the significant contributions that TSA personnel have made in protecting America (e.g., intercepting weapons, actual or potential), nor to downplay the real difficulties experienced by TSA officers (especially when dealing with rude and surly rude passengers), but simply to document the most salient complaints and some of the unintended consequences.

In order to contextualize the growth and development of the controversial security-related TSA policies and practices over the past six years, this chapter follows a relatively simple chronology, tracing the events that passengers might experience from getting to an airport to deplaning. It then briefly reviews the different kinds of theories of bureaucratic decision making that are applied to policy making, and concludes that to all intents and purposes, the TSA has been operating on an incremental decision-making basis.

THE TSA AND AVIATION SECURITY IN THE POST–SEPTEMBER 11 ERA

There are numerous vulnerabilities in airline and airport safety that necessitate safeguards. Concerns about our country's air safety as a result of criminals, hijackers, and terrorists did not begin with September 11. There is a long history of individuals, traditional criminals, and terrorists commandeering passenger airplanes, and/or placing explosive devices on planes.[3] Naturally, there has been a considerable amount of scholarly research that has examined these incidents and the government and industry responses to them.

Since September 11, the passenger airline industry has focused its security efforts on four areas: "Airport security; passenger identification and screening; airport proximity security: aircraft security during take off and landings, [and] in-flight security."[4] In short, since September 11, in most of the large airports in the United States, security procedures have become more rigorous. The following sections point out these areas of concern and the numerous inconveniences passengers have experienced as a result.

Dropping Off and Picking Up Passengers

Depending on the airport, picking up and dropping off passengers by car is now more inconvenient, and sometimes a more time-consuming and expensive venture than pre–September 11. Those wishing to pick up passengers who are arriving or drop off passengers who are departing are no longer allowed to stand (i.e., stay in the vehicle with the motor running), wait, or park their cars (i.e., leave the vehicle unattended). Most big-city airports (in Chicago, Los Angeles, New York, and elsewhere) use local police, state police/troopers, or airport police to constantly and vigorously monitor the traffic and dissuade drivers from waiting for passengers at the curbside by threatening ticketing or towing. Some airport authorities, recognizing the inconvenience of these practices, have negotiated with companies that have leased parking facilities to let drivers park free for the first half hour. Other airport authorities have established or constructed cell-phone waiting areas, where drivers can temporarily park their cars and wait (typically up to an hour), until their loved ones, friends, colleagues, or clients call to be picked up at a designated place. Negotiating the dropping off of a passenger is only the beginning. The inconveniences for travelers do not appreciably diminish from curbside to ticketing counter (another post–September 11 security point).

At the Ticketing Counter

Despite the advent of electronic ticketing, airline passengers are now required to check in at least an hour before their plane takes off for domestic flights and two hours for international flights. Unfortunately this practice can lead to inordinately long wait times. This is especially frustrating given the fact that in the past few years passengers have also witnessed significant increases in the number of late departures and/or cancellations. Once at the ticket counter, passengers must show more forms of identification and are still asked a number of security questions by airline personnel, such as, "Has anyone helped you pack your bag?" and "Has your bag been in your possession at all times?" These are not foolproof questions, as passengers can easily lie and there is little that airline personnel can do to detect this.

Because of increased baggage restrictions and screenings, checking baggage is more onerous. Airlines now restrict carry-on luggage to one item, either to increase their revenue by charging for baggage that passengers would in the past have normally taken as carry-on, or to minimize the items that could possibly be carried on to the plane and used as weapons. In another new measure, baggage handlers and screeners have been "federalized" and integrated into the TSA. In general, passenger and baggage screeners (there are now some 30,000 of them) are doing a more thorough job, including testing ticketed passengers' personal effects for gunpowder residue, using equipment with increased metal sensitivity, and making regular and random searches. In short, those responsible for baggage handling and inspection are said to be better trained and more experienced than pre–September 11 employees performing similar functions.

Security Processes before Entering a Terminal

Many people, from passengers to TSA workers, believe that the procedures for screening ticketed customers range somewhere along a scale from pointless to ridiculous.

Procedures such as having 80-year-old women turn over nail files or treating quadriplegics as would-be terrorists simply to demonstrate impartiality in screening annoy passengers far more than they convey any sense of safety. Meanwhile, there appears to be considerable inconsistency with respect to items that are considered to be potential weapons, for example, not allowing nail clippers but permitting disposable razors, or not being able to take cigarette lighters on board, but being permitted to take three boxes of matches. Documentary film director Michael Moore captured these ironies well in his controversial 2004 movie *Fahrenheit 911*, when he showed all the items that could not be brought aboard aircraft and those that were permissible. These contradictions helped to lead to the reversal of the ban on carrying cigarette lighters.[5]

Passenger Identification

Over the past six years, a number of different passenger prescreening programs have been implemented, often with little success. Many passengers have been unnecessarily searched and delayed because of ethnic profiling, being on watch lists because of certain types of employment, participation in public protests, and previous travel. The secret no-fly list once led to Senator Edward M. Kennedy (D-Mass.) being detained on his regular Washington to Boston flight and again on his attempt to fly back to Boston.

Baggage Handling and Screening/Clearing Security

Although failures to intercept weapons and properly vet TSA personnel have repeatedly garnered media attention,[6] some of the biggest passenger complaints are connected to the screening procedures they experience while trying to clear security to enter the terminals on the way to their gates. This is usually caused by the increasing number of banned items, and the apparent randomness of decisions connected to specific individuals and items that are subjected to increased security.

In December 2001, Richard Colvin Reid, a British citizen, a recent convert to Islam with nebulous ties to al Qaeda, the terrorist group responsible for the September 11 attack, tried to blow up an American Airlines flight en route from Paris to Miami. The primitive bomb was located in his shoes. Only when passengers noticed that he was trying to light his shoes was he overpowered and the bomb discovered. This led to a revision of policies such that airline passengers are now required to take off their shoes while going through a gate check and have them placed on the conveyor belts on their way to the X-ray machines. Then belts were targeted, with the occasional person seen walking through X-ray scanning devices grasping the waistband of his pants to prevent them from falling down around his shoeless feet. Passengers started to wonder what other kinds of clothing would be next.

Then, in August 2006, it was announced that al Qaeda was experimenting with carrying liquid explosives in water or perfume bottles. Almost immediately, the TSA banned passengers from carrying bottles in excess of four ounces, whether liquids, gels or pastes, in carry-on bags. In September 2006, the TSA lifted its ban on carrying liquids in favor of requiring travelers to carry only "travel-size toiletries (3.4 ounces or less) that fit comfortably in one quart-size, clear plastic, zip-top bag." Predictably, at least in the beginning, bags were not provided to passengers. And when travelers used wrong-size bags they were often chastised by TSA workers. Only later did the TSA or airport authorities start providing the bags. TSA workers who identify passengers carrying prohibited liquids and so on give travelers the opportunity to stow the items in their carry-on bags once the items have been thoroughly screened, but by that time most passengers are in a rush to board their planes, or do not want to incur the extra inconvenience of retrieving their bags, going back to the ticketing counter, and dealing with the airline personnel, and simply agree to have their prohibited items thrown in the garbage.

Waiting in the Terminal

Since September 11, airports have adopted a "standard concentric circle security design," featuring increased security checkpoints that ticketed passengers and authorized personnel must go through before they are allowed to enter the terminals and gate areas, and eventually board the planes. "Prior to September 11 many airports were designed as mini-shopping centers."[7] Since the new security restrictions were implemented, a number of retail businesses located in the terminals and the parking facilities (usually leased by the airport authorities to private companies) have incurred significant losses in revenue. Some terminals have resembled veritable ghost towns on the American landscape.

Revised Boarding Procedures

A number of changes have occurred with respect to boarding and onboard procedures as well. Nationwide, when boarding a plane, certain passengers can be taken aside to have their persons and their carry-on items completely searched.

Onboard Security Processes

In addition, after the September 11 attacks, because of Ronald Reagan National Airport's close proximity to the Pentagon (one of the sites of the September 11 attacks), flights out of this airport were initially suspended, then scaled back, and sky marshals were placed on all flights in and out of the airport. Moreover, passengers are not allowed to leave their seats for the first half hour after departure from or during the approach to Reagan Airport and nearby Dulles Airport in northern Virginia. In other decisions that were as arbitrary, in December 2003 the Federal Air Marshal Service was transferred from the TSA to the U.S. Bureau of Immigration and Customs Enforcement, and then in 2006 it was returned to the TSA.

Pilots are now allowed to carry guns (under the Federal Flight Deck Officer Program), and cockpit doors have been reinforced. The airlines no longer serve food on so-called short-haul trips; one would assume this last precaution has been introduced because utensils are potential weapons, and because not providing food makes up for the loss of income incurred immediately after September 11.

Remaining Gaps in Security Provision

Despite the increased security, there is no point-to-point baggage checking. In other words, in many airports once your bag comes off the conveyer belt almost anyone can pick it up. Rarely are airline personnel or security guards in attendance to make sure that the bag you retrieve is yours. And there is criticism of the fact that cargo placed in the airplane's hold is either never screened at all, or not properly screened.

Formal Responses to the Terrorist Threat: Passenger Identification Systems

One of the preferred measures to dealing with the evolving terrorist threat involves passenger identification systems.

1. CAPPS I. A considerable number of passenger identification procedures have been created that lie outside of the TSA's purview. "Recognizing the need for more effective screening and monitoring of foreign visitors, the United States has new visa requirements, new high-tech passport requirements, and the United States Visitor and Immigration Status Indicator Technology, or US VISIT program."[8] Within the TSA's domain, however, is the Computer Assisted Passenger Pre-screening System, or CAPPS.

As James A. Fagin points out, "In 1996, Northwest Airlines developed a refined system called Computer-Assisted Passenger Prescreening System or CAPPS. The system was operated by the airlines and based on their computer records about passengers. It did not compare passenger names to lists of potential terrorists kept by the State Department. In 1998, other airlines began to use CAPPS, as recommended by the White House Commission on Aviation Safety and Security. In 1999, CAPPS was no longer used to select passengers and their carry-on luggage for additional screening. After September 11 CAPPS was again used to screen passengers for additional security screening but was still not connected to State Department watch list which has now expanded to include people not necessarily connected to or a part of terrorist organizations. The data used by CAPPS to select passengers for additional security screening did not accurately discriminate between passengers who were potential security risks and those who were not. As a result CAPPS flagged about 50 percent of the passengers for additional security screening in short-haul flights."[9]

2. CAPPS II. CAPPS did not prevent the September 11 attacks, and this fact together with "its poor record in discriminating between potential hijackers and ordinary passengers resulted in Congress authorizing the creation of a new system for determining who should receive additional security screening at airport checkpoints."[10] The new system, named CAPPS II, examines a passenger's travel history to determine if there are any "unusual" patterns. CAPPS "uses airline reservation computers to identify passengers who may pose a higher risk of being terrorists and subjects them to additional scrutiny."[11] CAPPS II "examines 26 aspects of a passenger's travel history," but we don't know exactly what those items are because "details are classified."[12]

Apparently in order to determine the utility of this process, the country's airlines gave the Federal Bureau of Investigation information on 10 million passengers. When news of this came to public attention there were "complaints of privacy violation, lawsuits, and warnings of infringement on privacy rights by various civil rights watchdogs. . . . CAPPS II was criticized as being not only a significant intrusion into privacy rights but also being ineffective in screening for terrorists."[13]

3. Secure Flight. Although CAPPS II was to be introduced in fall 2004, by then the number of problems connected to protecting the privacy of citizens and to "mission creep" forced Congress and the DHS to terminate the program. By that time, the government had already invested over $100 million in it. In its place, the DHS created Secure Flight. "Preliminary details of Secure Flight indicate that it would narrowly focus on screening for potential terrorists and would not screen passengers wanted for violent crimes. Secure Flight would rely primarily on government databases rather than commercial databases for its data mining, but would make some use of the latter."[14]

In 2004, Secure Flight was criticized by the American Civil Liberties Union (ACLU) as a violation of passenger rights, because of the unreasonable search and seizure practices to which it exposed airline passengers. The TSA changed its procedures. "In 2005, Congress prohibited the use of appropriated funds for CAPPS II or its successor, Secure Flight, until the government could certify that privacy requirements were being met, largely related to false positives and the sharing of private information."[15]

4. STAR System. In July 2007, it was announced that the FBI "is developing a computer-profiling system that would enable investigators to target possible terror suspects. . . . The System to Assess Risk, or STAR, assigns risk scores to possible suspects, based on a variety of information, similar to the way a credit bureau assigns a rating based

on a consumer's spending behavior and debt. The program focuses on foreign suspects but also includes data about some U.S. residents. A prototype is expected to be tested this year."[16] "STAR is being developed by the FBI's Foreign Terrorist Tracking Task Force, which tracks suspected terrorists inside the country or as they enter."[17]

5. Other Problematic Passenger Identification Systems. In tandem with the Secure Flight program, the TSA has developed registered traveler programs, better technology to read travel documents, and a no-fly list. The last item has run into severe difficulties. "The no-fly list is the government's secret list of passengers who are not allowed to board a commercial aircraft or who must go through extensive screening before boarding. It differs from the CAPPS-type screening programs in that it uses government databases and intelligence data from federal law enforcement and intelligence agencies to compile a list of names."[18]

THEORIES OF DECISION MAKING

To better understand how TSA has evolved since its inception, it helps to look at the Agency's decision-making process. There are three major explanations of how people and by extension groups make decisions: rational, incremental, and cognitive. First, *rational* or *intellectual* approaches attempt to make broad-ranging diagnoses. This style of decision making involves obtaining definitions of the situation. Those using this style then attempt to collect a wide range of information. They tap different sources for information to minimize bias. Then they conduct an extensive search for policy options. These decision makers are open to new information, and they evaluate opportunity costs, compare costs and benefits, and estimate the usefulness of options. They choose the options that promise to give them the greatest benefits and the lowest costs. The rational process recognizes that it is difficult and to compare things of different magnitudes and to measure many constructs, and that the process is very time consuming. In reality people, from leaders to workers, have little time to make complicated decisions. Consequently, most people do not routinely engage in this sort of decision making, save for those paid to do it.[19]

The *incremental, mechanical, or cybernetic* approach involves the consideration of one option at a time.[20] This kind of decision making looks at the first available option that will satisfy the minimum needs. This process is also called *satisficing*. Options only differ to a small degree. This is why decision makers typically rely on standing operating procedures (SOPs). These may be set out in written form or may simply be informally accepted as the product of past experience. SOPs are usually based on trial and error experiences. The decision makers don't analyze, and don't weigh opportunity costs. The cybernetic model of decision making explains the phenomenon of conservatism (resistance to change). It assumes that decision makers have experience with situations and that crises are of a structured nature.

Finally, there are *cognitive* theories of decision making.[21] These show a better empirical fit between theory and practice. They compensate for weaknesses in the rational and cybernetic methods. Cognitive theories argue that decision makers are bounded by constraints. Those who follow cognitive theories diagnose problems with prevailing beliefs, search for information and options that confirm prevailing beliefs, and ignore information that disconfirms them. The decision makers then use techniques of inconsistency management to support their decisions. Only when they are overwhelmingly wrong do these people change their behavior. In general, these decision-makers do not consider trade-offs but argue that their option is to be preferred and will meet all the objectives.

While the TSA has only been in operation for seven years, it seems their decision is mainly incremental. That is, each new threat or event is dealt with almost totally separate and apart from other happenings. This leads to a scattershot approach to security where long-term planning is lacking. In the absence of some sort of strategic planning, it seems that the TSA is operating in an incremental fashion. The TSA's practice of dealing with crises as they develop and scrambling to set in place policies and practices inevitably frustrates the public in general and commercial air travelers in particular, whose patience has worn thin over the last six years, and it decreases public confidence in the agency.

NOTES

1. For a review of post–September 11 counterterrorism policies and practices, see, for example, Jeffrey Ian Ross, *Political Terrorism: An Interdisciplinary Approach* (New York: Peter Lang, 2006).

2. James A. Fagin, *When Terrorism Strikes Home: Defending the United States* (Boston, MA: Pearson Allyn & Bacon), 159.

3. See, for example, Edward McWhinney, *Aerial Piracy and International Terrorism: The Illegal Diversion of Aircraft and International Law*, 2nd rev. ed. (Chicago: Kluwer Law International, 1987).

4. Fagin, *When Terrorism Strikes Home*, 57.

5. Ryan Singel, *Airplane Lighter Ban Lifted; Michael Moore and Senate Democrats Crushed*, July 20, 2007, http://blog.wired.com/27bstroke6/2007/07/airplane-lighte. html.

6. Fagin, *When Terrorism Strikes Home*, 169.

7. Ibid., 158.

8. Ibid., 159.

9. Ibid., 160.

10. Ibid.

11. A. Levin and B. Morrison, "Security Plan Proposed Years Ago," *USA Today*, October 5, 0A.

12. Ibid.

13. Fagin, *When Terrorism Strikes Home*, 161.

14. Ibid., 162.

15. William Banks, Renee De Nevers, and Mitchel B. Wallerstein, *Combating Terrorism: Strategies and Approaches* (Washington, DC: CQ Press, 2008), 190.

16. Ellen Nakashima, "FBI Plans Initiative to Profile Terrorists," *Washington Post*, July 11, A8.

17. Ibid.

18. Fagin, *When Terrorism Strikes Home*, 163–64.

19. Max Weber, *Economy and Society* (Los Angeles: University of California Press, 1921/1978).

20. C. E. Lindblom, "The Science of Muddling Through," *Public Administration Review* 19, no. 2 (1959): 79–88.

21. John D. Steinbruner, *The Cybernetic Theory of Decision: New Dimensions of Political Analysis* (Princeton, NJ: Princeton University Press, 1974).

CHAPTER 8

In-Cabin Security

David E. Forbes

This chapter will present a picture of aviation security issues today and also predict what we can expect to experience in the future. It touches upon the effort to protect commercial airliners from terrorists, considering what can occur and how we might counter potentially lethal assaults within the passenger cabin environment. It also examines the current state of preparedness in this environment. As of this writing, November 2007, the public and private dialogue and the often contentious debate between the parties with an interest in commercial airline security are unceasing.

A REACTIVE PROTECTION HISTORY

When we pose investigative questions about the security of the airliner cabin, it becomes clear that this is an area that is sorely neglected. Moreover, we are now in a period when our guard, specifically in the context of in-cabin security, is gradually slipping, going back to the self-deception of the "comfort zone" that has historically created opportunities for successful terror attacks.

Experience shows, and there is no greater example than that of the pivotal events of September 11, 2001, that it is the action of the aggressor, not the defender, that leads to changes in commercial aviation security. This pattern is demonstrated by the series of hijacking and bombing events that have spanned more than 70 years, starting with the first recorded hijacking in May of 1930, when a Pan American mail-carrying aircraft was seized and commandeered by revolutionaries in the skies over Peru. Since that time, with the exception of a limited number of acts designed for personal criminal gain, unlawful interference with commercial airliners has placed passengers and crew at the mercy of terrorist groups.

When we examine the more intense periods of concentrated action against aviation, we can see that surges of activity and varied forms of assault generate two outcomes: first, the creation of new domestic and international regulations, protocols, and security processes; and second, a comparative lull of five to seven years in terrorist attacks on civil aviation. There is generally a third outcome, however—the surprise, dramatic, and usually lethal end to that lull.

In his book *Blind Spot—The Secret History of American Counter Terrorism*, Timothy Naftali claimed that in the 1960s

The American public and US Government were willing to put up with a monthly rate of hijacking that appears almost absurd in the context of the post-9/11 world. At the time, all of the private-sector lobbies, including initially the Air Line Pilots Association, opposed even the most limited security measures.[1]

In the early 1960s, we saw a wave of hijackings, mostly affecting American air carriers, when would-be "escapees" from Castro's Cuban regime easily used aviation. When the United States introduced armed guards and the death penalty for hijackings in late 1961, this seemed to address the threat, but from 1968 through 1972 an epidemic of more than 350 hijackings occurred. International conventions, which were negotiated and ratified during the early 1970s to address criminal acts against civil aircraft, appeared to have the desired deterrent effect, in spite of lethal attacks in the years up to 1976. Such large numbers and such a high frequency of hijacking events have not been witnessed since. In 1985, however, the hijacking of a TWA plane between Athens and Beirut, and the Atlantic Ocean bombing of an Air India Boeing 747 that had originated in Vancouver, Canada, brought the world a rude reminder that the terrorist threat had not abated, at least not to such an extent that air travel could return to the relatively relaxed era of the previous 10 years.

The horror of the Pan Am Flight 103 Boeing 747 bombing over Lockerbie, Scotland, in December 1988 was followed by yet more energy and effort dedicated to international regulation and protection upgrades. There was also a renewed impetus to develop technological countermeasures to protect civil aviation, notwithstanding the false hopes generated by the rhetoric of a presidential commission.

In 2001, a Scottish court convicted a Libyan national in connection with the Pan Am 103 bombing. Later that year, the world witnessed the worst terrorist atrocity in commercial aviation history.

After September 11

The National Commission on Terrorist Attacks on the United States, generally known as the 9/11 Commission, included remarks in its chapter titled

"Foresight and Hindsight" that are very pertinent to today's in-cabin security vulnerabilities:

We believe the 9/11 attacks revealed four kinds of failure: imagination, policy, capabilities and management.[2]

Later in the same chapter we find further comments that continue to apply today:

Neither the intelligence community nor aviation security experts analyzed systemic defenses within an aircraft or against terrorist-controlled aircraft, suicidal or otherwise. The many threat reports were passed to the FAA. While that agency continued to react to specific, credible threats, it did not try to perform the broader warning functions we describe here. No one in the government was taking on that role for domestic vulnerabilities.[3]

Threats from Passengers

While researching this chapter, I spoke with many flight attendants. During one trans-Pacific crossing in July 2007, a senior cabin crew member told me that the short term emphasis on security issues has moved away from security knowledge and training, and that there are gaps in the teaching of countermeasure capabilities. This long-serving flight attendant supervisor said that cost and customer service pressures are dictating priorities, that competitive airlines are hyping service expectations, and that consequently growing percentages of passengers have become very demanding. This is creating difficulties that sometimes translate into physical security threats to the safety of the aircraft, passengers, and crew. My informant said that a combination of alcohol, consumed on board or before boarding, with drugs, prescribed medications, or substances of unknown legal status, is contributing to confrontational events in flight.

Coping with violent passengers is causing more than event-specific concern for the crew. Whereas occurrences involving irrational spontaneous conduct are not frequent, they highlight the even weaker position of cabin attendants in the circumstance of facing a premeditated and orchestrated attack from within the passenger cabin. The assertion that a dedicated custom-designed security training and technological support requirement is not being offered or met was consistent across a range of cabin crew, domestic and international, in Australia and the United States.

The Neglect of Flight Attendant Security Training

On November 1, 2007, Patricia A. Friend, international president of the Association of Flight Attendants—Communications Workers of America (CWA), part of the American Federation of Labor—Congress of Industrial Organizations (AFL-CIO) gave testimony before the Subcommittee on Transportation Security and Infrastructure, Protection of the Homeland

Security Committee, U.S. House of Representatives. Ms. Friend pulled no punches when she effectively (albeit coincidentally) confirmed the cabin crew members' assertion:

I'm here to tell you that for the over 100,000 flight attendants in this country, very little has changed since the attacks of September 11th. While this Congress and the Administration have taken steps for airline pilots, who are now safely barricaded behind reinforced doors and are in some cases armed with guns, and air marshals are on a higher percentage of flights than before September 11th, flight attendants are left in the cabin with no meaningful training or tools. This is an unacceptable situation and one which we, many aviation security experts and the 9–11 Commission have been urging a change to for well over six years now.[4]

I will return to Patricia Friend's testimony later in a discussion about the absence of, the potential for, and the apparent obstacles to flight attendant security training and tools. In addition, I will comment on what I believe to be the fallacy of Friend's perception that pilots are "safely barricaded behind reinforced doors."

Given the serious disquiet about the ability and even the willingness of government regulators and airlines to improve in-cabin security, students and practitioners might pause to cast a questioning glance at the better established, parallel, and security-convergent discipline of aviation safety. Why is security a poor cousin in relation to safety?

Safety and Security—The Relationship

A long-standing, constantly evolving, and largely successful regulatory safety culture in air transportation has endured the complication of responding to the threat of terrorist attack over more than five decades. As blurred as the line may sometimes seem, the distinction between safety and security is important. The author is working from several basic assumptions:

- Multiple airline operations scenarios, technical, physical, and procedural, individually or in combination, including security occurrences, produce a safety threat outcome.

- In much smaller measure, limited in frequency, the converse position is true, that is, safety concerns may create security vulnerabilities. For example, a commercial airliner loaded with passengers, crew, baggage, cargo, and fuel, diverted or temporarily held on the ground due to technical safety checks, may be exposed to security vulnerabilities.

- Thus, exposure to safety vulnerability due to security-related events represents a relatively small percentage of all safety threat eventualities.

- Generally, and with considerable success, the aviation safety regulatory regime is respected, supported, and enforced on a significant scale.

- Security as a discipline or as a mandated compliance requirement is prone to arbitrary interpretation and discretion. The depth of knowledge and application detail, notwithstanding the need for confidentiality, does not match that within safety disciplines. The penalty exposure for safety violations is subject to qualitative performance measurement of security. It is consequently elusive. Its effectiveness is constantly questionable by a much larger population compared with aviation safety.

• The audit and inspection systems applied by regulators throughout the world are more predictable and consistent for safety standards enforcement than the equivalent resources for maintenance of security protocols are. One factor playing into the security issue is that there is a larger and more diverse range, not always coordinated, of security audit, inspection, and enforcement agencies with sufficient counterterrorism jurisdiction and responsibilities to justify involvement with aviation security.

For the purpose of investment in "in-cabin security," passenger and crew safety is the assumed goal. Security measures consisting of policy practice and equipment applications make up the tool-kit for achieving that goal. The security system—and the threat dimension—is a blend of four components:

• People
• Equipment
• Regulation
• Processes

This is an expansive subject deserving of and unquestionably receiving longer and deeper discussion than this chapter will allow. Each of the four components delineates a key critical area for focused study and development of in-cabin security standards. Any expectation of improvement, for example, to the satisfaction of the cabin attendant community, can only be achieved by starting from an assessment of the status quo. Why do I not include pilots and passengers here? From constant conversations and e-mails with both groups over the past few years, it seems that only the flight attendants are prepared to be persistently vocal about inadequate in-cabin security. I have yet to meet a pilot who is passionate about the subject, and of the numerous private individuals I have engaged on this topic, none are prepared to dedicate any worthwhile effort toward improving security. I will not waste space here explaining my interpretation of the reasons for this apparent incongruity, except to say that the demand for affordable air travel and the convenience that this represents are dominant, diminishing daily the images of September 11.

People and Equipment

The determinants of cabin security conditions are influenced by several categories of people including those who may remain physically "outside" the cabin. Some of these are dealt with peripherally later, but for the most part this section concerns the people who are present in the passenger cabin of a commercial aircraft. Most of my attention is given over to the front line of protection—the flight attendant. This means no disrespect to the air or sky marshals, to whom I refer later in brief when discussing equipment. Flight attendants are always there, on every scheduled commercial flight. In my eyes, they are foremost in any analysis of in-cabin security. First, though, there is a category that we cannot ignore: the most influential category, both inside and outside the cabin, is that of the terrorist.

The Specter of Terrorism

Using the CIT formula—capabilities, intention, timing—we apply a combination of historical indicators and human intelligence to try to determine what it is we are protecting the aviation system against, and how we can prevent a successful assault by motivated and organized aggressors. Unfortunately our prognostications have fallen short too often. We are left to intelligently estimate, or guess, terrorist group capabilities, that is, the weaponry they have and their ability to use it. We cannot absolutely and confidently provide an accurate accounting of terrorist capabilities worldwide at any given moment.

We can generalize about terror group aims, but we cannot be assured of specific detailed operational intentions 100 percent of the time, notwithstanding some impressive counterterrorism intelligence operations that have led to arrests in France, Germany, Spain, the United Kingdom, and the United States.

In March 2007, it was reported that the British authorities had discovered that al Qaeda had obtained fake identity papers when an estimated 10,000 passports had been issued to fraudsters between October 2005 and September 2006.[5] Close to 16,500 fraudulent applications had been received; therefore there was a criminal success rate of more than 30 percent. Dhiren Barot, a senior member of al Qaeda and a British national, had obtained two of these passports; a Moroccan national now serving 18 years imprisonment for terrorist offences had also obtained two. Barot actually had seven passports with his true identity and two false passports when he was arrested. In 2006, he pleaded guilty to conspiracy to murder, having planned to launch attacks in Washington, DC, New York, and Newark, NJ, as well as in Britain. It is unlikely that we will ever know the precise details of his intentions or the identities of the other people he would have relied on to carry out the attacks. We can only speculate on the intent of those who possess fake passports and have not been arrested. That also brings us to the question of timing, an equally elusive, unpredictable factor in any threat assessment. When and where might those passports be used and with what objective?

Why is the foregoing important in a discussion about in-cabin security? Because advance planning by terrorists takes account of and is designed to circumnavigate "No-Fly" lists, and because a successful hijacking attack can depend upon strategic seating arrangements intended to ensure a "position of dominance." This favors the first class, business class, and other front-end seat assignments; early seating assignment may not occur if certain names are used. A great deal of useful information can be gained by probing techniques, including checking names from boarding passes, to ensure that the false name adopted is not on a restrictions list.

The persistent challenge is to identify the terrorist within the multitudinous ranks of ticketed passengers and crew, and thereby prevent access to the aviation system by an aggressor. Other people with preflight access to the aircraft, including caterers, cleaners, and ramp workers, add to the exposure and vulnerability of the flight.

Optimism Keeps Us Flying—For Now

Setting the voluminous topic of airport security aside, the in-flight crew complement is made up of air crew on the flight deck and flight attendants and passengers in the passenger cabin. In relation to the passenger cabin, the optimistic assumption on the part of legitimate travelers and crew is that armed sky marshals are on board, that passengers and carry-on bags have been screened, and that baggage and cargo have been screened. This provides an assurance of safety through effective counterterrorism procedures. This may not be true; any one of the protective measures may be less than perfect; but the absence of events challenging the assumptions of passengers and crew suggests that optimism is warranted for a time at least. Cynically stated, the lull involving a false sense of security, which was so horrifically demolished on September 11, 2001, has returned.

The word "facade" is a fairly common term used in Web blogs and occasionally in media articles referring to aviation security rules and their implementation. With large segments of developed world populations traveling by air, opinions about security are never in short supply. In my continual conversations with other passengers, mostly within the United States, it has been striking how often individuals have offered suggestions on gaps in the system, even improvised onboard weapons, that can still be used by terrorists. The submissive resignation witnessed in the lines of shoeless passengers heading into the walk-through at the security checkpoint and the steadily growing numbers of airline passengers worldwide tend to show that market forces are also contributing to a desire to believe that the terrorist threat is being safely contained. A deeper examination, however, brings the serious student back to the cold reality that terrorists are biding their time, watching, waiting, and planning.

Some of the measures brought in through post–September 11 regulation may actually contribute to the degree of shock and surprise that inevitably accompanies a lethal terrorist assault. Specifically, the physical and procedural restriction of access via the cockpit door has changed the dynamics of in-cabin and aircraft security. This is discussed later. For the purpose of this section, in the human context, the effect of the changed in-flight environment due to the separation of the flight deck from the passenger cabin is of significant interest. It also crosses over into an analysis of regulation and process components. The prospect of an attacker overcoming preflight countermeasures and being on board for more than the objective of probing for in-flight security weaknesses is frightening. It is the ultimate threat of a person-to-person, face-to-face physical confrontation. If equipment, regulation, and processes are defeated, this is the cabin crew's most dreaded nightmare realized, broken down to minutes and seconds of survival decisions and actions.

In September 2005, with an independent authorized remit to review government program progress, the United States Government Accountability Office (GAO) published a 45-page report to congressional requesters on aviation security, focusing on the training of flight and cabin crew in the handling of potential threats against domestic aircraft.[6] The report's introduction made it clear that this is a responsibility that is shared between air carriers and the federal government. Many of the conclusions about unsatisfactory performance expressed in the report were directed at the Transportation Security Administration (TSA). The GAO recommended the establishment of strategic goals for crew security training, written procedures for monitoring air carriers' crew security training, and performance measures and a time frame for evaluating the effectiveness of voluntary self-defense training.

Communications *and* Training?

More than two years after the GAO report cited above, on November 1, 2007, Patricia Friend was giving testimony to Congress, representing the views of flight attendants. In addition to the remarks quoted earlier, she told the House committee that in spite of several recommendations from various influential sources, including the Rapid Response Team for Aircraft Security, of which she had been an appointed member, security loopholes stemming from outdated and inadequate airline security training from before September 11 had not been remedied. She said that the flight attendants had repeatedly asked for training updates to include basic self-defense maneuvers and crew communications and coordination. In a damning statement she declared that

Currently, there is no comprehensive training or explanation of what the three components of in-flight security—flight attendants, pilots and air marshals—are trained to do in case of an attack. Clearly, these three groups must be trained on how to work together as a team to be as effective as possible. Unfortunately, this is not happening.[7]

Ms. Friend went on to describe how varied and limited the carrier' security training was, with discrepancies that left many flight attendants unprepared for any future terrorist attack. She also alleged that airline management had been instrumental in attempting to sabotage flight attendant security training, especially during the 2003 federal legislative term, when various related bills were being prepared for passage. In one reference she talked of interference with the FAA reauthorization of Vision 100, when

At the last minute, Continental Airlines went to Republican House Leader Tom DeLay and had him change one word in the security training provisions. He had the provision that said "TSA *shall* issue guidelines" changed to "TSA *may* issue guidelines." By changing this one word, he took away the ability to force TSA to issue these guidelines.[8]

This troubling picture is compounded by Ms. Friend's further statement that the current status (November 2007) of flight attendant security training programs remains unsatisfactory: these consist of an advanced, voluntary program provided by TSA, and basic mandatory training provided by the airlines. Reports from the air safety, health, and security representatives at her organization, drawn from carriers of all sizes, indicated that *"security training has been watered down year after year."*[9]

Cabin Crew and New Technologies

Based on my study of flight attendant training course content, I have my own concerns that can be added to those of the GAO, the flight attendants' representatives, and others. The in-flight world is morphing into a smart, convenient, cylindrical travel machine. The changing environment, new airlines, new aircraft, new materials inside and out, new interiors, new technologies, and the world shortage of pilots, engineers, and experienced flight attendants are being used to justify a low standard of cabin crew security training that the industry has not even begun to remedy.

Some of the new technologies are not unique to aviation. Electronic devices carried by passengers can easily become the new threat, joining the restriction on gels and liquids set in place by the regulators following the findings of the August 2006 terrorist plot investigations in the United Kingdom. Radio frequency devices, cell phones, remote model car and boat controls, garage door openers, and other types of apparatus ubiquitously employed in improvised explosive device (IED) bombings around the world are easily accessible to terrorists, who have a propensity to defeat sophisticated high technology defenses with low tech and sometimes crude weapons of mass destruction. With the constant interest in improving in-flight entertainment and communications options, do we have here a potential Trojan horse, in which in-hold bomb detonations and cabin fires can be induced by the action of a passenger? We are surely left with a choice, to train and equip flight attendants to recognize and somehow neutralize a suspect device, or to prohibit all electronic devices from being carried on to an aircraft? The former is unlikely to be a realistic or effective option; the latter, as tough a restriction as it sounds, is a distinct possibility.

Although international and domestic protocols still place the responsibility for safety of the aircraft passengers and crew with the pilot in charge (PIC), the secure cockpit door and separation from the passenger cabin imposes a much greater burden of responsibility, capability, and know-how on the cabin crew for security risk management. That fact is not reflected in the quality and content of flight attendant training.

What of the passengers? Is the "legitimate" passenger a dependable part of the layers of defense, a measurable asset to in-flight response to a terrorist attack? If we sensibly acknowledge the need for training but we are not training our flight attendants for security in their regular work environment, what chance is there that a passenger or passengers will take effective action?

Untrained intervention may actually increase the dangers to others. The romantic belief in passengers rising up to defeat an aggressor, while understandable, is not a security strategy to be recommended. Least of all does it excuse a lack of investment in flight attendant security training?

Some novel, strange, and almost laughable ideas have been floated about as countermeasures since September 11. I once received a suggestion that the captain of the flight upon becoming aware of an attack mounted in or from the cabin should release an anesthetic vapor or gas into the passenger cabin. Asked about the threat to passengers with heart conditions, asthma, and similar health issues, the person proffering the suggestion declared that this should be treated as acceptable collateral damage. Just as oddly, in her book *Jetliner Cabins*, Jennifer Coutts Clay wrote the following under the heading "Tableware":

Following the 11 September 2001 terrorist attacks, for security reasons many airlines stopped carrying implements, such as ice picks and carving knives. They have also withdrawn all metal knives and forks, and are now flying plastic cutlery in all classes of service. Even in many gate lounge hospitality areas plastic cutlery is now the norm. There is, however an argument in favour of issuing metal steak knives to all adult passengers at the time of boarding: would potential hijackers with box-cutter blades dare to attack a crew member if they knew that large groups of passengers could, in a crisis situation, use their knives to fight back in a concerted way?[10]

Ms. Coutts Clay may have intended this to be a tongue-in-cheek inclusion. I certainly hope so.

Cabin Crew Fatigue and Security

A special note is warranted here on those very important people, the flight attendants. The gradual increase in cabin crew fatigue is going to reveal itself in the not too distant future unless the regulators step in to mitigate the risks associated with this growing problem. This is a subject worthy of more detailed explanation, but I will leave it at this point by saying that the safety and security duties, passenger expectations, and effectiveness of flight attendants depend on the vigilance that comes from their good health, proper rest, and refreshment.

Security-Relevant Equipment Knowledge

The commercial aircraft itself is often referred to as a piece of "equipment." In the context of in-cabin security, we will remain figuratively inside that upper part of the tubular section of the fuselage where the passengers sit, where the lavatories/washrooms are located, and where the flight attendants work from their galleys and flight jump seats. While some brand new, state-of-the-art aircraft are introduced, many older commercial airliners undergo an full or partial interior refit every five to seven years. Judging the in-cabin security features and improvements may not therefore depend on the age of the originally manufactured airframe alone. Improvements in teaching flight crew about security risk can aid in carrying out duties which help to make the cabin safer. A pervasive, nagging impression from my years of study of threats against aviation is the inferiority of the equipment-related knowledge of the cabin crew, which increases their vulnerability when compared with the target-focused facts gathered by terrorist planners.

In 1997, a paper titled "Evaluation of Cabin Crew Technical Knowledge" was presented at an international symposium in Columbus, Ohio. The paper cites examples of aviation accidents that illustrate inadequate communications between the cabin crew and the flight deck, largely influenced by flight attendants' lack of knowledge about the aircraft and the airlines' lack of concern about cabin crew ignorance of the equipment. Two strong points were raised to justify closer examination of operating and training standards. The audience was reminded of the changes in flight operations that necessitate this action:

First, automation has led to the proliferation of 2-pilot aircraft. As the position of flight engineer has been replaced by advanced technology, the flight crew has also lost the trained eyes and ears of an intermediary to information beyond the cockpit door. Second, flight attendants have not been trained to be technically aware nor articulate in order to facilitate effective information transfer.[11]

While the presentation did not specifically address security considerations, it offered a glimpse of the weaknesses in operational in-flight security communications practices that persist today. Although the paper discussed specific safety threats arising from excessively rigid application of the "sterile cockpit" restrictions on communications during takeoff and landing, the presenters did not know what would lead to the introduction of the secure cockpit. The post–September 11 separation of flight and cabin crew unquestionably strengthens the 1997 message on flight attendant awareness training.

The prospect of hijackers being able to modify standard aircraft interior fittings such as latches, handles, sections of plastic panel, and so forth, in order to conceal assault weapons is being addressed in modern aircraft through the use of new materials, and the softening, blending, and smoothing of openers and closers. The design of lavatory compartments, besides embracing improved aesthetics and user convenience, is taking into account the need to prevent the concealment of a device or weapon while also facilitating the efficient and speedy search protocols required of the crew. Current International Civil Aviation Organization (ICAO) protocols require a preflight search that includes life vest pouches, lavatories, and areas above stowage compartments.

Fire is one of the threats that air carriers have good reason to fear. This chapter will not enter into the detail of yet another large topic, but in addressing the security of the cabin and concerns about flight attendant training, we cannot ignore the fact that weapons available to terrorists include self-igniting flammable materials. Behavioral observation by the cabin crew through trained situational awareness becomes vital when in flight. It is not sufficient to assume that the antihazard safety testing of cabin construction materials will prevent a significant fire on board. Wires concealed behind interior panels carry electric power, control systems, and signaling capabilities. The most advanced composite materials, engineering thermoplastics, make up the floor and ceiling panels, bulkheads, stowage bins, window surrounds, galley, and lavatory modular paneling, and even the food and drink carts.

On the ground at least, professional firefighters are training for faster response and special skills when called to an aircraft fire, because of the shift to the composite material construction of the airframe. It has been claimed that firefighters at Atlanta's Hartsfield–Jackson International Airport have three minutes to reach passengers in a fire on board a jet on the ground. The article explained that planes are now built from a composite material instead of aluminum; the outer skin is a five-layer composite material both lighter and stronger than aluminum. It does not perform in the manner of aluminum in a fire, expelling hydrogen cyanide when it burns. In a quoted comment about the very short response time, which should provoke questions about preventing and fighting a deliberately set fire on board and in flight, firefighter Rodney Cook told *USA Today:* "You train, you prepare, so that in an incident I don't freeze up."[12]

An interesting development presently still in the early stages of trial application is the introduction of intelligent fasteners. These are mechanical devices with security-encrypted embedded electronics. A large commercial aircraft is constructed with several hundred thousand variable but conventional mechanical fasteners. The potential of the intelligent fastener for the cabin is that maintenance panels and other equipment in aircraft interiors can be speedily secured and opened electronically, and may offer remote status diagnostics, thereby reducing the frequency of the need for close-up physical inspection. In October 2007, one manufacturer reported a successful flight trial of an intelligent fastener stowage application on a Boeing 737 customized business jet.

When such technological advances are applied to interior stowage areas, crew quarters and galleys, and even washrooms, it becomes possible to maintain an electronic audit record of openings and closings to enhance the security and integrity of cabin crew–managed equipment. It is believed that the removal of passenger seats for repair or replacement will in the near future be a task accomplished in about 2 minutes using intelligent fasteners, as opposed to 45 minutes using conventional tools to remove metal screws, bolts, and nuts. Advances of this nature, however, validate the question—do we need to train the cabin crew so that all are sufficiently aware of the technological makeup of their environment and are able to interpret circumstantial implications for in-cabin security?

The Cockpit—Separation, Not Protection?

The so-called hardened cockpit door is something of an anachronism, in that it is an afterthought, compromise retrofit development not entirely congruous with its airframe and functional surroundings. It has long been taught in crime prevention circles that there is little purpose in fitting a locking mechanism that is physically stronger than the door it is meant to secure, or where the adjacent wall is weaker than the lock or door. By smashing through the wall, an intruder defeats the investment in the lock or the door. The bulkhead walls on either side of the locked door are frequently constructed of plastic or board, penetrable not only by bullets but by lightweight tools, and in some aircraft types via the forward lavatory. Penetration does not necessarily mean immediate bodily entry by an aggressor. The insertion of a tube pushed through from the lavatory and the use of an aerosol device can introduce a noxious vapor sufficient to adversely affect operations on the flight deck.

The foregoing assumes that the assailant has bypassed the screening controls intended to prevent the vaporized chemicals from being taken on board. Unfortunately this assumption has some merit. Between March 2007 and July 2007, in the course of a GAO system test, government investigators were able to take identifiable risk liquids unchallenged on board aircraft on several occasions.[13] The liquids and other bomb-making formulas designed formula information were found through easily accessible Web sources; and controlled tests later demonstrated that the offending test materials did indeed produce a lethal detonation. The resourcefulness of terrorist entities, however, should cause us to remember that there is more than one route to bringing lethal materials onto a commercial airplane.

Returning to the "hardened" cockpit, some airlines, notably United, have taken a further step and introduced a secondary barrier, which acts as a buffer zone on selected aircraft. This is a system of steel wires extending from the top of the cabin down to the floor, and then locked in place by a metal bar.

Some, if not most experts, in aviation security would remove the passenger access to a forward lavatory or even remove the lavatory entirely for reasons illustrated above, and also because it has already compromised the security of the cockpit. A Turkish Boeing 737 en route from Tirana, Albania, to Istanbul, Turkey, in March 2006 was hijacked when a large man forced his way into the cockpit just as a flight attendant was entering the flight deck. This access can be gained without the presence of a lavatory. The area of the cabin adjacent to the cockpit door requires best-quality surveillance, so that the door is opened only when there is no unauthorized person present or imminently able to gain access.

Underpinning the relatively primitive treatment of cockpit protection within a high-asset-value, sophisticated machine is the failure to mandate and provide best-quality crew communications and risk management surveillance options. There has been and continues to be much debate and formal examination of the implications of regulatory or voluntary decisions arising from both needs. Little credit can be justifiably awarded to American carriers when their attitudes on this come under scrutiny, with some exceptions. Jet Blue, for example, has not waited for mandates to introduce in-cabin video surveillance. But when the exceptions are so limited, the serious security practitioner and the curious student are entitled to inquire as to the reasons.

In the United States, an FAA notice of proposed rulemaking (NRPM) and then the final rules published in the Federal Register are accompanied by explanations of the contributory opinions from the industry. The 9/11 Commission, berating the absence of imagination, capabilities, policy, and management, should perhaps send a copy of that statement each year to each of the negotiating parties—the FAA and the Air Transport Association, representing the airlines, for starters. Those who have knowledge in the field of security and communications technologies and who take time to read some of the NPRMs may be amused and more than disappointed at the lack of understanding of what good, homegrown, patriot-driven, technological products have to offer.

One example of the many sources of September 11–triggered solutions is CAPS, a discreet, wireless alert communications device. In a two-hour test flight aboard a Boeing 747–400, it performed perfectly and sent signals from transmission locations throughout the aircraft. It was developed by Capitol Electronics of St. Paul, Minnesota, and the owner of this company, Jane Pahl, spent years trying to persuade the industry and its regulators that this was a good investment for in-cabin security. The culmination of the process came in October 2007 with the Federal Aviation Regulations (FAR) "Final Rule on Flightdeck Door Monitoring and Crew Discreet Alerting Systems."

The final rule concerned procedures for and means of compliance with surveillance near and safe opening of the locked cockpit door. My interest is, however, drawn toward the part of the rule concerning crew discreet alerting systems. In the published explanation of current practice, in which the crew interphone is the method of communication, and in remarks addressing more discreet smart systems of communications, I found the following excerpts incredible to read:

The FAA notes that the interphone system is not intended to be an encrypted or a secure communications means, rather it is a way for all crewmembers to be able to communicate among themselves throughout the passenger cabin and the flight deck. Nevertheless, if a crewmember uses the existing technology of the interphone systems while adhering to the procedures, discreet communication may be maintained.[14]

The FAA acknowledged the fact that "some commenters, including the Professional Flight Attendants Association and the Association of Professional Flight Attendants, recommended that flight attendants carry or have in their possession a wireless device to contact the flight deck."[15]

Then came an astonishing statement: "The FAA does not believe requiring flight attendants to carry or have in their possession a wireless device to contact the flight deck is a good idea. A wireless device that is carried on the person (in a pocket or around the neck) may be problematic because an attacker could threaten or assault the flight attendant in order to obtain the wireless device and then use the device fraudulently to gain access to the flight deck."[16]

This extraordinary display of ignorance of capabilities, disdain for the "can-do" spirit, and further evidence of "failed imagination" yet again validates the conclusions of the September 11 Commission. In her November 2007 testimony cited earlier, Patricia Friend criticized the limitations of the interphone for use in security emergencies:

when various federal agencies conducted a mock terrorist attack onboard an aircraft in June of 2005, referred to as "Operation Atlas," one of the first things that the mock terrorists did was to cut the phone cord on the aft interphone, thereby restricting communication between the cabin and cockpit.[17]

She added that

AFA-CWA, along with other unions representing flight attendants at major carriers in this country have repeatedly called for a cost effective, wireless communication device for flight attendants to use onboard the aircraft. . . . AFA-CWA believes that it is well past time that hands-free, discreet, wireless devices should be made mandatory for all flight attendants.[18]

This demand for discreet wireless alert communications equipment also surfaced during the ICAO's 36th Assembly in September 2007.

Hope from the Rest of the Aviation World?

After being immersed in the mire of U.S. aviation security, it is somewhat refreshing to realize that there is another, potentially more progressive galvanization of the future aviation security scene. Global growth in aviation, as seen in new aircraft orders, new airlines, new routes, and the accompanying infrastructure planning dynamics, suggests in 2007 that American dominance of commercial aviation may be waning. Industry operators, carrier and aviation sector employee associations, regulators, and air frame manufacturers are beginning to offer different perspectives on the future of safe and efficient air travel.

The European Union (EU) and non-American Asia Pacific players are taking the lead in many aspects of aviation; and we have some indications of the creativity and energy devoted to aviation security. Specifically related to in-cabin security, the work of the National Aerospace Laboratory (NLR) in Amsterdam, the Netherlands, is encouraging. At the European Aircraft Cabin Safety Symposium, held in Prague in June of 2006, three contributors from

NLR presented their report on onboard security and interaction with the cabin crew. The presenters showed that leading European companies and institutes joined forces on the Security of Aircraft in the Future European Environment (SAFEE) project: "SAFEE envisages constructing advanced aircraft security systems designed to assess on-board threats and to provide a response advice to the flight crew."[19]

Their report also included a reference to the threat assessment and response management system (TARMS). This concept is designed to gather information from onboard sensors and databases. The SAFEE program and the development of TARMS appear to restore faith in the imagination factor.

SAFEE is offered as a modular system, with subsystems available for short-term installation. TARMS is designed to provide an onboard decision support system. It offers high quality connectivity and process flow capability that will bring greater efficacy, uniting the security preparedness and response coordination of the flight crew, the cabin crew, and where applicable, sky marshals. TARMS, however, has been developed without the need to rely on a sky marshal. The following is a brief summary of TARMS:

TARMS plays a central role in the analysis of threat identification since it is of direct influence to the user response. Three successive stages can be distinguished in the information processing by TARMS: information analysis, scenario analysis and response management. All these steps require external knowledge from databases and sensors. The outcome of these stages is communicated to relevant connected systems, to onboard users and in some cases to external actors (e.g. Air Traffic Control or Airline Operations Centre). TARMS can thus be considered as the coordinating component for the interaction between the sensors, the acting systems, the primary users and the external actors.[20]

Completing the Blend—Regulations and Processes

While aboard aircraft in flight, cabin crews are virtually alone with their security responsibilities for the safety of the flight, each time getting to know from scratch the security status of the equipment—the plane and its interior and the passengers and crew. The security status cannot be safely assumed as constantly stable. Regulation and the procedures mandated by governments and international protocols provide some security guidelines but there is undoubtedly a disconnect, demonstrated by the remarks of the FAA, cited earlier. Some processes are developed to a standard above the minimum regulatory requirements, but not many.

In a confidential exchange with a qualified regular aviation security surveillance expert, I posed this question: "If from your professional observations you were to categorize the contemporary status of three protective layer dimensions—cabin crew awareness, crew security application competence, and evidence of up-to-date security training preparedness, (a) what overall measure would you give these, say from 10 at best to 1 at worst? and (b) what descriptive words, stated honestly, adequately describe the present profile of in-cabin security when all human and technological conditions are considered? For example, viewing the range of variables, are the words "primitive" and/or "advanced" or "efficient" justifiable in this context?"

The response contained some sensitive comment that is not repeated here. The responder gave a security performance opinion rating of American carriers, applied to domestic operations. No carrier was awarded 10 points, and only two received a rating of 8 points. At the other end of the scale, two carriers each were given 2 points and were described as having "pathetic ground and in-flight security." The priorities suggested to bring standards up to an acceptable level were stated as follows:

1. Cabin crew awareness
2. Crew security application process
3. Up-to-date security awareness training

For the airlines at the top end of the rating, the descriptive words were as follows: "forward looking," "security conscious," "research development," and "efficient." For the airlines with the worst ratings, the descriptions were: "pathetic," "scary," "complacent," "rude," "counterproductive," and "arrogant."

Conclusions

This chapter contains less than 5 percent by volume and possibly less than 10 percent of potential analysis outcome from the research source material, constrained as it is, understandably, by practicalities and editorial direction. Overall, I conclude that there is an enormous gap between what the aviation regulators and operators consider acceptable for in-cabin security on the one hand and what cabin crew and security experts believe on the other.

In my discussions with my peers, and with technology developers, it is easy to conclude that involvement of the full range of stakeholders is more a token effort than an honorable, respectful appreciation of the front line—the flight attendants—and their credibility, opinion, and contributory worth. While this applies to other countries as well, the United States bears much responsibility for it because of its leading aviation position. ICAO Annex 6 (Safety and Security Training), and 17 (Security) appear to contain good foundation precepts that are weakened by cherry-picking among member states.

In an information paper presented to the ICAO's 36th Assembly in September 2007, the International Transport Workers' Federation (ITF) attempted to follow up on its submission to the 35th Assembly three years earlier. The ITF represents unionized aviation workers around the world and claims to speak for millions of aviation workers globally. The ITF's paper at the 36th Assembly dealt with cabin crew members as safety and security professionals. The principal objective of this submission was to seek further progress on an ITF proposition that cabin crew should be subject to certification, applying standardized training requirements. Reiterating its 2004 position, the paper stated that "The ITF continues to believe that licensing/certification in the aviation industry must include cabin crews to avoid one side of the safety triangle of parts, providers and personnel remaining vulnerable."[21]

In 2003, Andrew Thomas *Aviation Insecurity—The New Challenges of Air Travel* described flight attendant training, using words that still apply in 2007:

Nearly a year after the 9/11 attacks, the Association of Flight Attendants surveyed twenty-six airlines and found that training for flight crew ranged from two to sixteen hours. Sometimes the training involved little more than lectures or video tapes. One training program even taught "verbal judo" designed to redirect behavior through language.[22]

Most disturbing is the almost unassailable deduction that within the influential sphere of the U.S. aviation industry, the poor standard of in-cabin security preparedness will only be addressed after another significant terrorist attack on the passenger airline system. It is reasonable to hope that the good work now going on in Europe will help to redress the imbalances in global security and safety influences.

The prevailing image of procrastination and even obfuscation surrounding progress in in-cabin security is reminiscent of historical preparedness failings. In a 1935 speech to the British Parliament, Winston Churchill, later hailed as one of the world's great statesmen, warned an apparently naïve Europe:

Want of foresight, unwillingness to act when action would be simple and effective, lack of clear thinking, confusion of counsel until the emergency comes, until self-preservation strikes its jarring gong—these are the features which constitute the endless repetition of history.[23]

No further words seem necessary to describe the threatening status of in-cabin security, more than six years after an event that itself came about through the same lack of foresight.

NOTES

1. Timothy Naftali, *Blind Spot—The Secret History of American Counter Terrorism* (New York: Basic Books, 2005), 312.

2. *The 9/11 Commission Report Including Progress Reports by the 9/11 Pubic Discourse Project* (New York: Barnes & Noble Publishing, 2006), 339.

3. *The 9/11 Commission Report*, 347.

4. Patricia A. Friend, Testimony before the Subcommittee on Transportation Security and Infrastructure, Protection of the Homeland Security Committee, U.S. House of Representatives, November 1, 2007, http://homeland.house.gov/Site Documents/20071101164934–12623.pdf.

5. James Sturke and agencies, "Al-Qaida Gets Fake Papers as Home Office Issues 10,000 Passports to Fraudsters," *Guardian Unlimited*, March 20, 2007, http://www.guardian.co.uk/terrorism/story/0,,2038442,00.html.

6. General Accountability Office, GAO-05–781, *Aviation Security Flight and Cabin Crew Member Security Training Strengthened but Better Planning and Internal Controls Needed*, September 2005, http://www.gao.gov/new.items/d05781.pdf.

7. Friend, Testimony.

8. Ibid.

9. Ibid.

10. Jennifer Coutts Clay, *Jetliner Cabins*, 2nd ed. (Chichester, England: Wiley-Academy, 2006), 73.

11. Melisa G. Dunbar, Rebecca D. Chute, and Kevin Jordan, "Evaluation of Cabin Crew Technical Knowledge," *Proceedings of the 9th International Symposium on Aviation Psychology* (Columbus, OH: 1997), 527–31, http://www.cabinfactors.com/pages/FATechnical_Knowledgerev.htm.

12. Larry Copeland, "Fast Firefighting Required for New Jets," *USA Today*, September 16, 2007, http://www.usatoday.com/news/nation/2007–09–16-airportfires_N.htm.

13. General Accountability Office, GAO-08–48T, *Aviation Security Vulnerabilities Exposed through Covert Testing of TSA's Passenger Screening Process*, November 2007, http://www.gao.gov/new.items/d0848t.pdf.

14. Federal Aviation Administration, 14 CFR Part 121 (Docket No. FAA-2005–2249; Amendment No. 121–334), "Flightdeck Door Monitoring and Crew Discreet Alerting Systems," *Federal Register*, August 15, 2007, effective October 15, 2007, http://rgl.faa.gov/Regulatory_and_Guidance_Library/rgFinalRule.nsf/0/C953A8E95055FB988625733800517FE1?OpenDocument.

15. Ibid.

16. Ibid.

17. Friend, Testimony.

18. Ibid.

19. A.J.J. Lemmers, T.J.J. Bos, and L.J.P. Speijker, *An On-Board Security System and the Interactions with Cabin Crew*, Report NLR-TP-2006–378 (National Aerospace Laboratory, Amsterdam, The Netherlands: National Aerospace Laboratory, August 2007 (based on a presentation at the European Aircraft Cabin Safety Symposium, Prague, June 2006).

20. Lemmers, Bos, and Speijker, *On-Board Security System*, 7.

21. International Transport Workers' Federation, Agenda Item 30: Other Safety Matters, "Cabin Crew as Safety and Security Professionals," presented to the International Civil Aviation Organization Assembly, 36th Session, September 2007, http://www.icao.int/icao/en/assembl/a36/wp/wp164_en.pdf.

22. Andrew R. Thomas, *Aviation Insecurity—The New Challenges of Air Travel* (Amherst, NY: Prometheus Books, 2003), 177.

23. Winston Churchill, speech, House of Commons, May 2, 1935, *Winston S. Churchill: His Complete Speeches, 1897–1963*, ed. Robert Rhodes James, vol. 6, (New York: Penguin Books, 1974), 5592.

CHAPTER 9

Cabin Crew Functioning in a High-Stress Environment: Implications for Aircraft Safety and Security

Michael Tunnecliffe

The role of cabin crew and flight attendants in general has been given sporadic attention in the aviation literature. The portrayals of the flight attendant role have been largely left to pop culture, particularly movies and TV, where they have been many and varied. These have ranged from comedy to more malevolent roles, as in the Jodie Foster movie, *Flightplan*, in which a flight attendant is cast as the villain. This movie triggered a protest from the Association of Flight Attendants and the Transport Workers Union.[1] Few of the portrayals do justice to the diversity of roles and the variety of demands that cabin crew deal with on a regular basis.

An examination of the flight attendant role reveals one in which fatigue, interpersonal problems, airline requirements, passenger demands, medical emergencies, health consequences, and security threats all add up to a stressful work environment.[2] This notion is reinforced by a plethora of publications by former flight attendants giving anecdotal accounts of incidents that range from humorous to life-threatening. Titles such as *The Smile High Club*,[3] *Flying by the Seat of my Pants*,[4] and *Around the World in a Bad Mood*[5] convey a picture of a high-stress occupational role that can have significant consequences for flight attendants.

The increasingly stressful environment is exacerbated by the fact that commercial carriers worldwide are looking to cut costs. It's been reported that around 22 percent of all flight attendants in the United States have been laid off since September 11, 2001.[6] Yet carriers insist that flight attendants maintain even greater vigilance in relation to security and safety issues. The implications of the high-stress work environment are even more significant in the light of research, which suggests that there is a negative impact on tasks requiring high vigilance when motivation and choice are reduced.[7]

A general review of the literature reveals a number of key factors that impact on the functioning of flight attendants by increasing stress levels. These are as follows:

- The interpersonal relationships between all crew on board the aircraft
- The demands of the customer service role
- Medical emergencies and critical incidents
- The health and physical well-being of flight attendants
- Safety and security responsibilities.

INTERPERSONAL RELATIONSHIPS BETWEEN ALL CREW ON BOARD THE AIRCRAFT

While most air crews build good working relationships, the variance in role and long-standing traditions often promote some form of distancing between flight crews and cabin crews.[8] While most cabin crews tend to maintain good collegial relationships, it would be naive to suggest that flight attendants are immune to the conflicts and interpersonal pressures of any regular workplace. In fact, the enclosed space of the aircraft cabin, the nature of the customer service role, the time constraints within which duties need to be performed, and the rotation of colleagues suggest a work environment that has a greater propensity for conflict and disagreement than most others.

While there have often been anecdotal accounts of friction between flight crews and flight attendants,[9] in recent times similar comments have been made about the presence of air marshals traveling anonymously on flights. Many flight attendants have reported feeling devalued and expendable because of negative comments attributed to flight crew members and air marshals.[10]

The diversity of culture, educational background, personality, beliefs, values, and motivations is a prime factor in crew disharmony. Even a failed attempt at humor or a sarcastic remark can be the trigger for crew members to avoid duties or each other.[11] When these situations are combined with time pressures, demanding customers, and fatigue factors, incidents of displaced stress between flight attendants are not uncommon.[12] Displaced stress is the tendency to focus stress reactions on a third party, rather than address the issue directly with the person who is the source of the stress. Psychologists often characterize such reactions as passive-aggressive.[13] Given the work environment of flight attendants and the overt customer service function they perform, often for a demanding and sometimes belligerent clientele, it's not surprising that displaced stress can become a significant work pressure.

THE DEMANDS OF THE CUSTOMER SERVICE ROLE

In the early days of flights carrying paying passengers, the first flight attendants employed were nurses, such was the belief about the impact of flying on the average person and the need to be prepared for any untoward events.[14]

While flight attendants recognize the significance of their customer service role, the vast majority will cite the duties of safety, security, and the well-being of passengers over the importance of serving tea, coffee, and meals.[15] Yet airline advertising gives prominence to customer comfort and satisfaction rather than safety and security. In contrast, there are increasing numbers of low-cost and budget airlines around the world that have emphasized economy while glossing over the cuts in customer comforts. This can become a source of friction, especially when the traditionally free cup of coffee has to be paid for. The combination of factors likely to elevate levels of flight attendant stress and pressure becomes even more significant when cutbacks in cabin crews and increasing service demands from the passenger population are included.[16] Once more, anecdotal reports of difficult passenger behavior are numerous, and there is every reason to believe that incident reports detailing passenger misconduct are a significant underrepresentation of the true state of affairs.[17]

Episodes of customer service pressure are almost legend among cabin crew, with most flight attendants having their favorite story about the most obnoxious person they have dealt with. These range from passengers who come on board with well oversized hand luggage; passengers who refuse to take their allocated seats; or those who are a source of complaint from others on board because of intoxication, body odor, obscene language, or generally creating a nuisance to their fellow travelers when various problems are combined: the physical constraints of close proximity of the seating, inadequate legroom, and the claustrophobic environment, and the heightened anxiety of flying phobia or the emotional contagion that air travel may cause.[18]

Managing passenger complaints has become a major issue for flight attendants, and in many cases, the problem has escalated into the phenomenon generally referred to as "air rage."[19] Air rage, the direction of verbally or physically aggressive behavior toward airline staff or other passengers, is often triggered by general dissatisfaction with the service or flight conditions. The situation is frequently compounded by intoxication, mental health problems of passengers, or the air travel system, which tends to create passenger expectations that cabin crew cannot meet, often due to a lack of resources or factors outside of cabin crew control, such as flight cancellations due to weather conditions, malfunctioning entertainment systems, or changes in operational priorities.

Anecdotal reports describe numerous incidents of verbal abuse, food being thrown, sexual innuendo directed toward flight attendants, and, in more serious cases, incidents of passengers attacking each other and physically assaulting members of the cabin crew.[20] The source of such behavior is occasionally the behavior of celebrities or well-known people who see themselves as immune from consequences if they are unhappy about conditions onboard or an instruction from a flight attendant.[21] The situation becomes even more difficult when the flight attendant is caught between the pressure of delivering a high level of customer service to maintain the carrier's image and the need to deal with a situation that may create a risk to personal safety.[22] One comparative study found that female flight attendants were more likely to experience sexual harassment, bullying, violence, and threatening behavior than nurses or teachers.[23] Such behavior contributes to an increasing body of evidence suggesting that violence toward customer service personnel is escalating in most developed countries.[24] However, the increase in aggressive behavior toward staff in the airline industry may be more significant than in other customer service areas. Some writers contend that the real reason behind air rage is not the traditional explanations used by the airline industry management (intoxication and cigarette deprivation) but the cost-cutting practices of maintaining poor cabin air quality and decreasing leg room between seats.[25] Although no comparative data is available, it's not hard to speculate that the pressure on flight attendants has increased with the introduction of no-frills, budget airlines.

MEDICAL EMERGENCIES AND OTHER CRITICAL INCIDENTS

Flight attendants prefer trips that are uneventful, allowing them to do their job without disruption and delay while enjoying the interaction with passengers and fellow crew members.[26] Flights are not always uneventful, as medical emergencies and other critical incidents are bound to be part of an industry that transports large volumes of people over great distances each year. It's the flight attendant's role to deal with such situations, as an aircraft cabin at more than 30,000 feet above the ground is not a place where paramedics can be called to assist.

A 30-year review of medical events on aircraft revealed that more than a third (36 percent) involved musculo-skeletal or head injuries, usually resulting from falls, turbulence factors, luggage dislodged from lockers, or injuries caused by food carts. The next largest group of medical events involved heart attacks (15 percent), with fatalities resulting from only 3 percent of these events. While the study revealed that most recorded events would not be classified as emergencies, more than one-third led to aircraft diversions, causing disruption to schedules and pressure on passengers and crew.[27]

Another constant source of pressure for flight attendants is the presence of passengers who may have mental health issues.[28] Given that many people in society function well with underlying mental health challenges, it's important not to stigmatize passengers with mental health–related problems. With appropriate assistance, many people travel without difficulty. Problems may arise for cabin crew, however, when the combination of changes in routine, crowded conditions, the unfamiliar environment, and confusion about expectations result in behaviors that are demanding for flight attendants and passengers, most of whom expect the flight attendant to take control and manage the situation.[29]

Rough weather, thunderstorms, and midair turbulence caused by changes in temperature or wind, or sudden jolts caused by the wake of other aircraft, are significant factors in injuries to flight attendants.[30] This is especially so when the seatbelt rules for passengers and for cabin crew differ. In fact, some airlines insist that passengers must continue to be served unless a member of the flight crew actually instructs flight attendants to take their seats, regardless of the seatbelt sign being illuminated.[31] This policy has been a prime cause of serious injury to flight attendants and remains a continual source of concern for cabin crew with some carriers.[32]

Medical emergencies, episodes of air rage, weather, operational disruption, and a host of other critical incidents are all issues that have some potential to create undue stress on cabin crew and compromise the safety of passengers. What may be of greater stress to flight attendants is the feeling that their concerns about these issues are going unrecognized by their employers.[33]

HEALTH AND PHYSICAL WELL-BEING OF FLIGHT ATTENDANTS

Flight attendant concerns about lack of support with regard to in-flight stress factors, such as air rage and medical emergencies, are compounded by what the Association of Flight Attendants (AFA) sees as a lack of interest in the health challenges faced by their members. Various issues are cited as impacting on physical and mental well-being. These include cabin air quality and exposure to noise, temperature fluctuations, vibration, noxious odors, and concerns about the effects of solar radiation and exposure to radioactivity.

Perhaps the most common health risk referred to is fatigue.[34] Accounts of flight attendant fatigue are numerous, and almost every publication relating to stress and pressure among cabin crew makes mention of this factor. Airlines are in constant motion. In the United States alone, there are estimated to be between 2,000 and 4,000 commercial flights in operation at any one time.[35] Although not all of these flights carry cabin crew, many do.

Fatigue can come from many sources, not the least of which is the requirement to fly great distances across numerous time zones in a single shift.[36] Often referred to as jet lag, the impact of disruption to the circadian rhythm of the body can be highly debilitating.[37] There is now a significant body of research indicating that jet lag results in chronic sleep disturbances, irritability and mood swings, inattentiveness, and a host of potential ailments.[38] Sleep derivation alone has significant implications for both mental and physical health, and this is frequently underestimated when employers make demands upon personnel in occupations that require the disruption of normal sleep cycles.[39]

Compounding the problems caused by scheduling requirements is any disruption to those schedules. Flight cancellations, changes in turnaround times, forced layovers and short-notice crew changes are not uncommon in an industry that is subject to the demands of weather, equipment malfunction, personnel availability, industrial action, and commercial decisions. These factors can all have implications for flight attendant well-being that go well beyond the physical.[40] Social disruption and being away from home and family can result in a range of relationship issues, as many flight attendants struggle to maintain what most people would call a "normal life" and its parenting and family responsibilities. There is speculation that this disruption leaves flight attendants with greater risk of marital problems because of the time away from home.[41] Efforts to cope with such circumstances frequently involve potentially addictive habits, such as alcohol use. Evidence of lowered job satisfaction, resentment, and increasing lack of interest in customer service paints a picture consistent with a high level of cumulative stress. This trend is reinforced by reports of people leaving the industry and increased use of employee assistance counseling by airline personnel, including flight attendants.[42]

Another significant contributor to fatigue is the quality of air in the cabin, which has long been a source of complaint. The problems can range from hypoxia, the effects of lowered levels of oxygen on passengers and crew, to flight attendant illness generated by the toxicity of the cabin air. An example of the extreme impact of air quality problems occurred in 2000 among cabin crew operating BAE 146 passenger jets.[43] Some flight attendants experienced significant problems, including headaches, memory loss, lowered concentration, and coordination difficulties. The airline involved at first attempted to avoid any liability, until legal action taken by flight attendants forced the company to address the issue.

The overall concerns about the impact of hypoxia on flight attendants continue. The air quality in the cabin of the aircraft is regulated either by an automatic setting or by flight crew adjustment. It's been reported that the cockpit receives up to 10 times more oxygen than do passengers and flight attendants in the cabin.[44] The effects on the body can be serious, yet the individual may not immediately notice any change, as the onset of problems will vary from person to person. Given the brain impairment that can accompany hypoxia, the implications for alcohol-consuming passengers and fatigued flight attendants are significant and have led to numerous anecdotal reports by passengers and cabin crew. The outcomes in extreme cases can be disastrous. In August 2005, a Helios Airways Boeing 737 crashed in mountainous terrain north of Athens, Greece, resulting in the deaths of 121 passengers and crew. This tragedy occurred as a result of hypoxia, when all on board were rendered unconscious due to a switch on the flight deck, which controls the airflow, being left in the "manual" position.[45]

Claims by airline personnel that they have also been subjected to a range of noxious chemicals have been documented by major airlines worldwide and led to the emergence of the word "skypoxia," used by some flight attendants.[46] Weight is added to these contentions when it's appreciated that prior to starting work with an airline, flight attendants require a complete medical clearance. Concern is increased by the knowledge that the effect of toxins on the human organism is cumulative.

Added to the stress of physical demands is the concern that flight attendants generally have about how they are seen by their employer. Airline policies can be harsh and punitive. There have been many changes to the pay, conditions, and employment of flight attendants, involving moving jobs offshore and cost-saving restructuring within the commercial operations of carriers, as they seek to maintain services at reduced cost and their major concern becomes the business of flying.[47] The impact on cabin crew is particularly felt when the job role they originally took on no longer fits with their needs, ambitions, or lifestyle. This alone may prompt maladaptive coping behaviors, resulting in cumulative stress, which then triggers a wide range of physical and emotional problems.[48]

The fatigue issues of flight attendants have been recognized and discussed. A report by the NASA Ames Research Center concluded that data gathered on fatigue are generally ad hoc, with a lack of centralized collation within the industry. There also appears to be some confusion as to which factors are the major predictors of fatigue, resulting in recommendations for further research, validation of models for assessing flight attendant fatigue, review of international policies and practices on this issue, and consideration of further training requirements.[49]

SAFETY AND SECURITY RESPONSIBILITIES

Any discussion of health issues pertaining to a particular industry or occupational group is bound to illustrate a range of at-risk situations and potential areas of health concern. The implications of impaired functioning in flight attendants are likely to be particularly serious, because their role is seen by their employer and themselves as more than just ensuring good customer service and passenger comfort.

The training of flight attendants and in-flight protocols place emphasis on safety issues above all other cabin crew duties.[50] In the post–September 11 environment, this has been highlighted by the use of air marshals, the greatly increased security screening at airports, the restrictions on what passengers can carry on board, and the certification of flight attendants.

The industry now clearly expects flight attendants to act as safety professionals.[51] However, it has been claimed that the customer service role is often valued more than the safety role by some sections of the industry.[52] This point becomes especially important when the demands of passengers put pressure on flight attendants to forgo safety requirements. Again, numerous anecdotal accounts have been written about the experiences of cabin crew dealing with passengers who simply refuse to obey the airlines' safety procedures, often because the instruction comes from a flight attendant.[53] These incidents include passengers refusing to take their assigned seats, fasten seatbelts, secure hand luggage in overhead lockers, bring seats into an upright position for landing, return to their seats when the seatbelt sign is illuminated, or refrain from smoking in an aircraft toilet. The United Kingdom Department of Transport cited "smoking in the aircraft's toilet" as the most common significant incident reported by cabin crew.[54]

While alcohol is often cited as the cause of such problems, not all passengers who refuse to acknowledge a flight attendant's safety role are intoxicated or have any other contributory cause for their behavior, apart from not wanting to obey a legitimate instruction from an airline staff member. In fact, some passengers go so far as to take legal action against the airline when their name is cited in a complaint or incident report.[55] It causes significant frustration to flight attendants when it appears their role and viewpoint are ignored in favor of the paying passenger.[56]

The ultimate price airlines pay for poor safety is the loss of an aircraft and the deaths of passengers and crew. Air crashes are unforgiving in the toll taken on those who work in the industry and use its services. While, in comparative terms, aviation is a relatively safe form of transport, problems in the industry are continually highlighted but not all are acted upon.[57] As a number of accounts have illustrated, the experience of an air crash is the one flight attendants fear most.[58] This serves to highlight the frustration flight attendants experience when they believe their concerns are ignored, often by an administration more concerned about the immediate cost rather than dealing with the foreseeable risk.

Parallel to the important safety role of flight attendants are the more onerous responsibilities associated with security. After the aviation industry worldwide was stunned by the events of September 11, 2001, flight attendants acquired a new role, partly by carrier planning and partly assumed by the flight attendants themselves. Much of this was in response to what some in the industry describe as a "viral fear" of being victimized by terrorism.[59] It's believed that increasing global threats and heightened terror alerts are causing many to question aviation security.

On board an aircraft, security is not an activity confined to a single crew member. The tasks of screening, observing, and maintaining continual vigilance have become essential for cabin crew. This is because once passengers have boarded the aircraft and the door to the flight deck is locked, the flight attendants are the only staff members in a position to maintain the security of the aircraft. Incidents are recorded every year that reinforce the security role of the flight attendant. Rather than emanating from hijackers or terrorists, such events are more likely to come from an intoxicated passenger who attempts to open an aircraft door in flight, or someone who, in a state of mental disturbance, attacks and wounds cabin crew members, as happened in Australia on a Qantas domestic flight in 2003.[60] During this incident, two flight attendants were stabbed with wooden stakes by a passenger who attempted to break into the cockpit and attack the pilots. Although wounded, the flight attendants subdued their assailant and averted disaster with assistance from other passengers.

While significant incidents such as this receive ample attention, newspapers also highlight incidents of poor judgment,, such as the breastfeeding mother removed from a Delta Airlines flight for continuing to breastfeed her child, and claims of perceived bias[61] when six Muslim clerics claimed they were racially profiled, detained, and barred from boarding a US Airways flight in 2006. According to flight attendants, these incidents reinforce their claims that inadequate attention is given to the training needs and overall preparation of cabin crews that would assist them to meet the raised expectations of their employers and the traveling public. While most passengers take security on board for granted, there are some who question if flight attendants are as well equipped as one would hope to deal with any threat that may arise.[62]

Handling security requirements and dealing with suspicious passenger behavior has become an everyday part of the flight attendant role, yet there are claims by the Association of Flight Attendants that the Transport Security Administration (TSA) is overreliant on the air marshal program and flight deck partitioning, to the extent that comprehensive security and counterterrorism training for cabin crew has been slow to come into operation.[63] In 2005, an AFA-CWA–sponsored submission by Candace Kolander to the Subcommittee on Economic Security, Infrastructure Protection, and Cybersecurity of the Homeland Security Committee highlighted these same problems.[64] Numerous anecdotal accounts illustrate the ways in which FAA-certified flight attendants are subjected to excessive scrutiny at airports and not afforded the same level of speedy processing as their colleagues on the flight decks, despite having undergone the same level of background checks and receiving the same level of security clearances. Emphasis was placed on appropriate recognition for flight attendants and the need for training in counterterrorism, which would include extensive background information, self-defense skills, and first-responder expertise, which would allow flight attendants to become a fully integrated part of a team that would also include flight deck officers and air marshals.

There is ample evidence of the stressful nature of the flight attendant role. Yet flight attendants comprise an occupational group that has not been afforded a degree of scientific review similar to that provided by the appraisal of health and ergonomic factors impacting on flight deck officers. In a world where flight attendants are simply there to maintain a primary role of customer service to the paying public, this would be understandable. But this is not the real world of commercial air travel today.

There are three competing demands on flight attendants that airlines have to be able to balance. These are service, safety, and security. These tasks can only be undertaken by a workgroup that is healthy and well trained. Health concerns, risk exposure, and training requirements are areas where the various professional associations of flight attendants have sought attention from commercial carriers and government agencies, with varying degrees of success. The harsh realities of the business world are likely to produce inconsistencies in the ways the needs of flight attendants are addressed.

The task of setting health standards, reducing risk exposure, and mandating appropriate levels of training largely relies on legislative requirements, which can involve a slow and cumbersome process. To maintain attention to their needs, flight attendants will need to look at three key initiatives. First, they should continue to source good reliable data to reinforce their claims. Anecdotal information is interesting, descriptive, and helps to rouse sentiment, but it tends to be ignored when it's not supported by quantitative, scientific research. Second, they should continue to lobby for legal safeguards against exposure to risk from unhealthy aspects of their work conditions and physical environment, and from the threat posed by unruly or dangerous passengers. While various jurisdictions around the world have responded differently to these problems, the need to address the issues in a consistent, meaningful way still remains a priority. Third, those who set security policy should recognize the essential safety and security tasks within the flight attendant role and provide appropriate training to meet the requirements of that role. Many of the major commercial carriers have already gone a long way toward putting appropriate and consistent training in place. However, the economic reality is that unless forced by legislation, there are others who will cut cost sand the crew and the passengers will get only what their carrier is prepared to pay for.

More people than ever before are traveling around the globe by air, and carriers are expanding their fleets and purchasing bigger aircraft. It's important not to be seduced by size and speed. Airlines are staffed by people and achieving the safety, security, and overall integrity of the passenger-carrying aircraft is a team effort. It's essential that the role of the cabin crew members within that team is not overlooked or underestimated.

NOTES

1. Diane Clarkson, "Jodie Foster Movie Outrages Flight Attendants," *Jupiter Research*, September 29, 2005, http://weblogs.jupiterresearch.com/analysts/clarkson/archives.

2. Drew Whitelegg, *Working the Skies* (New York: New York University Press, 2007).

3. Allan Zullo and Kathy Nelson, *The Smile High Club* (Kansas City, MO: Andrews McMeel Publishing, 2002).

4. Marsha Marks, *Flying by the Seat of My Pants* (Colorado Springs, CO: Waterbrook Press, 2005).

5. Rene Foss, *Around the World in a Bad Mood* (New York: Hyperion, 2002).

6. Francine Parnes, "For Flight Attendants, Stress Comes with the Job," *New York Times*, August 12, 2003.

7. J. Szalma and P. Hancock, "Performance, Workload, and Stress in Vigilance: The Power of Choice," in Proceedings of the Human Factors and Ergonomics Society 50th Annual Meeting, Maui, Hawaii, 2006, p. 1609.

8. Whitelegg, *Working the Skies*, 106.

9. Elliott Hester, *Plane Insanity* (New York: St Martin's Griffin, 2001).

10. Whitelegg, *Working the Skies*, 110.

11. Nattanya Anderson, *Broken Wings* (Coquitlam, BC, Canada: Avia Publishing, 1997).

12. Foss, *Around the World in a Bad Mood*, 28.

13. Tim Murphy and Loriann Hoff Oberlin, *Overcoming Passive-Aggression* (New York, Marlow and Company, 2005).

14. Whitelegg, *Working the Skies*, 107.

15. Mark Coldebella, "Enroute Emergency," *Flight Safety Australia*, January–February 2000.

16. Caroline Kelleher and Sinead McGilloway, "Study Finds High Levels of Work-Related Stress among Flight Attendants," Flight Safety Foundation, *Cabin Crew Safety*, November–December 2005.

17. Gary Stoller, "Flight Attendants Feel the Wrath of Flyers," *USA Today*, October 6, 2007.

18. Geoffrey Thomas, Christine Forbes Smith, Guy Norris, and Tom Ballantyne, *Passengers Who Make Your Flight Hell* (Perth, Australia: APTI, 2007).

19. Anonymous and Andrew Thomas, *Air Rage, Crisis in the Skies* (Amherst, NY: Prometheus Books, 2001),

20. Marks, *Flying by the Seat of My Pants*, 116; Hester, *Plane Insanity*, 64.

21. Anderson, *Broken Wings*, 208.

22. Angela Dahlberg, *Air Rage, The Underestimated Safety Risk* (Aldershot, England: Ashgate, 2001).

23. Holmfridur Gunnarsdottir et al., "Lifestyle, Harassment at Work and Self-Assessed Health of Female Flight Attendants, Nurses and Teachers," *Work* 27 (2006): 165–72

24. Martin Gill, Bonnie Fisher, and Vaughan Bowie, *Violence at Work* (London: Willan Publishing, 2002),

25. Anderson, *Broken Wings*, 210; Thomas, *Air Rage*, 90.

26. Farrol Kahn, *Arrive in Better Shape: The Long-Haul Passenger Handbook* (San Francisco: Thorsens, 1995).

27. Rick Darby, "Is There a Doctor Aboard?" Flight Safety Foundation, *Aerosafety World*, March 2007.

28. Anonymous and Thomas, *Air Rage*, 70.

29. "Psychiatric Emergencies," *Flight Safety Australia*, March–April 2003.

30. Whitelegg, *Working the Skies*, 107.

31. Anderson, *Broken Wings*, 58.

32. Diana Fairechild, *Strategies for the Wise Passenger* (Anahola, HI: Flyana, 2003).

33. Whitelegg, *Working the Skies*, 115.

34. Corey Caldwell, "AFA-CWA Raises Awareness of Flight Attendant Fatigue in Congress," press release relating to the testimony of AFA-CWA International president, Patricia Friend, before the House Transportation and infrastructure Aviation Subcommittee, June 6, 2007.

35. Daniel Baker, "Did You Know You Can Find IFR Rules for an Upcoming Flight," July 22, 2006, http://www.flightaware.com.

36. Whitelegg, *Working the Skies*, 119.

37. Farrol Kahn, *The Curse of Icarus: The Health Factor in Air Travel* (London: Routledge, 1990).

38. Anderson, *Broken Wings*, 229.

39. William Avison and Ian Gotlib, *Stress and Mental Health* (New York: Plenum, 1994).

40. Whitelegg, *Working the Skies*, 173.

41. Annie Baxter, "Some Flight Attendants Wonder Whether the Job Is Worth It," *Minnesota Public Radio—Morning Edition*, August 7, 2006.

42. Barbara De Lollis, "Job Stress Beginning to Take Toll on Some Airline Workers," *USA Today*, November 29, 2004.

43. Adrienne Lowth, "CASA Attacked over Handling of Toxic Fume Complaints," transcript from press release, *Australian Broadcasting Commission*, October 12, 2000.

44. Diana Fairechild, *Air Travel Health News*, March 2003, http://www.flyana.com/air.html.

45. *Accident Database*, August, 2005, http://www.airdisaster.com.

46. Diana Fairechild, "Skypoxia: Toxins on Board," *Jet Smart Newsletter*, March, 2004.

47. "Qantas Strikes a Deal with FAAA," *MSN*, November 2007, http://money.ninemsn.com.au/article.

48. Michael Tunnecliffe, *How to Understand and Manage Stress* (Palmyra Australia: Bayside Books, 1999).

49. *Flight Attendant Fatigue*, report prepared by the Fatigue Countermeasures Group, Human Factors Research and Technology Division, NASA Ames Research Centre, Moffett Field, California, September 2005, http://stint.dtic.mil/oai/oaifuerb=getRecordmetadataprefix=html8identifier=ADA471470.

50. Anderson, *Broken Wings*, 77.

51. Kathleen Barry, *Femininity in Flight: A History of Flight Attendants* (Durham, NC: Duke University Press, 2007).

52. Whitelegg, *Working the Skies*, 114.

53. Anonymous and Thomas, *Air Rage*, 43.

54. Department of Transport (United Kingdom), *Disruptive Behaviour On Board UK Aircraft*, April 2002–March 2003, http://www.dft.gov.uk/pgr/aviation/hci/db/disruptivebehaviouronboarduk2954.

55. Hester, *Plane Insanity*, 61.

56. Whitelegg, *Working the Skies*, 117.

57. Stephen Barlay, *The Final Call: Air Disasters. When Will They Ever Learn?* (London: Arrow Books, 1991).

58. Sandy Purl, *Am I Alive? A Surviving Flight Attendant's Struggle and Inspiring Triumph over Tragedy* (Ellicott City, MD: Chevron Publishing, 1997).

59. Kathleen Hall, "Terrorist Stress Is Paralyzing Our Lives," media release, August 2006, http://wwwdrkathleenhall.com.

60. Padraic Murphy and Phillip Hudson, "Heroes Foil Qantas Hijack Attack," *The Age*, May 30, 2003.

61. Emily Bazar and Sam Hemingway, "Nursing Mom Files Complaint against Airlines," *USA Today*, November 16, 2006; Leslie Miller, "At National Airport, Prayers against Profiling," *Washington Post*, November 28, 2006.

62. Rick Guy, "Aviation Security—The Thinning Frontlines," *Jagwa Forbes Group*, June 2007, http://www.jagwaforbes.com.au/aviation-security-thinning-frontlines.

63. "Flight Attendants Lament Lack of Training, Poor Security," Transportation Security online exclusive, October 30, 2003, http://www.transportationsec.com/microsites/newsarticle.asp.

64. Candace Kolander, Association of Flight Attendants—CWA, Testimony before the Subcommittee on Economic Security, Infrastructure Protection and Cybersecurity of the Homeland Security Committee, House of Representatives, Washington DC, May 13, 2005.

CHAPTER 10

An Assessment of Aviation Security Costs and Funding in the United States

Clinton V. Oster, Jr., and John S. Strong

This chapter examines the costs of aviation security, both those borne by the federal government and those borne by airlines, airports, and travelers. It discusses how these activities are financed, and funding issues and options for the future.

FEDERAL POLICY AND SPENDING ON HOMELAND SECURITY

The terrorist attacks on September 11, 2001, prompted a fundamental change in how transportation security in the United States is organized and funded. On November 19, 2001, the Transportation Security Administration (TSA) was created within the U.S. Department of Transportation (DOT) by the Aviation and Transportation Security Act (Public Law 107–71). TSA took on responsibility for many aviation security activities, some of which had been housed elsewhere in government and some of which had previously been provided through private organizations under contract to airlines, airports, or aviation authorities. Passenger and baggage screening were the most visible of these activities, but TSA responsibilities also include air cargo security, the Federal Air Marshal Service, transportation employee background checks and roles, and the security of rail, urban transit, port, and maritime activities. On November 25, 2002, the Department of Homeland Security (DHS) was created by the Homeland Security Act of 2002 (Public Law 107–296), and in March 2003, TSA was moved from DOT to DHS. In addition, DHS also includes the Coast Guard, the Federal Emergency Management Agency (FEMA), Customs, Immigration, and Border Protection, and the U.S. Secret Service.

Federal spending on homeland security activities has grown from a little under $44 billion in FY 2002 to a little over $58 billion in FY 2007, as Figure 10.1 shows.[1] This spending is spread throughout the government, but the bulk of the activities are found in the recently formed Department of Homeland Security and the Department of Defense (DOD). Figure 10.2 shows the

Figure 10.1
Federal Funding of Homeland Security Activities

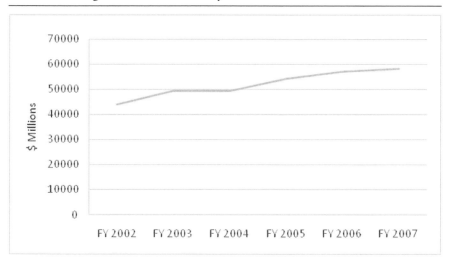

Figure 10.2
Federal Homeland Security Funding by Agency FY 2007

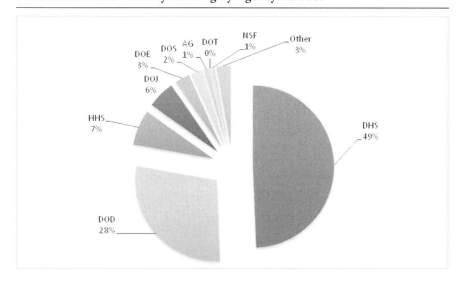

Figure 10.3
DHS Appropriations by Activity

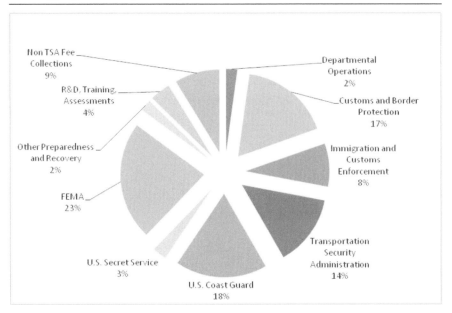

breakdown of federal funding of homeland security activities. As can be seen in the figure, nearly half the funding, 49 percent, is in DHS and another 28 percent is in DOD.

DHS responsibilities go well beyond both aviation security and the broader category of transportation security. Figure 10.3 shows the breakdown of DHS appropriations by activity. Within DHS, the Transportation Security Administration accounts for only 14 percent of the budget.

AVIATION SECURITY ACTIVITIES

TSA was given three initial mandates: (1) take responsibility for security for all modes of transportation; (2) recruit, assess, hire, train, and deploy security officers for 450 commercial airports from Guam to Alaska in 12 months; and (3) provide 100 percent screening of all checked luggage for explosives by December 31, 2002. Meeting these mandates was a difficult challenge, but TSA was able to hire, train, and deploy a federal workforce of over 50,000 passenger and baggage screeners and install equipment at more than 400 commercial airports to allow screening of all checked baggage.

As TSA has moved beyond its initial mandates, some of its other goals have proven more difficult to achieve. In August 2007, the Government Accountability Office (GAO) reported that DHS, through TSA, had generally achieved 17 of 24 of GAO's performance expectations in aviation security.[2] Among the expectations that had been met were those related to developing a strategic approach for aviation security functions; hiring, training, and deploying an aviation security workforce; developing and implementing checkpoint screening processes; and carrying out checked baggage screening. Among the expectations generally not achieved were those related to establishing effective airport perimeter security, controlling access to airport secured areas, developing the advanced prescreening system (Secure Flight, discussed below), and developing technologies to screen air cargo.

Table 10.1 shows the TSA's FY 2007 budget and the FY 2008 budget requested by the administration and passed by the House and Senate. The primary difference between the A\administration's FY 2008 request and the FY 2007 budget is the absence of the $250 million in funding for the Aviation Security Capital Fund that provided grants to airports for constructing in-line

Table 10.1
Transportation Security Administration Budget by category ($ million)

	FY 2007 Enacted	FY 2008 Administration	FY 2008 House	FY 2008 Senate
Aviation Security	5122	4953	5199	5043
Screening	3268	3266	3364	3262
Explosives Detection Systems/Explosives Trace Detection	786	704	824	786
Regulation and Other Enforcement	218	224	224	224
Airport Management, Information Technology, and Support	666	656	652	646
Air Cargo Security	135	56	73	66
Other	48	50	57	54
Aviation Security Capital Fund	250	0	0	0
Federal Air Marshal Service	719	722	722	722
Threat Assessment and Credentialing	40	78	64	67
Credentialing Fees	76	83	83	83
Surface Transportation Security	37	41	41	41
Transportation Security Support/Administration	525	525	527	522
Recision	−67			
Total	6702	6402	6636	6478

Note: FY 2007 Enacted column includes FY 2007 Supplemental.

Source: Authors' calculations, based on data from CRS Report for Congress, Homeland Security Department FY 2008 Appropriations, RL 3404, updated August 20, 2007.

explosives detection systems (EDS). The authority for this fund had been set to expire at the end of FY 2007, but a provision to extend it through 2028 was included in P.L. (Public Law) 110–53.[3] (The issue of EDS/ETD funding will be discussed below.) Another notable change in the administration's budget is an increase in funds for threat assessment and credentialing, intended to support the long-delayed Secure Flight program. Secure Flight is intended to establish a centralized system to prescreen airline passengers against terrorist watch lists. Finally, the administration budget proposes an increase in surface transportation security funding, intended for the hiring of additional inspectors and canine teams for both rail and mass transit.

The budgets passed by the House and Senate differ from the administration request in three major ways. First, both the House and Senate include substantially more for explosives detection and trace detection. As discussed later in this chapter, the United States faces a difficult challenge with regard to baggage explosives detection systems. Most of the systems currently in use were installed in 2002 and 2003. These systems are not as capable as the newer systems, either in terms of detection capability or in terms of baggage throughput. Given their age and level of utilization, they also are becoming increasingly expensive to maintain. At the same time, TSA has to evolve to respond to potential threats beyond those in checked baggage, and is field testing new technologies including whole body imaging, explosives trace detection portal machines, bottled liquid scanners, and improved X-ray and explosives detection systems for carry-on baggage. These new systems bring with them the challenge of how to fund their acquisition, installation, and operation at the nation's 500-plus commercial airports.

The second difference is that both the House and the Senate included significantly more for air cargo security. The basic dispute reflected in these budget differences is that the administration favors a risk-based targeting system based on the current known shipper program, while the House and to a lesser extent the Senate want to increase the share of air cargo that is physically inspected, particularly the cargo placed on passenger aircraft. Also, the House and Senate included funding to improve airport perimeter security, a program element that was not included in the administration's request.

The third difference is that neither the House nor the Senate has appropriated nearly as much for the Secure Flight program, reflecting frustration throughout Congress with TSA's failure "to fully articulate the goals, objectives, and requirements for the program."[4] Overall, the differences in budget proposals reflect different priorities as well as differences in defining fundamental approaches to aviation security policy.

FUNDING AVIATION SECURITY

The aviation security activities of TSA are funded by a combination of specific taxes and the general fund. Table 10.2 shows the amounts collected from

Table 10.2
Transportation Security Fee Collections ($ millions)

	2002	2003	2004	2005	2006	2007	2007 Share
September 11 Security Fee (Passengers)	1,000	1,200	1,600	1,750	1,600	1,900	76.3%
Aviation Security Infrastructure Fee (Air Carriers)	140	250	290	305	310	570	22.9%
Hazmat Threat Assessment				4.1	13	14	0.6%
Alien Flight Student Pilot Fee				1.8	2.3	3.3	0.1%
Indirect Air Carrier (Air Cargo)						3	0.1%
Registered Traveler Fee						0.6	0.0%

Source: Transportation Security Administration, http://www.tsa.gov/research/fees/fee_data.shtm.

the specific taxes used to fund TSA. By far the largest fee in terms of revenue is the September 11 Security Fee, which is imposed on airline passengers at the rate of $2.50 per enplanement with a maximum of two enplanements per one-way trip. Thus a passenger making a connection on both the outbound and inbound portions of a trip would pay a total fee of $10.00. As can be seen in the far right-hand column of the table, this fee accounted for over 76 percent of all transportation security fee collections in 2007. In the past, this fee has been a point of contention between Congress and the administration. Prior to the FY 2008 budget request, the administration had repeatedly sought an increase in this fee, but Congress had not supported the request. In the FY 2008 administration budget request, no increase in this fee was sought.

The other significant fee, in terms of revenue collected, is the Aviation Security Infrastructure Fee, which amounted to $570 million in 2007, or nearly 23 percent of the total collected. This fee is collected from the airlines and is intended to reflect costs related to functions taken over by TSA that had previously been provided by the airlines. The fee is designed to reflect the costs of passenger and baggage screening in 2000, to the extent that the September 11 Security Fee was insufficient to cover TSA's costs for aviation security.[5]

There are four other transportation security fees, three related to aviation and one to surface transport. Taken together, they amounted to less than 1 percent of all transportation security fees collected in 2007. The three aviation related fees are the Alien Flight Student Pilot Fee, a charge of $130 to conduct a background check for each non-U.S. citizen seeking flight training, the Indirect Air Carrier Management System Fee for freight forwarders, and the Registered Traveler Fee. The only transportation security fee not related to aviation is a fee to participate in the HAZMAT Endorsement Threat Assessment Program, which conducts threat assessments for any driver seeking to obtain a hazardous materials endorsement on a state-issued commercial driver's license.

COSTS BORNE BY AIRPORTS

The traffic declines in the wake of September 11 disrupted a long-sustained period of growth in airport volumes. This resulted in lower revenues and passenger facility charges. This had major effects on airport economics, as a successful airport business model combines a high rate of asset utilization with a strong nonaeronautical revenue stream. In 2000, the Airports Council International reported that average airport profits after tax were about 2 percent of gross operating revenues; in 2001, airports essentially broke even, with many airports reporting losses for the first time ever. In the United States, the FAA estimated that operating profit margins were cut in half at hub airports overall.[6] In monetary terms, this represented a decline of about $820 million in operating profits for the 508 commercial airports in the United States between 2000 and 2002. By 2004, however, traffic volumes had recovered, along with airport revenues.

However, airports have experienced higher ongoing security costs that have not been reimbursed by the federal government or recouped from airline charges.[7] Estimation of ongoing security operating costs for airports is made difficult because of the variety of organizational and financial structures under which they operate. For example, residual financing structures obligate the airlines to make payment of all costs not offset by nonairline revenue sources. Other airports operate on a not-for-profit status, in which public funds are appropriated to cover funding shortfalls, or charges are designed based on a pass-through basis. The ultimate incidence of security costs is sometimes difficult to identify.

Airport financial reports and associated press releases that attempt to separate out security-related costs indicate that such expenditures represent about one-fourth of major airports' income. The identified costs range from 3 percent to just over 7 percent of operating revenues. Data from the Federal Aviation Administration Compliance Activity Tracking System (CATS) reports show that the 508 commercial service airports in the United States had 2006 operating revenues of $13.5 billion.[8] A mid-point estimate of security costs of 5 percent indicates that operating expenses for security were approximately $675 million. It should be noted that this estimate does not represent incremental spending since September 11, but rather total amounts. While incremental costs are hard to calculate, industry analysts suggest that these costs are 30–50 percent higher than previously.

The other major effect on airports is the significant and ongoing capital expenditures required to meet new security regulations, including retrofits of terminal spaces for explosives screening equipment and efforts to make property perimeters and access points more secure. Historically, capital expenditures on security-related items had averaged about $50–$60 million per year; during FY 2002 (following September 11), security projects from the FAA's Airport Improvement Program (AIP) represented 17 percent of the total AIP grants, equal to $560 million.

For 2001–5, the FAA estimated that planned capital development at airports eligible for federal aid would total $46 billion or approximately $9 billion annually.[9] The Airports Council International—North America (ACI-NA) estimated that total capital spending during the 2002–6 period for all commercial airports (not just federally eligible ones) would total $75 billion, or about $15 billion per year.[10] On the basis of types of investments, ACI-NA estimates that 3 percent of capital spending is specifically for safety and security projects. This represents about $1.4 billion over 2002–6, or just under $300 million annually. This amount is likely understated, as many of the investments defined as capacity enhancements or to meet regulatory standards have a security component as well. If 5 percent of these other categories were of this type, it would indicate a security-related capital program on the order of $500 million annually. Looking ahead, ACI-NA estimates that airport capital spending will need to rise to $87.4 billion for 2007–11 ($17.5 billion annually) to meet industry growth and standards.[11] The security-related portion of this five-year sum is expected to rise to 5.3 percent of total capital spending, representing approximately $4.7 billion, or about $940 million annually.

COSTS BORNE BY AIRLINES

The airlines have served as intermediaries for many of the fees and charges levied for security. The direct charge for the September 11 fee on passengers was $1.9 billion in FY 2007, while the airline payment of the Aviation Security Infrastructure Fee (ASIF) had risen to $570 million in FY 2007. In addition, Immigration and Customs Inspection Fees paid by the airlines totaled approximately $1 billion in FY 2007. In total, direct fee payments were approximately $3.5 billion, having risen from $2.5 billion in FY 2004. The demand-reducing effect of these fees is also significant. Rossiter and Dresner indicate that in 2002, just over 2 million passengers diverted from air to auto travel as a result of the new security fee.[12] This represents approximately $380 million in lost airline revenues; at a 5 percent operating margin, this translates into foregone operating profits of about $20 million annually.

A second financial impact on airlines is the costs of certain security requirements, including freight and mail restrictions and the provision of seats for air marshals, that prevent air carriers from collecting these revenues from business operations. The Air Transport Association estimated these items at $518 million in FY 2004.[13] If we adjust for yield growth between 2004 and 2007 for cargo, mail, and passengers, we estimate that these foregone revenues totaled approximately $560 million in FY 2007. Since these services were already being performed, the incremental profits would be a significant proportion of these foregone revenues.

A third impact and financial burden on airlines is the cost of regulatory mandates that are not reimbursed. For example, the requirement to harden cockpit doors to restrict access to the flight decks has been estimated to cost $300 million, only about one-third of which was reimbursed. Additional ramp security, aircraft inspections, passenger document verification, and enhanced employee background screening added significant costs as well. The Air Transport Association estimated these additional expenditures at $739 million in calendar year 2004.[14] We estimate that more than half of these items are recurring expenses; with inflation, these costs are calculated at more than $400 million in FY 2007.

THE COST TO DOMESTIC TRAVELERS OF ENHANCED SECURITY MEASURES

Travelers have had to bear the costs of enhanced security in the wake of September 11 in a variety of forms. Perhaps the greatest cost component on travelers is the added time they must spend at airports in anticipation of the potential delays in going through security checkpoints. Passengers have always varied in their behavior in terms of how long before to their flight they arrived at the airport, with some tending to arrive just before departure and others arriving well in advance. Prior to September 11, a common rule of thumb for passengers was to arrive at the airport an hour before a domestic flight was scheduled to depart. After September 11, the Transportation Security Administration (TSA) recommendation was to arrive two hours before flight time.

Recently, TSA has worked to bring average security wait times down, but there is still considerable variability in how long passengers can expect to wait at any given airport. When TSA was formed within the Department of Transportation, the secretary established a goal that passengers be processed through passenger screening checkpoints in 10 minutes or less.[15] TSA has made progress in bringing down the waiting times at security checkpoints, and by FY 2006, the average peak wait time for all categories of airports was 8.2 minutes.[16]

However, this figure is misleading for travel planning purposes for several reasons. First, at large airports where most of the travel takes place, the wait times are longer. In FY 2006, the average peak wait time at so-called Category X airports was 12.6 minutes and at Category I airports it was 10.4 minutes.[17] Second, these averages conceal considerable variation from airport to airport, from day to day, and from hour to hour. Using TSA's website to check expected wait times, one finds that at almost all of the largest airports, there are maximum wait times on some days at some times that often exceed 25 to

Table 10.3
Time Costs for Domestic Travelers Because of Anticipated
Security Delays ($ million)

Year	Large Hub Originations	Medium Hub Originations	Delay Cost to Travelers (ATA VOT)	Delay Cost to Travelers (FAA VOT)	Delay Cost to Travelers (Minumum VOT)
2006	357,438,106	101,963,067	$ 24,391	$ 19,692	$13,312
2005	355,454,890	103,065,117	$ 23,588	$ 19,044	$ 12,874
2004	339,124,899	98,656,464	$ 21,713	$ 17,530	$ 11,851
2003	324,815,977	80,543,475	$ 19,536	$ 15,773	$ 10,662
2002	312,661,338	88,868,797	$ 18,582	$ 15,003	$ 10,142
Total	1,689,495,210	473,096,920	$ 107,809	$ 87,043	$ 58,841

Source: Authors' calculations.

40 minutes.[18] Finally, the time TSA measures as wait time is not the time it takes to get through the security checkpoint or even the time it takes to get to the screening equipment. Rather, it is the time that elapses between when a traveler gets in line at security and when the traveler reaches the point where he or she is assigned to a lane for screening. At many airports, the wait once you've been assigned to a lane can be considerable.

Table 10.3 summarizes an analysis of the costs imposed on travelers in domestic markets due to the added time they must spend at airports to allow for increased potential delays at security checkpoints. The goal of the analysis was to estimate the order of magnitude of these costs, and several assumptions were made in order to do that. The assumptions were intended to be conservative. First, it was assumed that there were additions to wait time only at large hub and medium hub airports and that the average added time spent at the airport at large hubs was 45 minutes and at medium hubs 30 minutes. In light of the actual experiences with delays at large and medium hub airports, these seem like conservative assumptions for the period. Second, it was assumed that the historical pattern that 70 percent of enplanements at large and medium hub airports were of passengers originating at that airport, as opposed to connecting passengers, prevailed during the years 2002 to 2006.[19]

The guidelines used by the U.S. Department of Transportation (DOT) for the value of time is to value time at the wage rate for intercity business travel and at 70 percent of the wage rate for intercity personal travel.[20] For domestic airline travel, the Air Transport Association assumes that 41 percent of travel is for business and 59 percent is for leisure or personal travel.[21] For the wage rates, three different approaches were taken in the table. The first was to use wage rates based on surveys done by the Air Transport Association in 1996 and then adjusted to 2006 using Bureau of Labor Statistics (BLS) Wage Indices. The second approach was to use the wage rates that the FAA used in 2006 in its analysis of congestion at LaGuardia airport. These wage rates were then adjusted for the prior years using the BLS Wage Indices.[22] This approach probably gives the best estimate of the costs to travelers. Finally, a third approach was taken to try to give a lower boundary by using the BLS hourly wage rate for the category of "management, professional, and related" for business travel and the category of "all civilians" for leisure travel. These figures almost certainly understate the average wage rates for business and leisure air travelers.

As can be seen in the table, the costs to travelers are substantial, even using the minimum value of the time figures. For 2006, these costs were at least $13 billion and could have been as high as $24 billion. For the entire five-year period from 2002 through 2006, the total costs ranged between $59 billion and $108 billion. Even the lowest of these figures is twice as large as the TSA budget during these years.

There are additional costs imposed on travelers due to enhanced security. One obvious cost is the added tax of $2.50 per flight segment (up to a maximum of $5.00 per one-way trip) discussed elsewhere in this chapter. The out-of-pocket costs for taxes are substantially less than the time costs. Another cost is the added inconvenience of travel because of the increased restrictions over what can be placed in carry-on luggage. Restrictions such as those on the quantity of liquids and gels that can be carried on have caused some travelers to check baggage that, absent those restrictions, they would have carried on.[23] Checking baggage, of course, incurs additional delays while waiting for it to be brought to baggage claim and still greater delays and inconvenience if the baggage is lost.

Because of the added time costs of air travel coupled with the added out-of-pocket costs in the form of security fees, some travelers have opted to substitute highway travel for air travel, particularly for relatively short-haul trips. Highway travel is less safe than air travel, and the result of these diversions could well be additional highway fatalities. Rossiter and Dresner have done a careful analysis of the potential added highway deaths from such passenger diversions.[24] They conclude that due to the segment fee of $2.50 and an added wait time at the airport of 20 minutes, there would be a little over three added deaths per year from the diversion from short haul air travel to auto travel. Even if their results were to be adjusted to the longer added wait times that we project, the effect of added security time and cost on transportation fatalities is likely to be quite small.

FINANCIAL IMPACTS OF SECURITY IMPROVEMENTS

The United States faces some significant financial investments if it's to improve the security of air travel. TSA has estimated that it will cost over $23 billion just to install inline explosives detection systems for checked baggage in the 250 largest airports in the United States.[25] Of this amount, about $6 billion is in capital costs while the remainder is in personnel, operations, and maintenance costs. Moreover, cost reductions are difficult to achieve even if implementation is scaled back. For example, were the scope of these installations to be reduced to only the top 100 airports, the costs would decrease by only about $120 million, less than 1 percent, over the life of the project.[26] Expenditures of this magnitude are not easily accommodated in TSA's budget. Indeed, if the current rate of spending is maintained, the completion of the installation of the systems would not occur until well after 2020.[27]

Explosives detection systems for checked baggage aren't the only investments that will be needed. Improved systems are needed for checking carry-on bags and passengers for explosives and weapons. It also seems likely in the future that there will be increased pressure to install biometric systems to screen passengers. These systems will also likely be expensive and further stretch TSA's capability to invest.

A contentious question is how the costs of these systems will be shared between airports and the federal government. In addition to purchasing the equipment, systems such as in-line explosives detection systems can have large up-front costs for the airport modifications needed to accommodate the systems. To help defray these costs, the initial approach, in 2003, was for Congress to authorize TSA to reimburse airports up to 75 percent of the cost to install these systems by entering "letter of intent" (LOI) agreements. An LOI was not a binding commitment of federal funding, but instead represented TSA's intent to provide the agreed-upon funds in future years if the agency receives sufficient appropriations to cover the agreement. TSA issued eight letters of intent, but has issued none since 2004. The process has not gone entirely smoothly. As GAO reported,

In September 2003, TSA and the City of Los Angeles signed an LOI and an attached memorandum of agreement (LOI/MOA) in which TSA agreed to pay an amount not to exceed 75 percent of the agreed upon estimated total project cost of $341 million (about $256 million) to install in-line checked baggage screening systems at both Los Angeles (LAX) and Ontario (ONT) International Airports. However, in December 2003, officials from the City of Los Angeles' airport authority—Los Angeles World Airports (LAWA)—informed TSA that aspects of the design concept were infeasible and that additional construction modifications would be needed. LAWA subsequently submitted a revised cost estimate to TSA in April 2005 and requested that TSA amend the LOI/MOA to increase the federal reimbursement by about $122 million. TSA has not amended the LOI to provide for additional reimbursements; however, as of February 2007, TSA had obligated the $256 million for the City of Los Angeles LOI/MOA in accordance with the schedule agreed to in the LOI and had reimbursed LAWA for about $26 million in expenses.[28]

The working group that advised TSA on baggage screening investment noted that checked baggage screening is a federal responsibility under the Aviation and Transportation Security Act of 2001 (ATSA) (Public Law 107–71). Not surprisingly, the airline and airport members of the group felt that the federal government should be responsible for all of the funding necessary to achieve this mandate, including replacing or upgrading the initially deployed systems that are not up to the desired standards. Others in the working group felt that there should be more cost sharing, and no agreement was reached on a specific cost-sharing formula. The working group's final report, however, showed the airports and airlines covering 12 percent of the capital costs and 53 percent of the operating and maintenance costs, or 15 percent of the overall costs of the projects.[29]

The airports' position on cost sharing is clear. Their trade organization, Airports Council International (ACI), takes the view that costs should be borne by the government agency and not the airport. ACI goes on to maintain that airports are within their rights to charge a rental fee to the government agencies for the use of airport facilities and infrastructure.[30] This view recognizes that airport space is scarce and valuable, in that it can be rented out for various concessions, and so there is an opportunity cost to the space occupied by security devices.

FUNDING OPTIONS FOR LARGE CAPITAL INVESTMENTS

Irrespective of what the federal government's precise share of these investments should be, the federal government is almost certain to have to shoulder the burden of paying for most of the security improvements, so it will be faced with having to make large capital investments. The methods used to finance large capital investments are typically very different in the private sector than in the federal government. Private-sector organizations typically finance large capital investments by borrowing some or all of the required funds from a bank or other lending institution, by using their own financial resources, or by using some form of third-party financing or equity arrangement. They may also use alliances with other firms, joint ventures, sale-and-leaseback, and public-private partnerships. All of these approaches involve varying levels of risk, and some incur debt.

In the federal government, significant capital or facilities investments are primarily funded from the annual budget. With very few exceptions, individual departments and agencies may not borrow funds or otherwise incur debt to finance facilities. They must receive authorization from Congress for up-front funding to cover the full design and construction or purchase costs in a specific fiscal year's budget. Similarly, leases can be used only under carefully controlled circumstances, which generally follow this same up-front funding approach.

From the federal budget perspective, the requirement for full, up-front funding of federal facilities is intended to do the following:

1. Give adequate scrutiny to the initial costs and proposed benefits of an investment;
2. Avoid the risk of allowing projects to be started through incremental funding before they are adequately scrutinized;
3. Give Congress the flexibility to respond to changing circumstances and priorities;

4. Provide for transparency in the budget by making sure the investment proposal is understandable to a range of constituencies; and

5. Allow for the informed participation of those constituencies.

Under current procedures, requests to design and construct a new facility, to fund the major renovation of an existing facility, or to purchase a facility outright are scored up front in the year requested, even though the actual costs may be incurred over several years. Thus, the projected costs are counted against the agency's overall budget request for a given fiscal year. The requirement for full, up-front funding typically results in a spike in a department's or agency's budget request. If the agency is subject to spending caps and if it is to stay within its cap, a request for a significant facility investment will force cuts in other programs or activities within the department or agency, causing tension among the various in-house decision-making and operating groups.

These scorekeeping procedures used by budget agencies may have some unintended consequences. In spite of the intentions of the budget agencies, up-front scoring of major capital projects does not typically disclose the full costs of these investment decisions. It only discloses the projected design and construction costs. Facilities operation, maintenance, repair, and disposal costs are accounted for in different functional areas of the budget and are not linked to the decision to build or acquire specific facilities. Scorekeeping procedures create incentives for agencies to drive down the initial costs of facilities investments—even at the expense of life-cycle costs—in order to lessen their apparent impact on the current year's budget. In rewarding such behavior, the scorekeeping procedures can indirectly increase the long-term operation and maintenance costs of facilities—which can account for 90 to 95 percent of their life-cycle costs—and decrease the operating efficiencies that might result from additional initial investment.[31]

Recognizing some of the difficulties of providing adequate funding for required facilities investments through the annual budget process, legislation has been enacted over the years on a case-by-case basis for individual departments and agencies to allow the use of alternative approaches to acquiring or making investments in facilities. Legislation allowing the use of these approaches on a government-wide basis has not occurred, largely because of the strong and continuing opposition of government-wide oversight groups—Office of Management and Budget (OMB), Congressional Budget Office (CBO), and Congress.

In this environment, it's not surprising that the working group that examined baggage screening investments leaned heavily toward pay-as-you-go financing in making four financing recommendations:

1. tax credit bonds;

2. continued appropriations for the procurement and installation of EDS machines;

3. combined line items for the purchase and installation of EDS machines in order to provide TSA with increased flexibility in directing the funding where it is most needed; and

4. enhanced eligibility for the Passenger Facility Charge (PFC).[32]

The last three options are essentially pay-as-you-go approaches. Only the first, tax credit bonds, would be considered an investment strategy in which the capital is installed up front but the payments to cover the cost of that capital are spread over the useful life of the investment. Tax credit bonds are a relatively new form of debt that has gained some favor as a means to finance public capital expenditures for transportation (and other programs). The bonds, whose use must be specifically authorized by Congress, allow investors to receive a nonrefundable tax credit against their federal income tax liability instead of a cash interest payment. In essence, these bonds would provide a federal subsidy outside of the normal budget process.

While using tax-credit bonds would be more expensive than borrowing from the Federal Financing Bank, they would be of the same or lower cost than tax-exempt municipal or authority bonds. (The cost would be lower because they would be issued at the federal rather than the state or local level.) Bondholders would report the tax credit as income, but then would subtract the amount of the credit from the tax due. While the issuer would not receive annual interest payments, it would be required to establish a reserve for eventual principal repayment.

Tax-credit bonds have been proposed for use in school modernization and for green space acquisition—two activities that may have understood benefits but lack clearly defined and secured revenue streams. They also were proposed for use by Amtrak and for investment in high-speed rail. However, they have been opposed by the Treasury, and the way they would be "scored" is not clear. The Federal Financing Bank has centralized control of agency borrowing through its on-lending policy. The FFB does offer cheaper terms than private capital markets, but it appears restricted in its availability to TSA. In order for TSA to be a significant user of the FFB facility, congressional authorization is likely to be required.

In the current environment, bond financing for transportation security investments does not appear to hold much promise. Direct access to private long-term debt markets by TSA or DHS is limited by congressional authority, by budget scoring rules, and by the lack of a bankable organizational and financial/economic structure. For TSA to have options in the bond market, key policy considerations would have to be met. In particular, there would be a need for a legally independent structure, the ability to transfer assets to serve as collateral, and the ability to dedicate clear funding streams. As a government agency with a largely regulatory function, it seems unlikely that TSA would be organized along these lines. As a result, funding the next generation of security technologies across the entire aviation system remains a huge and unsolved problem.

SUMMARY AND CONCLUSIONS

The costs and burdens of aviation security have been borne by a variety of stakeholders, including airlines, airports, and taxpayers through government fees and charges. We estimate that recurring capital and operating costs related to aviation security as of 2007 are on the order of $10–$15 billion annually. In addition, another major cost of additional security screening has been delay costs imposed on passengers, which we estimate at approximately $13–$24 billion annually. We would not expect any of these costs to decrease significantly in the medium term; in fact, replacement of screening and detection equipment and additional capacity to keep up with the growth in air commerce is likely to result in higher costs going forward.

However, we should note five important caveats with regard to our estimates. First, we have tried to focus on the ongoing costs of aviation security, rather than measure the shorter-term economic dislocations from September 11. Second, security is typically not a line item in budgets or in accounts, so that estimating such costs requires extensive assumptions. Even the Department of Homeland Security budget contains programs that cut across security and non-security-related activities. Third, security spending has both capital and operating components. We have attempted to estimate capital costs on an annual basis. However, the high technology component of much of the capital investment means that these are not assets with especially long lives. This implies that the costs of aviation security should include significant recurring capital expenditures. Fourth, the ultimate burden of aviation security costs may not be on the entity that actually makes the payment of a tax or charge. For example, the extent to which airline or airport security costs can be passed on to customers may vary both in degree and over time. This issue is at the heart of discussions of the appropriate allocation of security costs between industry, users, and society overall. Finally, the estimation of security costs here does not attempt to estimate corresponding benefits, or the degree to which enhanced activities have increased aviation security.[33]

NOTES

1. Year-to-year comparisons, particularly using FY 2002, may not be directly comparable, because over time, agencies have improved their ability to distinguish between homeland security and non–homeland security activities.

2. Government Accountability Office, *Aviation Security: DHS Has Made Progress in Securing the Commercial Aviation System, but Key Challenges Remain*, Statement of Cathleen A. Berrick, Director Homeland Security and Justice Issues, GAO-08–139T (Washington, DC: GAO, October 2007).

3. *CRS Report for Congress, Homeland Security Department: FY 2008 Appropriations*, updated August 20, 2007 (Washington, DC: Congressional Research Service, 2007), 42.

4. Ibid., 48.

5. For more detail on this fee, see Transportation Security Administration, http://www.tsa.gov/research/fees/aircarrier_fee.shtm.

6. Hub airports are defined as all airports enplaning more than .0 percent of total U.S. passenger traffic. This represents 134 airports that serve more than 90 percent of U.S. passenger traffic.

7. For a review of these issues from the industry perspective, see Airports Council International, *The Economic Impact of September 11 on Airports* (Geneva: ACI, January 2002).

8. See FAA, http://cats.airports.faa.gov/. The database reports financial statements for commercial airports for the 1996–2007 period.

9. See General Accountability Office, *Airport Finance: Observations on Planned Airport Development Costs and Funding Levels and the Administration's Proposed Changes in the Airport Improvement Program*, Report, GAO-07–885, (Washington, DC: GAO, June 2007).

10. See Airports Council International–North America, *Airport Capital Development Costs 2007–2011* (Washington, DC: ACI-NA, May 2007), http://www.aci-na.org/docs/Capital%20Needs%20Survey%20Report%202007%20FINAL.pdf.

11. Ibid.

12. Adrianna Rossiter and Martin Dresner, "The Impact of the September 11th Security Fee and Passenger Wait Time on Traffic Diversion and Highway Fatalities," *Journal of Air Transport Management* 10, no. 4 (July 2004): 225–30.

13. See *Statement of James C. May, President and CEO, Air Transport Association, before the United States Senate Commerce, Science, and Transportation Committee*, June 22, 2004, http://www.airlines.org/government/testimony/ATA+Testimony+-+Oral+Statement+from+ATA+President+and+CEO+James+C+May+Concerning+Aviation+Security.htm.

14. Ibid.

15. Government Accountability Office, *Aviation Security: TSA's Staffing Allocation Model Is Useful for Allocating Staff among Airports, but Its Assumptions Should Be Systematically Reassessed*, Report to Congressional Committees, GAO-07–299 (Washington, DC: U.S. GPO, February 2007), 26.

16. Ibid., Table 2.

17. Taken together, Category X and Category I airports are roughly equivalent to FAA-designated Large Hub and Medium Hub airports.

18. See Transportation Security Administration, "Security Checkpoint Wait Times," http://waittime.tsa.dhs.gov/index.html.

19. Bureau of Transportation Statistics, U. S. Department of Transportation, http://www.bts.gov/programs/airline_information/air_carrier_traffic_statistics/airtraffic/annual/1981–2001.html.

20. Bureau of Transportation Statistics, U. S. Department of Transportation, http://ostpxweb.ost.dot.gov/policy/Data/VOT97guid.pdf.

21. Bureau of Transportation Statistics, U. S. Department of Transportation, http://www.airlines.org/economics/specialtopics/Econ+FAQs.htm.

22. Bureau of Transportation Statistics, U. S. Department of Transportation, http://www.bls.gov/web/echistrynaics.pdf.

23. Bureau of Transportation Statistics, U. S. Department of Transportation, http://www.tsa.gov/travelers/airtravel/prohibited/permitted-prohibited-items.shtm.

24. See Rossiter and Dresner, "The Impact of the September 11th Security Fee and Passenger Wait Time on Traffic Diversion and Highway Fatalities."

25. United States Government Accountability Office, Testimony before the Subcommittee on Aviation, Committee on Transportation and Infrastructure, House of

Representatives, *AVIATION SECURITY: TSA Has Strengthened Efforts to Plan for the Optimal Deployment of Checked Baggage Screening Systems, but Funding Uncertainties Remain*, Statement of Cathleen A. Berrick, Director Homeland Security and Justice Issues, GAO-06–875T, June 29, 2006.

26. *Working Group Report, Baggage Screening Investment Study*, prepared for: Aviation Security Advisory Committee, prepared by Baggage Screening Investment Study Working Group, August 9, 2006, http://www.aci-na.org/docs/BSIS%20Working%20 Group%20Report_Final_080906%20wb.pdf.

27. "Airports Praise H.R.1 Language for More Security Funding," *Aviation Daily*, January 12, 2007, 6.

28. United States Government Accountability Office, GAO Report to Congressional Committees, *AVIATION SECURITY: Cost Estimates Related to TSA Funding of Checked Baggage Screening Systems at Los Angeles and Ontario Airports*, GAO-07–445, March 2007.

29. See Table 1–1 in *Working Group Report, Baggage Screening Investment Study*.

30. *The Application of Biometrics at Airports*, position paper (Geneva: ACI World Headquarters, November 2005).

31. National Research Council, *Investments in Federal Facilities: Asset Management Strategies for the 21st Century* (Washington, DC: National Academies Press, 2004).

32. *Working Group Report, Baggage Screening Investment Study*.

33. For a discussion of these issues, see General Accounting Office, *Aviation Security: Progress since September 11, 2001, and the Challenges Ahead*, Report, GAO-03–1150T (Washington, DC: GAO, September 9, 2003); General Accountability Office, *Aviation Security: DHS Has Made Progress in Securing the Commercial Aviation System, but Key Challenges Remain*, Report, GAO-08–139T (Washington, DC: GAO, October 16, 2007). For a critique of aviation security policy, see Robert Poole and James Carafano, *Time to Rethink Airport Security*, Backgrounder Report no. 1955 (Washington, DC: Heritage Foundation, July 26, 2006).

CHAPTER 11

Future of Aviation Security: "Fast, Cheap, and Out of Control"

Mark B. Salter

Fast, reliable, seamless, profitable, efficient, and secure mobility is a sine qua non of contemporary globalization. Civil aviation is a vital artery for global civil society, politics, diplomacy, international relations, and economics. Through exponential reductions in average transportation and communication costs, the aviation sector consistently trends toward growth. Passenger volumes have increased steadily across the twentieth century, taking massive leaps with each new generation of jetliner, wide-body, and stretch jets, jumbo jets, and new larger aircraft. Large amounts of high-value, low-weight cargo, as well as perishables, are shipped by global air freight. Passenger and cargo traffic are predicted to increase nearly 5 percent per year in the foreseeable future, according to IATA figures. The current civil aviation sector is operating at 80–90 percent capacity, and the imminent increases in passenger, cargo, and aircraft movements will necessitate a fundamental rethinking of business models, regulations, and infrastructure.[1] Global trends toward privatization, deregulation, and neoliberalism have led to a revolutionary decentralization of the sector, in an increasingly complex network of networks. These dynamics are structured by public norms, in other words, the balance of risk, freedom, mobility, rights, and privacy that the public is willing to accept. Aviation security is fundamental to the success of global civil aviation—without customers, there is no aviation sector.

Aviation security is a complex, interdependent system of systems, in which international, national, local, and commercial interests shape expectations, norms, measures, and policies. In an environment of incredible density, networked security is dependent on the least-equipped police force, the most over-taxed screener, the greediest operator, the least comprehensible regulations, and the most nefarious plans. The network is at once integrated and decentralized: air cargo system, civil aviation systems, and airports. We must also consider the integrity of the communication, information, and navigation systems that manage those flows. The primary historical driver of change in aviation security has been reaction to failure, and we cannot predict with any great success the place or kind of the next great failure. This chapter identifies three axes of change that will shape the future of aviation security: technology, governance, and public norms.

The history of aviation security measures clearly demonstrates the degree to which disasters, crises, and threats have driven innovation.[2] Successful and unsuccessful attacks can have an equal impact on policies, perceptions, and acceptable practices. Walk-through X-ray portals were adopted after widespread hijacking in the United States; explosive detection devices were implemented after the attempted bombing by Richard Reid; limits on liquid and gels were implemented after the planned transatlantic attacks. Since terrorists and criminals are faster entrepreneurs than governments and corporations, we cannot predict new attacks, the next generation of technologies, or the subsequent public responses.

Security has both objective and subjective conditions. We can objectively measure threats against civil aviation, the number and kind of system failures, and the number of failed or successful attacks. But equally important is the *subjective perception* of security by the general public, the flying public, commercial actors, corporate boards, shareholders, regulators, professional risk managers, insurers, and policing experts. It is important to understand that future aviation security will be determined not only by the limits of technology or governance, but also, importantly, by the limits of public acceptance and market tolerance of risk. When faced with invasive security screening, regulative strangulation, complexity or ambiguity, or impossibly thin profit margins, the aviation industry could suffer a death by a thousand cuts. To understand the future of aviation security, we must focus equally on the *objective* integrity of the system and the *imagined* or *perceived* integrity of the system. Within this chapter, we can lay out some of the determinants, some of the possible avenues of change.

KEY ISSUES

To plot the possible future of aviation security, we can point to three axes of change: technology, governance, and public norms. Technology is central for the detection of dangerous and prohibited items, the tracking and the identification of individuals and cargo, and the administration of the system as a whole. Private and public security regimes take their shape from corporate governance norms, national regulatory regimes, and international standards and recommended practices. And, as argued above, all of these factors are dependent on the needs and attitudes of the public.

Technology

There are three technological drivers of aviation security: miniaturization, radical increases in computing power and the ability to store and share data, and the predominance of flexible designs. We see an increasing trend of horizontal and vertical technological integration, where security systems increasingly talk to one another. Integrated gateways can use biometric authentication for frequent-flyer identification, travel authorization, document verification, and explosives and narcotics detection. Similarly, integrated baggage, millimeter-scan or backscatter X-rays, and document verification systems provide a single go/no go message for operators, based on a multilevel analysis of triggers.

One of the predominant trends in technological innovation has been miniaturization: the size of processors, memory, and detection equipment has decreased exponentially in the past decade. The new standards in biometric passports are possible because of advances in chip, RFID, and contactless reader technology, advances that have also been applied to airside security.[3] Rather than a simple machine-readable numerical code, today's passports contain a great deal of personal information. The trial of RFID chips in luggage handling is also made possible due to miniaturization, and allows a refined and robust tracking system,[4] including the policing of sterile areas. Similarly, miniaturization drives the new advances in millimeter-scan and backscatter X-rays, explosives detection systems, and CAT scanners. While of each of these technologies has improved the detection capacity of many nodes in aviation security, the human factor remains the slowest—but most flexible—part of the screening process.

One of the prime drivers of global integration, and one that is characteristic of contemporary globalization, is the increase in processing power and storage capacity, and the corresponding decrease in telecommunications costs. Governments, corporations, and private actors have access to much more data, which can be analyzed quickly and easily, and communicated across the globe instantaneously. In the new security environment, governments and even some airlines are generating "no-fly" or security watch lists, integrating public and government data.[5] The exchange of API/PNR (advance passenger information and passenger name record) data between the European Union and the United States is emblematic of these new trends. More data is being gathered and the ability of risk algorithms and "fuzzy-logic" programs to sift through this data is increasing.

A second key revolution in technology and design is the standardization of global regulations, practices, and policies, which allows for flexibility and intelligent designs. For example, the standardization of the shipping container led to a dramatic reduction in global transportation costs. E-mail and "Voice over Internet Protocols" have led to a dramatic reduction in global communication costs. While airports are fixed nodes in the global civil aviation system, within those sites, airport and security authorities are becoming increasingly flexible in the way they arrange screening points and other security measures. Along with legacy hub-and-spoke systems, new point-to-point systems are emerging that make the aviation network more flexible and more adaptable. There is a problem corresponding to this integration of transportation, information, communication, and infrastructure networks. The greater the integration of systems, the greater the efficiency, the less slack, but also the more vulnerable the systems are. A tight transportation network will suffer more greatly from a single attack than a loose network.[6] In legacy systems or designs, one could designate a single clear chokepoint at which to complete security screening. Within a complex system, there is no single chokepoint, which makes the system more robust but more vulnerable. Technological change, changes in regulations, and market imperatives are driving the global aviation system toward more efficiency and more flexibility, which makes the task of aviation security that much more difficult.

Governance

The international civil aviation system has always been governed by sovereign states, who agree by necessity on certain global "standards and recommended practices" (SARPs) set by the International Civil Aviation Organization (ICAO). ICAO is the organization formed by the Chicago Treaty, consisting of 188 contracting states. It is a functional international organization aimed at facilitating global travel, rather than a political organization such as the United Nations Security Council or the World Trade Organization, both of which may impose sanctions.[7] The standards for global aviation security are set in Annex 17 of the Chicago Treaty, which has been amended 11 times and explained in the *ICAO Security Manual* (Doc. 8973).[8] Two crucial innovations in the description and governing of aviation have come about as a result of major disasters. After the successful bombing of Pan Am 103 over Lockerbie, Scotland, ICAO convened the Aviation Security Panel of Experts. The panel reports to the ICAO Secretariat and Council on the risks, threats, and trends in aviation security. The *Aviation Security Plan of Action*, resolved and implemented after the September 11 attacks, established the ICAO Universal Security Audit Program. Under this program, all contracting states are audited by an international ICAO team of security experts, although at present the results are confidential and shared only with the designated national aviation security authority. Sovereign states also have the absolute right to deviate from the Annex 17 SARPs with a notification of noncompliance. Within these dynamics, sovereign states are exclusively responsible for aviation security, although ICAO establishes global norms. The aviation system regime is consequently based on a foundation of similar norms, but in practice is composed of a set of over 200 different systems, each with national variations according to culture, language, capacity, and inclination. Accepting that the ICAO SARPs are norms, rather than laws, we can still make some generalizations about the national regulation of aviation security.

From the patchwork of national regulations, we can identify neoliberalism as the dominant trend in the governance of aviation security. Neoliberalism is a method of governance assuming that the government itself is less efficient than the marketplace at providing services. While government intervention is needed in areas of market failure, such as education, environmental protection, judicial processes, and national security, the market is better at providing health, insurance, natural resources management, infrastructure, and so forth. Within aviation security, examples of this are the privatization of air traffic control in Canada or the pre–September 11 privatization of airport security in the United States.[9] This follows the deregulation and privatization of national aviation infrastructures. American airspace deregulated in 1978, European in 1997, and major Asian markets, such as China, India, New Zealand, Japan, and Australia have deregulated in turn to varying degrees. The privatization of airports themselves has also accelerated in recent years.[10] As a consequence, a number of important airport, airside services, and information/communications management companies are coming to dominate the global market.[11]

These trends have two consequences for aviation security, demonstrating both centrifugal and centripetal forces. Aviation security is a service, and subject to the same pressures and tensions of the global marketplace as any other international service (such as insurance, banking, or consulting). Ownership of key airports and airlines is both consolidating and proliferating. While the privatization of the industry is allowing for more varied and diffuse ownership, key service providers are consolidating in dominant firms like Fraport/British Airport Authorities, Swissport, SITA/General Electric, Smiths, or L3. Because aviation security is provided at catering facilities, airside checkpoints, fixed-base operations such as aviation fuel farms, air traffic installations, and various cargo and off-site check-in locations, we see an increase in the number of sites of security. In this delocalization of the airport/aviation security, the behavior of governments, firms, and the public becomes a crucial variable.

Public Behavior

The aviation sector can succeed only with the cooperation and support of the general and flying public: people must be willing to fly, to ship by air freight, and to accept the risks of civil aviation. Despite advances in communication and information technology, global business still depends on the mobility of the transnational business elite (whose members account for a large proportion of regular passenger numbers). Passenger numbers dropped radically after the September 11 attacks because of a perceived decrease in security (even if the actual statistical risk of flying remained lower than that of similar travel by automobile).[12] Three segments of the public need to be convinced that aviation security works: the business elite, the general flying public, and the experts (insurers, risk managers, regulators, etc.).

The global "road warrior" or business elite provides a constant motor for wide-scale international travel. Though counting for only 10 percent of the total volume of international travel, business travelers were responsible for 28 percent of total revenue in 2002.[13] We must also take note that there is no divide between legacy and budget carriers in their dependence on business travel: 40–80 percent of all budget travelers were on business.[14] The demand has remained relatively static, or at least has been following sector-wide demand, since the 1980s. Thus, while we can expect that demand will remain consistent with general trends (to increase 5 percent over the next 10 years). Despite the rise of teleconferencing and virtual offices, there is a still a persistent culture of face-to-face business that is indispensable to doing business. Aviation security does not rank highly among business travelers' concerns, since their primary drivers are economic—in terms of cost and convenience. And, since there is no additional security premium attached to sitting in first or business class, the price differential is accounted for by other means. Demographically, nearly 90 percent of business travelers are men, although there is not a great deal of data to examine whether this proportion is changing.[15]

The rise of the jet, the long-haul jet, and more recently budget carriers has led to a variable demand for the use of air travel for tourism among the general public. Successful terror attacks have had effects on the overall use of air travel and on willingness to endure long-haul travel. Again, cost and convenience are the main drivers of tourist demand.

A final category of the public that must be convinced of the security of the civil aviation system is that of experts, namely, insurers, risk managers, regulators, economists, and so forth. It is these experts who determine rates of insurance, appropriate risk management or security management systems, and national standards for aviation security.[16] They are influenced by statistical data, industry norms, and ultimately the appetite for risk/cost/security of the regulators and markets.

A major issue in the public's perception of aviation security is that of cost and risk. In no other sector do passengers pay such a large proportion of the security costs, and so visibly (the various aviation security charges). It is a fundamental challenge to sell the public on aviation security. In addition, operators are reluctant to reveal security data—spending, services, or performance—for fear of alienating customers or informing potential attackers. There is an unfortunate silence in the public debate about airport security, which is dominated by post-facto audits of disasters.[17]

We can point to three general trends in the public face of aviation security: the move toward self-service, the rise of registered traveler services, and the use of prescreening. The underlying logic of these developments is risk management: the apportioning of resources (human, capital, and technological) to those elements of the system that pose the most risk (either because of known risk factors or precisely because the information is unknown). Since airport and aviation security is a complex network of interdependent systems, the central chokepoints, such as passenger, baggage, or cargo screening, establish the efficiency and effectiveness of the system. In an effort to systematically distribute the stress on these chokepoints, by weeding out the vast majority of travelers and the vast bulk of cargo and bags that pose no risk whatsoever, operators throughout the aviation sector are attempting to delocalize security operations. The use of off-site check-in and self-service counters attempts to avoid the peaks and valleys of passenger/cargo transit. Registered traveler programs (such as Privium at Schiphol, Clear in the United States, or the NEXUS program across the Canada-U.S. border) channel low-risk passengers into dedicated pathways that rely on preclearance (usually with additional security checks). Prescreening of passengers through carrier sanctions and remote visa approval systems (such as the Australian Advance Passenger Program or the U.S.-Canada preclearanc' agreement) locates the board/no board decision in the country of origin rather than at the destination. Thus, air carriers and customs and immigration agents make preemptive decisions about admissibility and security risk.

The dark counterpart to these programs, which rely on self-policing and self-registration, are the "no-fly" lists that have proliferated since September 11. Setting aside the actual efficacy of these programs, the confidence of the public in them is a necessary part of the public perception of aviation security. The rise and fall of the proposed CAPPS II system (Computer Assisted Passenger Prescreening System) provides an illustration.[18] Public resistance to no-fly lists and to additional screening measures imposed by governments is a liability for the aviation sector. Again, the same fundamental problem reappears: air operators do not wish to discuss security with their investors and their customers, and so the public debate is driven by anecdote or by failure.

The key dynamic is that security accounts for a significant proportion of costs in the aviation sector, but none of the important actors wish to engage in public discussion about the efficiency, efficacy, or risk associated with security measures. In this, the aviation sector is lagging behind other sectors of the economy, such as communications technology, insurance, or banking. The public must be educated about risk and threat in aviation security if costs continually increase without tangible benefit. Over the past few years, there has been an emerging consensus that security and facilitation are not competing goals but rather complementary aims, demonstrated by the success of the Simplifying Passenger Travel Interest Group. But, this needs to be further promoted.

PROBLEMS AND OPPORTUNITIES

Under the umbrella of Annex 17 of the Chicago Treaty and the ICAO security manual, there are of course fundamental national differences. Because of the slow speed of change in ICAO's SARPs (standards and recommended practices), aviation security is most often reactive and based on the lowest common denominator of acceptance. In the future of aviation security, three areas of current friction could intensify. There are fundamental problems in the areas of capacity, technology, and regulation and enforcement. These problem areas arise in the interface between the four major geographical centers of civil aviation: the United States, the European Union, Asia, and the rest of the world (RoW).

In terms of capacity, the American civil aviation market processes 1.3 billion passengers per year, with Europe trailing slightly at 989 million. The Asian market is expanding extremely rapidly. China alone is predicted to reach 950 million passengers within 15 years—comparable to the current European market. There are 133 large airports in China with 55 more anticipated to open before 2020.[19] There is a general concern that passenger volumes will exceed global capacity, especially at hub airports and within high-growth areas like East and South-East Asia.

In terms of technology and regulation, a core concern for the integrity of the global civil aviation security regime has to be the limited technological and governmental capacity of developing states, a central concern for ICAO. The results of ICAO's Universal Security Audit Program are confidential, but one of the reasons for covering all parts of the world was a specific concern about the global uniformity of security standards.

Technologies are not standard, despite the increasing concentration among security technology providers. The differing standards are most easily demonstrated in the current difference between American and European models of hold baggage screening. ICAO made 100 percent hold baggage screening mandatory by January 1, 2006 (Annex 17, Standard 4.4.8). The American policy is to screen each bag with a computed tomography–based, automated explosive detection system.[20] The European model uses a five-level system in which alarms trigger more intense scrutiny. Even with some consensus on the type of detection technology, U.S. and European regulators have different ways of managing risk, and different ways of interpreting the same data. The cultural differences between European and American regulators are minor, however. Equally pressing is the ability of governments to purchase the required technology and provide the required bureaucratic support for civil aviation security. While technology has the potential to be a force multiplier, without the governmental capacity to purchase, manage, and maintain technological systems, the resulting security will be thin.

FAST, CHEAP, AND OUT OF CONTROL

Brooks and Flynn, both MIT professors of robotics, propose that (to investigate other planets, for example) we should build robots that are "fast, cheap, and out of control," instead of single, complex, expensive, and delicate robots.[21] They argue that in the past we have been fascinated by the idea of creating a simulacrum of the perfect human—focusing on bipedal, autonomous robots—and we have ignored less ambitious projects that would be more efficient, feasible, and robust. We must fundamentally rethink our assumptions about the goals of innovation. Brooks realizes one day that the ants that are successfully invading his picnic are not superintelligent, stable, or strategic: they are fast, cheap, and out of control. Fast, because they are concerned with flexibility and not stability; cheap because they are small, disposable, and have a single function; and out of control because they are not centrally coordinated but rather function as a self-organizing system with a shared purpose but no prescribed solutions. Rather than adding more and more complex technologies, systems of remote control and surveillance, and redundancy and multiple checks in our security systems, we should understand that "Simplicity increases reliability."[22] In this spirit, we can imagine a future for aviation security that is flexible, decentralized, and self-organizing.

To date, however, aviation security has proceeded in fits and starts, driven by a short public attention span and spectacular failures. Innovations in organizational risk management, screening technologies, and business practices have the potential to harness the best aspects of governmental and corporate governance to provide a distributed, secure global civil aviation system. Crucial to this success will be the education of the flying public and its members' inclusion as active participants in aviation security.

NOTES

1. For example, see the American government's "Next Generation Air Transportation System" project, headed by the Joint Planning and Development Office, and the European Union's "Single European Sky" project.

2. M. H. Bazerman and M. Watkins, "Airline Security, the Failure of 9/11, and Predictable Surprises," *International Public Management Journal* 8 (2005): 376–77.

3. The Canadian Air Transport Security Authority and Transport Canada have recently implemented the RAIC (Restricted Area Identity Card), which uses biometrics to authenticate access to sterile areas at Canada's chief airports.

4. This system is currently in place at McCarran Airport in Las Vegas, Hanover Germany, and Pudong Airport in Shanghai, among others.

5. C. J. Bennett, "Comparative Politics of No-Fly Lists in the United States and Canada," in *Politics at the Airport*, ed. M. B. Salter (Minneapolis, MN: University of Minnesota Press, 2008), 88–122.

6. This is evident when a key global airport (such as O'Hare, New York, Heathrow, or Changi) suffers weather, air traffic control, or other problems. See N. Elhefnawy, "Societal Complexity and Diminishing Returns in Security," *International Security* 29 (2004): 152–74.

7. M. Zacher with B. Sutton, *Governing Global Networks: International Regimes for Transportation and Communications* (Cambridge: Cambridge University Press, 1996).

8. P. S. Dempsey, "Aviation Security: The Role of Law in the War on Terror," *Columbia Journal of Transnational Law* 41 (2003): 649–733.

9. J. Hainmüller and J. M. Lemnitzer, "Why Do Europeans Fly Safer? The Politics of Airport Security in Europe and the US," *Terrorism and Political Violence* 15 (2003): 1–36.

10. A. Advani and A. Borins, "Managing Airports: A Test of the New Public Management," *International Public Management Journal* 4 (2001): 91–107.

11. British Airport Authorities, Fraport, Swissport, and Vancouver International Airport, among others, all operate foreign airports in whole or in part. M. B. Salter, "Managing the Global Airport," in *Politics at the Airport*, ed. M. B. Salter (Minneapolis, MN: University of Minnesota Press, 2008).

12. A. Ghobrial and W. A. Irvin, "Combating Air Terrorism: Some Implications for the Aviation Industry," *Journal of Air Transportation* 9 (2004): 75.

13. K. J. Mason, "Observations of Fundamental Changes in the Demand for Aviation Services," *Journal of Air Transport Management* 11 (2005): 19–25.

14. Ibid., 21.

15. K. J. Mason, "Marketing Low-Cost Airline Services to Business Travelers," *Journal of Air Transport Management* 7 (2001): 105.

16. M. B. Salter, "SeMS and Sensibility: Security Management Systems and the Management of Risk in the Canadian Air Transport Security Authority," *Journal of Air Transport Management* 13 (2007): 389–98.

17. Standing Senate Committee on National Security and Defence, *The Myth of Security at Canada's Airports* (Ottawa: Senate of Canada, 2003); Standing Senate Committee on National Security and Defence, *Canadian Security Guidebook: An Update of Security Problems in Search of Solutions. Airports* (Ottawa: Senate of Canada, 2007); J. Wheeler, A*n Independent Review of Airport Security and Policing for the Government of Australia* (Melbourne: Commonwealth of Australia, 2005); G. D. Kutz and J. W. Cooney, *Aviation Security: Vulnerabilities Exposed through Covert Testing of TSA's Passenger Screening Process*, Testimony before the Committee on Oversight and Government Reform, House of Representatives, Government Accountability Office, GAO-08–48T, 2007.

18. A. Barnett, "CAPPS II: The Foundation of Aviation Security? *Risk Analysis* 24 (2004): 909–16; see also Bennett, "Comparative Politics of No-Fly Lists in the United States and Canada."

19. Aviation Technology.com, *Creating Capacity in China*, http://www.airport-technology.com/features/feature560/.

20. See G. Kauvar, B. Rostker, and R. Shaver, *Safer Skies: Baggage Screening and Beyond with Supporting Analyses* (Santa Monica, CA: Rand Corporation, 2002).

21. R. A. Brooks and A. M. Flynn, "Fast, Cheap and Out of Control: A Robot Invasion of the Solar System." *Journal of the British Interplanetary Society* 42 (1989): 478–85.

22. Ibid., 478.

REFERENCES

Advani, A., and A. Borins. 2001. "Managing Airports: A Test of the New Public Management." *International Public Management Journal* 4: 91–107.

Barnett, A. 2004. "CAPPS II: The Foundation of Aviation Security?" *Risk Analysis* 24: 909–16.

Bazerman, M. H., and M. Watkins. 2005. "Airline Security, the Failure of 9/11, and Predictable Surprises." *International Public Management Journal* 8: 376–77.

Bennett, C. J. 2008. "Comparative Politics of No-Fly Lists in the United States and Canada." In *Politics at the Airport*, ed. M. B. Salter, 88–122. Minneapolis, MN: University of Minneapolis Press.

Brooks, R. A., and A .M. Flynn. 1989. "Fast, Cheap and Out of Control: A Robot Invasion of the Solar System." *Journal of the British Interplanetary Society* 42: 478–85.

"Creating Capacity in China." 2005. Aviation Technology.com. Available at: http://www.airport-technology.com/features/feature560/.

Dempsey, P. S. 2003. "Aviation Security: The Role of Law in the War on Terror." *Columbia Journal of Transnational Law* 41: 649–733.

Elhefnawy, N. 2004. "Societal Complexity and Diminishing Returns in Security." *International Security* 29: 152–74.

Ghobrial, A., and W. A. Irvin. 2004. "Combating Air Terrorism: Some Implications for the Aviation Industry." *Journal of Air Transportation* 9: 67–86.

Hainmüller, J., and J. M. Lemnitzer. 2003. "Why Do Europeans Fly Safer? The Politics of Airport Security in Europe and the US." *Terrorism and Political Violence* 15: 1–36.

Kauvar, G., B. Rostker, and R. Shaver. 2002. *Safer Skies: Baggage Screening and Beyond with Supporting Analyses.* Santa Monica: Rand Corporation.

Kutz, G. D., and J. W. Cooney. 2007. "Aviation Security: Vulnerabilities Exposed through Covert Testing of TSA's Passenger Screening Process." Testimony before the Committee on Oversight and Government Reform, House of Representatives. Government Accountability Office (GAO-08–48T).

Mason, K. J. 2005. "Observations of Fundamental Changes in the Demand for Aviation Services." *Journal of Air Transport Management* 11: 19–25.

Mason., K. J. 2001. "Marketing Low-Cost Airline Services to Business Travelers." *Journal of Air Transport Management* 7: 103–9.

Salter, M .B. 2007. "SeMS and Sensibility: Security Management Systems and the Management of Risk in the Canadian Air Transport Security Authority." *Journal of Air Transport Management* 13: 389–98.

Salter, M. B. 2008. "Managing the Global Airport." In *Politics at the Airport*, ed. M. B. Salter, 25–71. Minneapolis, MN: University of Minnesota Press, 25–71.

Standing Senate Committee on National Security and Defence. 2003. *The Myth of Security at Canada's Airports.* Ottawa: Senate of Canada.

Standing Senate Committee on National Security and Defence. 2007. *Canadian Security Guidebook: An Update of Security Problems in Search of Solutions. Airports.* Ottawa: Senate of Canada.

Wheeler, J. 2005. *An Independent Review of Airport Security and Policing for the Government of Australia.* Melbourne: Commonwealth of Australia.

Zacher, M., with B. Sutton. 1996. *Governing Global Networks: International Regimes for Transportation and Communications.* Cambridge: Cambridge University Press.

DHS Has Made Progress in Securing the Commercial Aviation System, but Key Challenges Remain

Statement of Cathleen A. Berrick, Director
Homeland Security and Justice Issues

Madam Chair and Members of the Subcommittee:

I appreciate the opportunity to participate in today's hearing to discuss the Department of Homeland Security's (DHS) progress and challenges in securing our nation's aviation system. The Transportation Security Administration (TSA), originally established as an agency within the Department of Transportation in 2001 but now a component within DHS, is charged with securing the transportation network while also ensuring the free movement of people and commerce. TSA has primary responsibility for security in all modes of transportation and since its inception has developed and implemented a variety of programs and procedures to secure the commercial aviation system. Other DHS components, federal agencies, state and local governments, and the private sector also play a role in aviation security. For example, the U.S. Customs and Border Protection (CBP) has responsibility for conducting passenger prescreening—in general, the matching of passenger information against terrorist watch lists prior to an aircraft's departure—for international flights operating to or from the United States, as well as inspecting inbound air cargo upon its arrival in the United States. In accordance with TSA requirements, airport authorities are responsible for implementing measures to secure access to restricted airport areas as well as airport perimeters, while air carriers are responsible for inspecting air cargo, among other things.

My testimony today will focus on: (1) the progress TSA and other DHS components have made in securing the nation's commercial aviation system and (2) challenges that have impeded DHS's (and, as they relate to transportation security, TSA) efforts to implement its mission and management functions. My comments are based on issued GAO reports and testimonies addressing the security of the nation's aviation system, including an August 2007 report that highlights the progress DHS has made in implementing its mission and management functions.[1] In this report, we reviewed the extent to which DHS has taken actions to achieve performance expectations in each of its mission and management areas that we identified from legislation, Homeland Security Presidential Directives, and DHS strategic planning documents. Based primarily on our past work, we made a determination regarding whether DHS generally achieved or generally did not achieve the key elements of each performance expectation. An assessment of "generally achieved" indicates that DHS has taken sufficient actions to satisfy most elements of the expectation; however, an assessment of "generally achieved" does not signify that no further action is required of DHS or that functions covered by the expectation cannot be further improved or enhanced. Conversely, an assessment of "generally not achieved" indicates that DHS has not yet taken actions to satisfy most elements of the performance expectation. In determining the department's overall level of progress in achieving performance expectations in each of its mission and management areas, we concluded whether the department had made limited, modest, moderate, or substantial progress.[2] These assessments of progress do not reflect, nor are they intended to reflect, the extent to which actions by DHS and its components have made the nation more secure. We conducted our work in accordance with generally accepted government auditing standards.

SUMMARY

Within DHS, TSA is the agency with primary responsibility for securing the transportation sector and has undertaken a number of initiatives to strengthen the security of the nation's commercial aviation system. In large part, these efforts have been driven by legislative mandates designed to strengthen the security of commercial aviation following the September 11, 2001, terrorist attacks. In August 2007, we reported that DHS had made moderate progress in securing the aviation transportation network, but that more work remains.[3] Specifically, of the 24 performance expectations we identified for DHS in the

---

1. GAO, *Department of Homeland Security: Progress Report on Implementation of Mission and Management Functions*, GAO-07-454 (Washington, D.C.: August 2007); GAO, *Department of Homeland Security: Progress Report on Implementation of Mission and Management Functions*, GAO-07-1081T (Washington, D.C.: September 2007); and GAO, *Department of Homeland Security: Progress Report on Implementation of Mission and Management Functions*, GAO-07-1240T (Washington, D.C.: September 2007).
2. Limited progress: DHS has taken actions to generally achieve 25 percent or less of the identified performance expectations. Modest progress: DHS has taken actions to generally achieve more than 25 percent but 50 percent or less of the identified performance expectations. Moderate progress: DHS has taken actions to generally achieve more than 50 percent but 75 percent or less of the identified performance expectations. Substantial progress: DHS has taken actions to generally achieve more than 75 percent of the identified performance expectations.
3. GAO-07-454.

area of aviation security, we reported that it has generally achieved 17 of these expectations and has generally not achieved 7 expectations.

DHS, primarily through TSA, has made progress in many areas related to securing commercial aviation, and their efforts should be commended. Meeting statutory mandates to screen airline passengers and 100 percent of checked baggage alone was a tremendous challenge. To do this, TSA initially hired and deployed a federal workforce of over 50,000 passenger and checked baggage screeners, and installed equipment at the nation's more than 400 commercial airports to provide the capability to screen all checked baggage using explosive detection systems, as mandated by law. TSA has since turned its attention to, among other things, strengthening passenger prescreening—in general, the matching of passenger information against terrorist watch lists prior to an aircraft's departure; more efficiently allocating, deploying, and managing the transportation security officer (TSO)—formerly known as screener—workforce; strengthening screening procedures; developing and deploying more effective and efficient screening technologies; and improving domestic air cargo security. In addition to TSA, CBP has also taken steps to strengthen passenger prescreening for passengers on international flights operating to or from the United States, as well as inspecting inbound air cargo upon its arrival in the United States. DHS's Science and Technology (S&T) Directorate has also taken actions to research and develop aviation security technologies.

While these efforts have helped to strengthen the security of the commercial aviation system, DHS still faces a number of key challenges that need to be addressed to meet expectations set out for them by the Congress, the Administration, and the Department itself. For example, TSA has faced challenges in developing and implementing its passenger prescreening system, known as Secure Flight, and has not yet completed development efforts. As planned, this program would initially assume from air carriers the responsibility for matching information on airline passengers traveling domestically against terrorists watch lists. In addition, while TSA has taken actions to enhance perimeter security at airports, these actions may not be sufficient to provide for effective security. TSA has also begun efforts to evaluate the effectiveness of security-related technologies, such as biometric identification systems. However, TSA has not developed a plan for implementing new technologies to meet the security needs of individual airports and the commercial airport system as a whole. Further, TSA has not yet deployed checkpoint technologies to address key existing vulnerabilities, and has not yet developed and implemented technologies needed to screen air cargo.

A variety of cross-cutting issues have affected DHS's and, as they relate to transportation security, TSA's efforts in implementing its mission and management functions. These key issues include agency transformation, strategic planning and results management, risk management, information sharing, and stakeholder coordination. In working towards transforming the department into an effective and efficient organization, DHS and its components have not always been transparent, which has affected our ability to perform our oversight responsibilities in a timely manner. They have also not always implemented effective strategic planning efforts, fully developed performance measures, or put into place structures to help ensure that they are managing for results. In addition, DHS and its components can more fully adopt and apply a risk management approach in implementing its security mission and core management functions.[4] They could also better share information with federal, state, and local governments and private sector entities, and more fully coordinate its activities with key stakeholders.

BACKGROUND

The Aviation and Transportation Security Act (ATSA), enacted in November 2001, created TSA and gave it responsibility for securing all modes of transportation.[5] TSA's aviation security mission includes strengthening the security of airport perimeters and restricted airport areas; hiring and training a screening workforce; prescreening passengers against terrorist watch lists; and screening passengers, baggage, and cargo at the over 400 commercial airports nation-wide, among other responsibilities. While TSA has operational responsibility for physically screening passengers and their baggage, TSA exercises regulatory, or oversight, responsibility for the security of airports and air cargo. Specifically, airports, air carriers, and other entities are required to implement security measures in accordance with TSA-issued security requirements, against which TSA evaluates their compliance efforts.

TSA also oversees air carriers' efforts to prescreen passengers—in general, the matching of passenger information against terrorist watch lists—prior to an aircraft's departure. TSA plans to take over operational responsibility for this function with the implementation of its Secure Flight program initially for passengers traveling domestically. CBP has responsibility for conducting passenger prescreening for airline passengers on international flights departing from and bound for the United States,[6] while DHS's Science and Technology Directorate is responsible for researching and developing technologies to secure the transportation sector.

---

4. A risk management approach entails a continuous process of managing risk through a series of actions, including setting strategic goals and objectives, assessing risk, evaluating alternatives, selecting initiatives to undertake, and implementing and monitoring those initiatives.

5. Pub. L. No. 107-71, 115 Stat. 597 (2001).

6. Currently, air carriers departing the United States are required to transmit passenger manifest information to CBP no later than 15 minutes prior to departure but, for flights bound for the United States, air carriers are not required to transmit the information until 15 minutes after the flight's departure (in general, after the aircraft is in flight). See 19 C.F.R. §§ 122.49a, 122.75a. In a final rule published in the *Federal Register* on August 23, 2007, CBP established a requirement for all air carriers to either transmit the passenger manifest information to CBP no later than 30 minutes prior to the securing of the aircraft doors (that is, prior to the flight being airborne), or transmit manifest information on an individual basis as each passenger checks in for the flight up to but no later than the securing of the aircraft. See 72 Fed. Reg. 48,320 (Aug. 23, 2007). This requirement is to take effect on February 19, 2008.

DHS Has Made Progress in Securing the Nation's Commercial Aviation System, but More Work Remains

DHS, primarily through the efforts of TSA, has undertaken numerous initiatives since its inception to strengthen the security of the nation's commercial aviation system. In large part, these efforts have been affected by legislative mandates designed to strengthen the security of commercial aviation following the September 11, 2001 terrorist attacks. These efforts have also been affected by events external to the department, including the alleged August 2006 terrorist plot to blow up commercial aircraft bound from London to the United States. For example, TSA has undertaken efforts to hire, train, and deploy a screening workforce; and screen passengers, baggage, and cargo. Although TSA has taken important actions to strengthen aviation security, the agency has faced difficulties in implementing an advanced, government-run passenger prescreening program for domestic flights, and in developing and implementing technology to screen passengers at security checkpoints and cargo placed on aircraft, among other areas. As shown in table 1, we identified 24 performance expectations for DHS in the area of aviation security, and found that overall, DHS has made moderate progress in meeting these expectations. Specifically, we found that DHS has generally achieved 17 performance expectations and has generally not achieved 7 performance expectations. We identified these performance expectations through reviews of key legislation, Homeland Security Presidential Directives, and DHS strategic planning documents.

Aviation Security Strategic Approach

We concluded that DHS has generally achieved this performance expectation. In our past work, we reported that TSA identified and implemented a wide range of initiatives to strengthen the security of key components of the commercial aviation system. These components are interconnected and each is critical to the overall security of commercial aviation.[7] More recently, in March 2007, TSA released its National Strategy on Aviation Security and six supporting plans that provided more detailed strategic planning guidance in the areas of systems security; operational threat response; systems recovery; domain surveillance; and intelligence integration and domestic and international outreach. According to TSA officials, an Interagency Implementation Working Group was established under TSA leadership in January 2007 to initiate implementation efforts for the 112 actions outlined in the supporting plans.

---

7. For more information, see GAO, *Aviation Security: Enhancements Made in Passenger and Checked Baggage Screening, but Challenges Remain*, GAO-06-371T (Washington, D.C: April 2006).

Table 1
Performance Expectations and Progress Made in Aviation Security

Performance expectation	Assessment		
	Generally achieved	*Generally not achieved*	*No assessment made*
Aviation security strategic approach			
Implement a strategic approach for aviation security functions			
Airport perimeter security and access controls			
Establish standards and procedures for effective airport perimeter security			
Establish standards and procedures to effectively control access to airport secured areas			
Establish procedures for implementing biometric identifier systems for airport secured areas access control			
Ensure the screening of airport employees against terrorist watch lists			
Aviation security workforce			
Hire and deploy a federal screening workforce			
Develop standards for determining aviation security staffing at airports			
Establish standards for training and testing the performance of airport screener staff			
Establish a program and requirements to allow eligible airports to use a private screening workforce			
Train and deploy federal air marshals on high-risk flights			
Establish standards for training flight and cabin crews			
Establish a program to allow authorized flight deck officers to use firearms to defend against any terrorist or criminal acts			

Passenger prescreening
Establish policies and procedures to ensure that individuals known to pose, or suspected of posing, a risk or threat to security are identified and subjected to appropriate action
Develop and implement an advanced prescreening system t o allow DHS to com-pare domestic passenger information to the Selectee List and No Fly List
Develop and implement an international passenger prescreening process to compare passenger information to terrorist watch lists before aircraft departure

Checkpoint screening
Develop and implement processes and procedures for physically screening passengers at airport checkpoints
Develop and test checkpoint technologies to address vulnerabilities
Deploy checkpoint technologies to address vulnerabilities

Checked Baggage screening
Deploy explosive detection systems (EDS) and explosive trace detection (ETD) systems to screen checked baggage for explosives
Develop a plan to deploy in-line baggage screening equipment at airports
Pursue the deployment and use of in-line baggage screening equipment at airports

Air cargo security
Develop a plan for air cargo security
Develop and implement procedures to screen air cargo
Develop and implement technologies to screen air cargo

Total   17   7   0

Source: GAO analysis.

207

Airport Perimeter Security and Access Controls

We concluded that DHS has generally achieved one, and has generally not achieved three, of the performance expectations in this area. For example, TSA has taken action to ensure the screening of airport employees against terrorist watch lists by requiring airport operators to compare applicants' names against the No Fly and Selectee Lists.[8] However, in June 2004, we reported that although TSA had begun evaluating commercial airport perimeter and access control security through regulatory compliance inspections, covert testing of selected access procedures, and vulnerability assessments at selected airports, TSA had not determined how the results of these evaluations could be used to make improvements to the nation's airport system as a whole. We further reported that although TSA had begun evaluating the controls that limit access into secured airport areas, it had not completed actions to ensure that all airport workers in these areas were vetted prior to being hired and trained.[9] More recently, in March 2007, the DHS Office of Inspector General, based on the results of its access control testing at 14 domestic airports across the nation, made various recommendations to enhance the overall effectiveness of controls that limit access to airport secured areas.[10] In March through July 2007, DHS provided us with updated information on procedures, plans, and other efforts it had implemented to secure airport perimeters and strengthen access controls, including a description of its Aviation Direct Access Screening Program. This program provides for TSOs to randomly screen airport and airline employees and employees' property and vehicles as they enter the secured areas of airports for the presence of explosives, incendiaries, weapons, and other items of interest as well as improper airport identification. However, DHS did not provide us with evidence that these actions provide for effective airport perimeter security, nor information on how the actions addressed all relevant requirements established by law and in our prior recommendations.

Regarding procedures for implementing biometric identification systems, we reported that TSA had not developed a plan for implementing new technologies to meet the security needs of individual airports and the commercial airport system as a whole.[11]

---

8. For more information, see GAO, Aviation Security: Transportation Security Administration Has Made Progress in Managing a Federal Security Workforce and Ensuring Security at U.S. Airports, but Challenges Remain, GAO-06-597T (Washington, D.C.: April 2006) and GAO, Aviation Security: Further Steps Needed to Strengthen the Security of Commercial Airport Perimeters and Access Controls, GAO-04-728 (Washington, D.C.: June 2004).

9. GAO-06-597T and GAO-04-728.

10. Department of Homeland Security Office of Inspector General, Audit of Access to Airport Secured Areas (Unclassified Summary), OIG-07-35 (Washington, D.C.: March 2007).

11. GAO-06-597T and GAO-04-728.

In December 2004 and September 2006, we reported on the status of the development and testing of the Transportation Worker Identification Credential program (TWIC)[12]—DHS's effort to develop biometric access control systems to verify the identity of individuals accessing secure transportation areas. Our 2004 report identified challenges that TSA faced in developing regulations and a comprehensive plan for managing the program, as well as several factors that caused TSA to miss initial deadlines for issuing TWIC cards. In our September 2006 report, we identified the challenges that TSA encountered during TWIC program testing, and several problems related to contract planning and oversight. Specifically, we reported that DHS and industry stakeholders faced difficult challenges in ensuring that biometric access control technologies will work effectively in the maritime environment where the Transportation Worker Identification Credential program is being initially tested. In October 2007, we testified that TSA had made progress in implementing the program and addressing our recommendations regarding contract planning and oversight and coordination with stakeholders. For example, TSA reported that it added staff with program and contract management expertise to help oversee the contract and developed plans for conducting public outreach and education efforts.[13] However, DHS has not yet determined how and when it will implement a biometric identification system for access controls at commercials airports. We have initiated ongoing work to further assess DHS's efforts to establish procedures for implementing biometric identifier systems for airport secured areas access control.

Aviation Security Workforce

We concluded that DHS has generally achieved all 7 performance expectations in this area. For example, TSA has hired and deployed a federal screening workforce at over 400 commercial airports nationwide, and has developed standards for determining TSO staffing levels at airports. TSA also established numerous programs to train and test the performance of its TSO workforce, although we reported that improvements in these efforts can be made. Among other efforts, in December 2005, TSA reported completing enhanced explosives detection training for over 18,000 TSOs, and increased its use of covert testing to assess vulnerabilities of existing screening systems. TSA also established the Screening Partnership Program which allows eligible airports to apply to TSA to use a private screening workforce. In addition, TSA has trained and deployed federal air marshals on high-risk flights; established standards for training flight

12. GAO, *Port Security: Better Planning Needed to Develop and Operate Maritime Worker Identification Card Program*, GAO-05-106 (Washington, D.C.: December 2004), and *Transportation Security: DHS Should Address Key Challenges before Implementing the Transportation Worker Identification Credential Program*, GAO-06-982 (Washington, D.C.: September 2006).
13. GAO, *Maritime Security: The SAFE Port Act and Efforts to Secure Our Nation's Seaports*, GAO-08-86T (Washington, D.C. October 4, 2007).

and cabin crews; and established a Federal Flight Deck Officer program to select, train, and allow authorized flight deck officers to use firearms to defend
against any terrorist or criminal acts. Related to flight and cabin crew training,
TSA revised its guidance and standards to include additional training elements
required by law and improve the organization and clarity of the training. TSA
also increased its efforts to measure the performance of its TSO workforce
through recertification testing and other measures.

Passenger Prescreening

We reported that DHS has generally achieved one, and has not generally
achieved two, of the performance expectations in this area. For example, TSA
established policies and procedures to ensure that individuals known to pose, or
suspected of posing, a risk or threat to security are identified and subjected to appropriate action. Specifically, TSA requires that air carriers check all passengers
against the Selectee List, which identifies individuals that represent a higher
than normal security risk and therefore require additional security screening,
and the No Fly List, which identifies individuals who are not allowed to fly.[14]
However, TSA has faced a number of challenges in developing and implementing an advanced prescreening system, known as Secure Flight, which will allow
TSA to take over the matching of passenger information against the No Fly
and Selectee lists from air carriers, as required by law.[15] In 2006, we reported
that TSA had not conducted critical activities in accordance with best practices
for large-scale information technology programs and had not followed a disciplined life cycle approach in developing Secure Flight.[16] In March 2007, DHS
reported that as a result of its rebaselining efforts, more effective government
controls were developed to implement Secure Flight and that TSA was following a more disciplined development process. DHS further reported that it plans
to begin parallel operations with the first group of domestic air carriers during
fiscal year 2009 and to take over full responsibility for watch list matching in
fiscal year 2010. We are continuing to assess TSA's efforts in developing and
implementing the Secure Flight program. We have also reported that DHS has
not yet implemented enhancements to its passenger prescreening process for
passengers on international flights departing from and bound for the United
States.[17] Although CBP recently issued a final rule that will require air carriers

---

14. In accordance with TSA-issued security requirements, passengers on the No Fly List are
denied boarding passes and are not permitted to fly unless cleared by law enforcement officers.
Similarly, passengers who are on the Selectee List are issued boarding passes, and they and their
baggage undergo additional security measures.

15. See 49 U.S.C. § 44903(j)(2)(C).

16. GAO, *Aviation Security: Management Challenges Remain for the Transportation Security Administration's Secure Flight Program*, GAO-06-864T (Washington, D.C.: June 2006).

17. GAO, *Aviation Security: Progress Made in Systematic Planning to Guide Key Investment Deci-
sions, but More Work Remains*, GAO-07-448T (Washington, D.C.: February 2007) and GAO,
*Aviation Security: Efforts to Strengthen International Passenger Prescreening Are Under Way, but
Planning and Implementation Issues Remain*, GAO-07-346 (Washington, D.C.: May 2007).

to provide passenger information to CBP prior to a flight's departure so that CBP can compare passenger information to the terrorist watch lists before a flight takes off, this requirement is not scheduled to take effect until February 2008. In addition, while DHS plans to align its international and domestic passenger prescreening programs under TSA, full implementation of an integrated system will not occur for several years.

Checkpoint Screening

We reported that DHS has generally achieved two, and has not generally achieved one, of the performance expectations in this area. For example, we reported that TSA has developed processes and procedures for screening passengers at security checkpoints and has worked to balance security needs with efficiency and customer service considerations.[18] More specifically, in April 2007, we reported that modifications to standard operating procedures were proposed based on the professional judgment of TSA senior-level officials and program-level staff, as well as threat information and the results of covert testing. However, we found that TSA's data collection and analyses could be improved to help TSA determine whether proposed procedures that are operationally tested would achieve their intended purpose. We also reported that DHS and its component agencies have taken steps to improve the screening of passengers to address new and emerging threats. For example, TSA established two recent initiatives intended to strengthen the passenger checkpoint screening process: (1) the Screening Passenger by Observation Technique program, which is a behavior observation and analysis program designed to provide TSA with a nonintrusive means of identifying potentially high-risk individuals; and the (2) Travel Document Checker program which replaces current travel document checkers with TSOs who have access to sensitive security information on the threats facing the aviation industry and check for fraudulent documents. However, we found that while TSA has developed and tested checkpoint technologies to address vulnerabilities that may be exploited by identified threats such as improvised explosive devices, it has not yet effectively deployed such technologies. In July 2006, TSA reported that it installed 97 explosives trace portal machines—which use puffs of air to dislodge and detect trace amounts of explosives on persons—at 37 airports. However, DHS identified problems

---

18. For more information, see GAO, Aviation Security: Risk, Experience, and Customer Concerns Drive Changes to Airline Passenger Screening Procedures, but Evaluation and Documentation of Proposed Changes Could Be Improved, GAO-07-634 (Washington, D.C.: May 2007); GAO, Aviation Security: TSA's Change to Its Prohibited Items List Has Not Resulted in Any Reported Security Incidents, but the Impact of the Change on Screening Operations Is Inconclusive, GAO-07-623R (Washington, D.C.: April 2007); GAO, Airport Passenger Screening: Preliminary Observations on Progress Made and Challenges Remaining, GAO-03-1173 (Washington, D.C.: September 2003); and GAO, Aviation Security: Enhancements Made in Passenger and Checked Baggage Screening, but Challenges Remain, GAO-06-371T (Washington, D.C.: April 2006).

with these machines and has halted their deployment. TSA is also developing backscatter technology, which identifies explosives, plastics and metals, giving them shape and form and allowing them to be visually interpreted.[19] However, limited progress has been made in fielding this technology at passenger screening checkpoints. The Implementing Recommendations of the 9/11 Commission Act of 2007 (9/11 Commission Act), enacted in August 2007, restates and amends a requirement that DHS issue a strategic plan for deploying explosive detection equipment at airport checkpoints and requires DHS to expedite research and develop efforts to protect passenger aircraft from explosives devices.[20] We are currently reviewing DHS and TSA's efforts to develop, test and deploy airport checkpoint technologies.[21]

Checked Baggage Screening

We concluded that DHS has generally achieved all three performance expectations in this area. Specifically, from November 2001 through June 2006, TSA procured and installed about 1,600 Explosive Detection Systems (EDS) and about 7,200 Explosive Trace Detection (ETD) machines to screen checked baggage for explosives at over 400 commercial airports.[22] In response to mandates to field the equipment quickly and to account for limitations in airport design, TSA generally placed this equipment in a stand-alone mode—usually in airport lobbies—to conduct the primary screening of checked baggage for explosives.[23] Based in part on our previous recommendations, TSA later developed a plan to integrate EDS and ETD machines in-line with airport baggage conveyor systems. The installation of in-line systems can result in considerable savings to TSA through the reduction of TSOs needed to operate the equipment, as well as increased security. Despite delays in the widespread deployment of in-line systems due to the high upfront capital investment required, TSA is pursuing the installation of these systems and is seeking creative financing solutions to fund their deployment. In March 2007, DHS reported that it is working with airport and air carrier stakeholders to improve checked baggage screening solutions to enhance security and free up lobby space at airports. The installation of in-line baggage screening systems continues to be an issue

---

19. GAO-06-371T

20. See Pub. L. No. 110-53, §§1607, 1610, 121 Stat. 266, 483-85 (2007).

21. For more information, see GAO-06-371T.

22. Explosive detection systems (EDS) use specialized X-rays to detect characteristics of explosives that may be contained in baggage as it moves along a conveyor belt. Explosive trace detection (ETD) works by detecting vapors and residues of explosives. Human operators collect samples by rubbing swabs along the interior and exterior of an object that TSOs determine to be suspicious, and place the swabs in the ETD machine, which then chemically analyzes the swabs to identify any traces of explosive materials.

23. For more information, see GAO, *Aviation Security: TSA Oversight of Checked Baggage Screening Procedures Could Be Strengthened*, GAO-06-869 (Washington, D.C.: July 2006), GAO-06-371T, and GAO-07-448T.

of congressional concern. For example, the 9/11 Commission Act reiterates a requirement that DHS submit a cost-sharing study along with a plan and schedule for implementing provisions of the study, and requires TSA to establish a prioritization schedule for airport improvement projects such as the installation of in-line baggage screening systems.[24]

Air Cargo Security

We reported that TSA has generally achieved two, and has not generally achieved one, of the performance expectations in this area. Specifically, TSA has developed a strategic plan for domestic air cargo security and has taken actions to use risk management principles to guide investment decisions related to air cargo bound for the United States from a foreign country, referred to as inbound air cargo, but these actions are not yet complete. For example, TSA plans to assess inbound air cargo vulnerabilities and critical assets—two crucial elements of a risk-based management approach—but has not yet established a methodology or time frame for how and when these assessments will be completed.[25] TSA has also developed and implemented procedures to screen domestic and inbound air cargo. We reported in October 2005 that TSA had significantly increased the number of domestic air cargo inspections conducted of air carrier and indirect air carrier compliance with security requirements. However, we also reported that TSA exempted certain cargo from random inspection because it did not view the exempted cargo as posing a significant security risk, although air cargo stakeholders noted that such exemptions may create potential security risks and vulnerabilities since shippers may know how to package their cargo to avoid inspection.[26] In part based on a recommendation we made, TSA is evaluating existing exemptions to determine whether they pose a security risk, and has removed some exemptions that were previously allowed. The 9/11 Commission Act requires, no later than 3 years after its enactment, that DHS have a system in place to screen 100 percent of cargo transported on passenger aircraft.[27] Although TSA has taken action to develop plans for securing air cargo and establishing and implementing procedures to

---

24. See Pub. L. No. 110-53, § 1603-04, 121 Stat. at 480-81.

25. For more information, see GAO, Aviation Security: Federal Action Needed to Strengthen Domestic Air Cargo Security (Washington, D.C.: October 2005) and GAO, Aviation Security: Federal Efforts GAO-06-76 to Secure U.S.-Bound Air Cargo Are in the Early Stages and Could Be Strengthened, GAO-07-660 (Washington, D.C.: April 2007).

26. GAO-06-76.

27. See Pub. L. No. 110-53, § 1602, 121 Stat. at 477-79. This provision defines screening as a physical examination or non-intrusive method of assessing whether cargo poses a threat to transportation security that includes the use of technology, procedures, personnel, or other methods to provide a level of security commensurate with the level of security for the screening of passenger checked baggage. Methods such as solely performing a review of information about the contents of cargo or verifying the identity of a shipper of the cargo, including whether a known shipper is registered in TSA's known shipper database, do not constitute screening under this provision.

screen air cargo, DHS has not yet developed and implemented screening technologies. DHS is pursuing multiple technologies to automate the detection of explosives in the types and quantities that would cause catastrophic damage to an aircraft in flight. However, TSA acknowledged that full development of these technologies may take 5 to 7 years. In April 2007, we reported that TSA and DHS's S&T Directorate were in the early stages of evaluating and piloting available aviation security technologies to determine their applicability to the domestic air cargo environment. We further reported that although TSA anticipates completing its pilot tests by 2008, it has not yet established time frames for when it might implement these methods or technologies for the inbound air cargo system.[28]

Cross-cutting Issues Have Hindered DHS's Efforts in Implementing Its Mission and Management Functions

Our work has identified homeland security challenges that cut across DHS's mission and core management functions. These issues have impeded the department's progress since its inception and will continue as DHS moves forward. While it is important that DHS continue to work to strengthen each of its mission and core management functions, to include aviation security, it is equally important that these key issues be addressed from a comprehensive, department-wide perspective to help ensure that the department has the structure and processes in place to effectively address the threats and vulnerabilities that face the nation. These issues include: (1) transforming and integrating DHS's management functions; (2) establishing baseline performance goals and measures and engaging in effective strategic planning efforts; (3) applying and strengthening a risk management approach for implementing missions and making resource allocation decisions; (4) sharing information with key stakeholders; and (5) coordinating and partnering with federal, state and local, and private sector agencies. We have made numerous recommendations to DHS to strengthen these efforts, and the department has made progress in implementing some of these recommendations.

DHS has faced a variety of difficulties in its efforts to transform into a fully functioning department. We designated DHS's implementation and transformation as high-risk in part because failure to effectively address this challenge could have serious consequences for our security and economy. DHS continues to face challenges in key areas, including acquisition, financial, human capital, and information technology management. This array of management and programmatic challenges continues to limit DHS's ability to effectively and efficiently carry out its mission. In addition, transparency plays an important role in helping to ensure effective and efficient transformation efforts. We have reported that DHS has not made its management or operational decisions

---

28. GAO-07-660.

transparent enough so that Congress can be sure it is effectively, efficiently, and economically using the billions of dollars in funding it receives annually. More specifically, in April 2007, we testified that we have encountered access issues during numerous engagements at DHS, including significant delays in obtaining requested documents that have affected our ability to do our work in a timely manner.[29] The Secretary of DHS and the Under Secretary for Management have stated their desire to work with us to resolve access issues and to provide greater transparency. It will be important for DHS and its components to become more transparent and minimize recurring delays in providing access to information on its programs and operations so that Congress, GAO, and others can independently assess its efforts.

In addition, DHS has not always implemented effective strategic planning efforts and has not yet fully developed performance measures or put into place structures to help ensure that the agency is managing for results. We have identified strategic planning as one of the critical success factors for new organizations, and reported that both DHS's and TSA's efforts in this area have been mixed. For example, with regards to TSA's efforts to secure air cargo, we reported that TSA completed an Air Cargo Strategic Plan in November 2003 that outlined a threat-based risk management approach to securing the nation's domestic air cargo system, and that this plan identified strategic objectives and priority actions for enhancing air cargo security based on risk, cost, and deadlines. However, we reported that TSA had not developed a similar strategy for addressing the security of inbound air cargo—cargo transported into the United States from foreign countries, including how best to partner with CBP and international air cargo stakeholders. In another example, we reported that TSA had not yet developed outcome-based performance measures for its foreign airport assessment and air carrier inspection programs, such as the percentage of security deficiencies that were addressed as a result of TSA's on-site assistance and recommendations, to identify any aspects of these programs that may need attention. We recommended that DHS direct TSA and CBP to develop a risk-based strategy, including specific goals and objectives, for securing air cargo;[30] and develop outcome-based performance measures for its foreign airport assessment and air carrier inspection programs.[31] DHS generally concurred with GAO's recommendations.

DHS has also not fully adopted and applied a risk management approach in implementing its mission and core management functions. Risk management has been widely supported by the President and Congress as an approach for

29. GAO, *Department of Homeland Security: Observations on GAO Access to Information on Programs and Activities*, GAO-07-700T (Washington, D.C.: April 2007).
30. GAO-07-660.
31. GAO, *Aviation Security: Foreign Airport Assessments and Air Carrier Inspections Help Enhance Security, but Oversight of These Efforts Can Be Strengthened*, GAO-07-729 (Washington, D.C.: May 11, 2007).

allocating resources to the highest priority homeland security investments, and the Secretary of Homeland Security and the Assistant Secretary for Transportation Security have made it a centerpiece of DHS and TSA policy. Several DHS component agencies and TSA have worked towards integrating risk-based decision making into their security efforts, but we reported that these efforts can be strengthened. For example, TSA has incorporated certain risk management principles into securing air cargo, but has not completed assessments of air cargo vulnerabilities or critical assets—two crucial elements of a risk-based approach without which TSA may not be able to appropriately focus its resources on the most critical security needs. TSA has also incorporated risk-based decision making when making modifications to airport checkpoint screening procedures, to include modifying procedures based on intelligence information and vulnerabilities identified through covert testing at airport checkpoints. However, in April 2007 we reported that TSA's analyses that supported screening procedural changes could be strengthened. For example, TSA officials decided to allow passengers to carry small scissors and tools onto aircraft based on their review of threat information—which indicated that these items do not pose a high risk to the aviation system—so that TSOs could concentrate on higher threat items.[32] However, TSA officials did not conduct the analysis necessary to help them determine whether this screening change would affect TSO's ability to focus on higher-risk threats.[33]

We have further reported that opportunities exist to enhance the effectiveness of information sharing among federal agencies, state and local governments, and private sector entities. In August 2003, we reported that efforts to improve intelligence and information sharing need to be strengthened, and in 2005, we designated information sharing for homeland security as high-risk.[34] In January 2005, we reported that the nation still lacked an implemented set of government-wide policies and processes for sharing terrorism-information, but DHS has issued a strategy on how it will put in place the overall framework, policies, and architecture for sharing information with all critical partners—actions that we and others have recommended.[35] DHS has taken some steps to implement its information sharing responsibilities. States and localities are also creating their own information "fusion" centers, some with DHS support. With respect to aviation security, the importance of information sharing was recently highlighted in the 9/11 Commission Act, which requires DHS to establish a plan to promote the sharing of transportation security

32. GAO, *Aviation Security: Risk, Experience, and Customer Concerns*, GAO-07-634 (Washington, D.C.: May 2007).

33. GAO, *Aviation Security: Risk, Experience, and Customer Concerns Drive Changes to Airline Passenger Screening Procedures, but Evaluation and Documentation of Proposed Changes Could Be Improved*, GAO-07-634 (Washington, D.C.: April 16, 2007).

34. GAO, *Homeland Security: Efforts to Improve Information Sharing Need to Be Strengthened*, GAO-03-760 (Washington, D.C.: August 2003) and GAO, *HIGH-RISK SERIES: An Update* GAO-05-207 (Washington, D.C.: January 2005).

35. GAO-07-454.

information among DHS and federal, state and local agencies, tribal governments, and appropriate private entities.[36] The Act also requires that DHS provide timely threat information to carriers and operators that are preparing and submitting a vulnerability assessment and security plan, including an assessment of the most likely methods that could be used by terrorists to exploit weaknesses in their security.[37]

In addition to providing federal leadership with respect to homeland security, DHS also plays a large role in coordinating the activities of key stakeholders, but has faced challenges in this regard. To secure the nation, DHS must form effective and sustained partnerships between legacy component agencies and a range of other entities, including other federal agencies, state and local governments, the private and nonprofit sectors, and international partners. We have reported that successful partnering and coordination involves collaborating and consulting with stakeholders to develop and agree on goals, strategies, and roles to achieve a common purpose; identify resource needs; establish a means to operate across agency boundaries, such as compatible procedures, measures, data, and systems; and agree upon and document mechanisms to monitor, evaluate, and report to the public on the results of joint efforts.[38] We have found that the appropriate homeland security roles and responsibilities within and between the levels of government, and with the private sector, are evolving and need to be clarified. For example, we reported that opportunities exists for TSA to work with foreign governments and industry to identify best practices for securing air cargo, and recommended that TSA systematically compile and analyze information on practices used abroad to identify those that may strengthen the department's overall security efforts.[39] Further, regarding efforts to respond to in-flight security threats, which—depending on the nature of the threat—could involve 15 federal agencies and agency components, we recommended that DHS and other departments document and share their respective coordination and communication strategies and response procedures.[40]

CONCLUDING OBSERVATIONS

The magnitude of DHS's and more specifically TSA's responsibilities in securing the nation's commercial aviation system is significant, and we commend the department on the work it has done and is currently doing to secure this network. Nevertheless, given the dominant role that TSA plays in securing the

---

36. See Pub. L. No. 110-53, § 1203, 121 Stat. at 383-86.
37. See Pub. L. No. 110-53, §§ 1512(d)(2), 1531(d)(2), 121 Stat. at 430, 455.
38. GAO, *Homeland Security: Management and Programmatic Challenges Facing the Department of Homeland Security*, GAO-07-833T (Washington, D.C.: May 2007).
39. GAO-07-660.
40. GAO, Aviation Security: Federal Coordination for Responding to In-flight Security Threats Has Matured, but Procedures Can Be Strengthened (Washington, D.C.: July 31, 2007). GAO-07-891R

homeland, it is critical that its programs and initiatives operate as efficiently and effectively as possible. In the almost 6 years since its creation, TSA has had to undertake its critical mission while also establishing and forming a new agency. At the same time, a variety of factors, including threats to and attacks on aviation systems around the world, as well as new legislative requirements, has led the agency to reassess its priorities and reallocate resources to address key events, and to respond to emerging threats. Although TSA has made considerable progress in addressing key aspects of commercial aviation security, more work remains in the areas of checkpoint and air cargo technology, airport security, and passenger prescreening. As DHS and TSA and other components move forward, it will be important for the department to work to address the challenges that have affected its operations thus far, including developing results-oriented goals and measures to assess performance; developing and implementing a risk-based approach to guide resource decisions; and establishing effective frameworks and mechanisms for sharing information and coordinating with homeland security partners. A well-managed, high-performing TSA is essential to meeting the significant challenge of securing the transportation network. As TSA continues to evolve, implement its programs, and integrate its functions, we will continue to review its progress and performance and provide information to Congress and the public on its efforts.

Madam Chair, this concludes my statement. I would be pleased to answer any questions that you or other members of the Subcommittee may have at this time.

GAO CONTACT AND STAFF ACKNOWLEDGMENTS

For further information on this testimony, please contact Cathleen Berrick at (202) 512-3404 or at berrickc@gao.gov. Individuals making key contributions to this testimony include Steve D. Morris, Assistant Director, Gary Malavenda, Susan Langley, and Linda Miller.

October 16, 2007.

Index

About the Editor and Contributors

ANDREW R. THOMAS is assistant professor of marketing and international business and associate director of the Taylor Institute for Direct Marketing at the University of Akron. He is founding editor-in-chief of the *Journal of Transportation Security*, the first peer-reviewed journal dedicated to the study and practice of this critical business component. A *New York Times* best-selling writer, Dr. Thomas is author, coauthor, or editor of:

- *Supply Chain Security and Innovation*
- *The Distribution Trap!*
- *Global Manifest Destiny: Growing Your Business in a Borderless Economy*
- *Direct Marketing in Action: Proven Strategies for Finding and Keeping Your Best Customers*
- *The New World Marketing*
- *Growing Your Business in Emerging Markets: Promise & Perils*
- *The Rise of Women Entrepreneurs: People, Processes, and Global Trends*
- *Defining the Really Great Boss*
- *Managing by Accountability: What Every Leader Needs to Know About Responsibility, Integrity—and Results*
- *Change or Die! How to Transform Your Organization from the Inside Out*
- *Aviation Security Management*
- *Aviation Insecurity: The New Challenges of Air Travel*
- *Air Rage: Crisis in the Skies*

Dr. Thomas has published articles in leading management journals such as *MIT Sloan Management Review*, *Business Horizons*, and *Marketing Management*.

He is a regularly featured analyst for BBC, UNIVISION, FOX NEWS, and CNBC. He has been interviewed by more than 800 television and radio stations around the world. A successful global entrepreneur, Professor Thomas has traveled to and done business in more than 120 countries on all seven continents.

GARY E. ELPHINSTONE, adviser to the editor, is currently managing director of AVSEC AusAsia Pty Ltd., an international aviation security consultancy. Elphinstone's distinguished career in aviation began with the Royal Australian Air Force, where he specialized in signals intelligence and communications. During his service, he was promoted to serve at the British GCHQ, Hong Kong, for two and half years and, later, served as a fully rated flight services officer with the then Australian Department of Civil Aviation (DCA), working out of Sydney International Airport, Airways Operations. This was followed with an engagement to NASA at the deep space tracking station DSS 42, participating as electronics communications technician in a support role for the Apollo missions 8–13 and other NASA Deep Space Network programs. He rejoined the Federal Department of Aviation's Security Branch in 1978 and subsequently was chosen for an assignment with ICAO (the International Civil Aviation Organization) as aviation security adviser team leader with the aviation security project team, based in Thailand. The ICAO project (RAS 087/003) provided assistance to some 23 countries with a purpose of enhancing the capabilities of the governments in the region to minimize acts of unlawful interference against civil aviation. This was the forerunner to the current ICAO USAP (Universal Security Audit Programme). Elphinstone retired from government service in 1997 as superintendent AVSEC Western Region, after 19 years. He resides with his family in Perth, Australia.

RUWANTISSA I. R. ABEYRATNE, FRAeS, DCL, PhD, LLM, LLB,. is coordinator, Air Transport Programmes, at the International Civil Aviation Organization in Montreal.

ANTON BOLFING is a doctoral student at Max Planck Institute for Biological Cybernetics, Tübingen, Germany, and the University of Zurich, Switzerland. His main research topics are human factors in aviation security, applied vision research, psychophysics, digital image processing, and statistical modeling.

CHARLES M. BUMSTEAD has been involved in aviation affairs for 60 years, having spent a career as a fighter pilot in the U.S. military (USAF) and 27 years with the FAA, and a short seven-year career with ICAO (Bangkok) and IATA(Bangkok). He has specialized in international relations and international terrorism. His most publicized work was a paper on terrorism, "Selective Assassination: An Instrument of National Policy." An additional major publication was a treatise titled *Air Traffic Control in the 1990s*, produced in 1972. He is currently retired but is still deeply involved with international affairs. Educated at the University of Alabama, Troy University (summa cum laude), and Inter-American University, he is a charter member of the Alpha Phi Chapter of Alpha Sigma Lambda (NHS) and is a distinguished graduate of the USAF Air War College.

ANTHONY T. H. CHIN. Prior to his return to the Department of Economics at the National University of Singapore in July 2004, Professor Chin was appointed as lead economist in the Economist Service at the Ministry of Trade and Industry. An NUS overseas merit scholar, he completed his PhD at Macquarie University, Australia, in discrete continuous choice methods. He is currently a member of the Public Transport Council and the Government Parliamentary Committee on Transport in Singapore and a fellow of AirNeth of the Netherlands. He is editor-in-chief of the *Journal of Logistics and Sustainable Transport* of the European Society of Logistics and Sustainable Transport and serves on the editorial boards of the *Journal of Air Transport Management, Asian Economy and Social Environment*, and the *Singapore Economic Review*. Among his areas of research specialization are consumer choice behavior (travel and crime); aviation economics; demand management and strategic planning of air hubs; and the economics of deviant behavior and personnel security. He has contributed articles to academic journals and presented papers at academic conferences and is a member of several international committees.

DAVID E. FORBES is a security analyst, having worked as an industry-based student of and advisor on aviation security since 1983. He has published a number of articles and white papers including the January 2004 paper, "Missing in Action—Aviation Security in America." His business and research work is conducted from bases in Denver, Colorado, and Perth, Western Australia. He is the cofounder and a director of Jagwa Forbes Group Pty. Ltd., an Australian consulting and training company specializing in emergency preparedness, safety training, and security risk management, with a major focus on aviation.

SASKIA M. KOLLER is a PhD student with the Visual Cognition Research Group of Prof. Dr. Adrian Schwaninger at the University of Zurich. In 2006, she finished her studies in psychology, business management, and criminology at the University of Zurich and is now writing her doctoral thesis in the field of airport security.

CHIEN-TSUNG LU teaches aviation system safety and risk management at the University of Central Missouri, Warrensburg, Missouri. He earned his PhD from the University of Nebraska and his MS from the University of Central Missouri. He is an FAA-certified aviation maintenance technician (A&P) and Federal Communication Commission licensee. Dr. Lu has numerous publications in aviation-related journals. His research and teaching interests are in the areas of aviation safety analysis, management models, and performance measurement.

CLINTON V. OSTER, JR., is professor and associate dean of the School of Public and Environmental Affairs, Indiana University. Professor Oster's current research centers on air traffic management and aviation infrastructure, aviation safety, and airline economics and competition policy. His most recent book is *Managing the Skies: Public Policy, Organization, and Financing of Air Navigation*, with John S. Strong (Ashgate Press, 2008). He has also coauthored four books and numerous articles on aviation safety and various aspects of the U.S. airline industry. Professor Oster has served on multiple special study committees and expert panels for the National Academy of Sciences. He has been a consultant on aviation and other transportation issues to national governments, multilateral institutions, state and local governments, and private sector companies in the United States, Canada, the United Kingdom, Russia, and Australia. Professor Oster received a BSE from Princeton University, an MS from Carnegie-Mellon University, and a PhD from Harvard University.

JEFFREY IAN ROSS, PhD, is an associate professor in the Division of Criminology, Criminal Justice, and Social Policy, and a fellow of the Center for International and Comparative Law at the University of Baltimore. He has researched, written, and lectured on national security, political violence, political crime, violent crime, corrections, and policing for over two decades. Ross's work has appeared in many academic journals and books, as well as popular outlets. He is the author, coauthor, editor and coeditor of 12 books including most recently *Special Problems in Corrections* (Prentice Hall, 2008). Ross is a respected and frequent source of scholarly and scientific information for local, regional, national, and international news media, including interviews with newspapers and magazines and radio and television stations. Ross has also been featured on CNN and on the Fox News Network. Additionally Ross has written op-eds for the *Baltimore Sun*, the *Maryland Daily Record*, the *Baltimore Examiner*, and the *Tampa Tribune*. From 1995 to 1998, Ross was a social science analyst with the National Institute of Justice, a division of the U.S. Department of Justice. In 2003, he was awarded the University of Baltimore's Distinguished Chair in Research Award.

MARK B. SALTER is associate professor at the School of Political Studies, University of Ottawa. He received a master's degree from the London School of Economics and a doctorate from the University of British Columbia. He is currently associate editor of the *Journal of Transportation Security*, and has edited two books on airports, borders, and security: *Politics at the Airport* and *Global Policing and Surveillance* (with Elia Zureik). He is the author of *Rights of Passage: The Passport in International Relations* and has also published articles in *International Political Sociology*, *Alternatives*, *Security Dialogue*, and the *Journal of Air Transport Management*. Salter has acted as a consultant for the Canadian Air Transport Security Authority, Transport Canada, and the Canadian Human Rights Commission, and has presented papers at numerous conferences, including AVSEC World and the Canadian Aviation Security Conference. In 2007, he was the recipient of the National Capital Educator's Award and the Excellence in Education Prize at the University of Ottawa.

Prof. Dr. ADRIAN SCHWANINGER has lectured at the University of Zurich and at the Federal Institute of Technology (ETH) in Zurich since 1999 and at the University of Applied Sciences Northwestern Switzerland since 2008. He is a member of the Training and Technical Task Forces of the European Civil Aviation Conference (ECAC), the moderator of the ECAC Technical Task Force TIP Study Group, and the chairman of the InterTAG ad hoc Working Group on Competency Assessment. In 1999, he received the Young Researcher Award in Psychology. In 2003 he received the ASI International Award of Excellence in Aviation Security: Enhancement of Human Factors. Together with his Visual Cognition Research Group (VICOREG) he is in charge of several aviation security projects in Belgium, Bulgaria, Canada, France, Germany, Greece, Norway, Romania, Sweden, Switzerland, the Netherlands, and the United States of America.

TERRY A. SHERIDAN, MA, AFAIM, MRCSA, is managing director and founder of Guardian Angel, an employment service with offices in Australia and Singapore, which uses a unique emotional energy based methodology to assist employers and employees in the workplace. Originally, the business was set up in 2002 to assist the mature aged unemployed, specializing in managers and executives. Other services have been added that are more preventative in approach, for example, counseling, employee-retention programs, and executive screening services. More recently, her methodology has been applied in a number of different areas, including aviation security and financial fraud detection. Her clients are from North America, Europe, Asia, and Australia. Ms. Sheridan has a background in human services and business management; her past roles include those of CEO of an employment service for people with disabilities, financial and management services director of a large superannuation fund, and director of a university commercial arm. She has presented over 30 papers at national and international academic conferences and forums on a variety of topics. In 2005, she undertook a national investigation of unemployed women managers for the Australian Commonwealth Government. Her professional affiliations include the following: she is an associate fellow of the Australian Institute of Management, and holds professional memberships of the United Kingdom Institute of Career Guidance and the Australian Association of Career Counsellors. Ms. Sheridan is currently completing her PhD, on the impression management techniques of executive fraudsters, at the Graduate School of Business, Curtin University of Technology, Western Australia.

JOHN S. STRONG is the CSX Professor of Finance and Economics at the Mason School of Business, College of William and Mary. Strong's research interests are in aviation policy and transport finance. He has coauthored five books and many articles on air transport finance, operations, safety, and infrastructure. His most recent book is *Managing the Skies: Public Policy, Organization, and Financing of Air Navigation*, with Clinton V. Oster, Jr. (Ashgate Press, 2008). He has served as a consultant on aviation issues to multilateral institutions and governments in the United States, Southeast Asia, China, Russia, India, Latin America, Africa, and Europe. Professor Strong received a BA from Washington and Lee University, and an MPP and PhD from Harvard University.

MICHAEL TUNNECLIFFE is an adjunct senior lecturer in counseling at the University of Notre Dame, Australia. In his professional practice, Michael is a clinical psychologist, specializing in crisis intervention and human behavioral issues, especially in relation to people in high-demand occupations with significant stress potential. As well as working with international and domestic airlines, he provides psychological support and educational services to law enforcement officers, emergency workers, and security personnel throughout Australia and New Zealand. Tunnecliffe is the author of *How to Understand and Manage Stress*, *How to Manage the Stress of Traumatic Incidents*, and *A Life in Crisis*. He is also the coauthor of *Emergency Support* and *Risky Practices*.